ETHNIC BOUNDARIES IN TURKISH POLITICS

Ethnic Boundaries in Turkish Politics

The Secular Kurdish Movement and Islam

Zeki Sarigil

NEW YORK UNIVERSITY PRESS

New York

NEW YORK UNIVERSITY PRESS
New York

www.nyupress.org

© 2018 by New York University

All rights reserved

References to Internet websites (URLs) were accurate at the time of writing. Neither the author nor New York University Press is responsible for URLs that may have expired or changed since the manuscript was prepared.

ISBN: 978-1-4798-8216-8

For Library of Congress Cataloging-in-Publication data, please contact the Library of Congress.

New York University Press books are printed on acid-free paper, and their binding materials are chosen for strength and durability. We strive to use environmentally responsible suppliers and materials to the greatest extent possible in publishing our books.

Manufactured in the United States of America

10 9 8 7 6 5 4 3 2 1

Also available as an ebook

CONTENTS

Introduction

In March 2011, Kurdish *meles*[1] led "civilian Friday prayers" as part of a larger civil disobedience campaign (*sivil itaatsizlik*) in the main public square of Diyarbakır, Turkey. Organized and sponsored by the secular Kurdish movement, which was represented in Parliament at that time by the Peace and Democracy Party (Barış ve Demokrasi Partisi, BDP), civilian Friday prayers aimed to boycott regular Friday prayers at state-controlled mosques. Party officials stated that they did not want to stand behind state-appointed imams arguing that state imams propagate prostate and progovernment views as well as Turkishness among Kurds in the region. Party coleader Selahattin Demirtaş, for instance, claimed the following: "Imams are selected by the National Security Council [Milli Güvenlik Kurulu, MGK] and then sent here [the Kurdish regions]. We ask our people not to pray behind those state imams who are sent here with a special mission. . . . We know that some of the state imams in the region are working for the government [run by the conservative Justice and Development Party]. They are here to impose Turkishness and statism on the people."[2]

Such an unexpected initiative by a secular, left-oriented political movement sparked huge controversy and heated debates in Turkish politics. The government, run by the conservative Justice and Development Party (Adalet ve Kalkınma Partisi, AKP), harshly criticized this initiative. Highly disturbed by the BDP-promoted civilian Friday prayers, then–prime minister Recep Tayyip Erdoğan condemned them on several occasions. He asserted that the pro-Kurdish party was exploiting religion to gain votes. To degrade the secular Kurdish movement in the eyes of conservative Kurds, Erdoğan further claimed that Kurdish ethnonationalists consider Abdullah Öcalan (the imprisoned Kurdish leader) as a prophet.[3] On one occasion, Erdoğan gratingly reacted to this initiative as follows: "Now, they organize alternative Friday prayers. But they do not really respect our sacred, religious values. For instance, there are females among those who participate in their Friday prayers. . . . They also consider Apo [Abdullah Öcalan] as a Prophet. . . . They still follow Marxist-Leninist understandings, which do not have anything to do with Islam and Islamic values."[4]

Civilian Friday prayers were part of a broader transformation in the secular Kurdish movement in Turkey in the past decades: the rise of a friendlier approach and attitude toward Islam. As this book's empirical chapters present in detail, we see many other similar initiatives by the Kurdish ethnonationalist movement, such as welcoming and co-opting conservative political figures and civil society organizations; assembling the Democratic Islam Congress in Diyarbakır and Istanbul; organizing mass meetings to celebrate the anniversary of the Prophet Muhammad's birthday (*mawlid* meetings) and public *iftar*[5] dinners during Ramadan; and increasing references to Islamic ideas, principles, and practices (e.g., frequently citing verses from the Koran and proposing the Charter of Medina as a social model for contemporary Turkey).

These unprecedented initiatives constitute a conundrum because it is widely acknowledged that one of the fault lines of Turkish politics is the divide between religious and secular (e.g., see Göle 1997; Cizre 2008; Yavuz 1997, 2003, and 2009). While most rightist political formations have been associated with the religious camp and advocate and promote conservative or Islamic ideas and values in society and politics, most leftist circles have sided with the secular camp, generally skeptical toward the role of religion and religious actors and movements in sociopolitical life. This observation is also valid for the PKK-led Kurdish ethnonationalist movement, which emerged in the second half of the 1970s. As chapter 2 depicts, the Kurdish ethnonationalist movement in Turkey, rooted in strong secularism and socialist, Marxist ideology, initially adopted a strongly anti-religious stance (see also van Bruinessen 2000b, 54–55; Romano 2006, 134). However, the movement has taken a much more moderate and lenient attitude in regard to Islam and Islamic actors over the past few decades, particularly since the early 2000s. As a result, Islam has become part of the movement's political discourse, strategies, and actions. I define such a transformation or evolution in leftist, secular Kurdish ethnopolitics as the *Islamic opening*. The term *Islamic opening* in this study, however, does not mean that a secular ethononationalist movement is turning into an Islamic one. Instead, it refers to the approval and endorsement of Islam and Islamic actors by the secular, leftist Kurdish ethnonationalist movement, which is a novel phenomenon in modern Kurdish ethnopolitics in the Turkish setting.

From a broader perspective, the increasing role of religion in sociopolitical life in the Middle East and across the world in the post–Cold War context is a widely acknowledged phenomenon (e.g., see Almond, Appleby, and Sivan 2003; Roy 2004; Emerson and Hartman 2006; Meijer 2009). In line with this religious revival or resurgence (i.e., the rise of Islamic movements and political parties), several nationalist groups or movements in the region, such as the Palestine Liberation Organization (PLO), have accommodated Islam.[6] As a result, we see the entanglement of nationalist and religious identifications and attachments in various nationalist movements (see also Juergensmeyer 1993, 2006, 2008; Rieffer 2003; Smith 2008; Barker 2009; Gorski and Türkmen-Dervişoğlu 2013).

One might expect that similar developments and processes have taken place in the Turkish polity. Indeed, several political formations and movements have adopted a more Islamic discourse and position in the post-1980 period, partly because of the declining influence of ideology politics (i.e., left-right divisions and polarization) in the Turkish polity and the increasingly welcoming attitude of the Turkish state toward Islam and religious orders. Within such a political environment, a shift toward Islam among right-oriented political formations is not that surprising. It is much more striking, however, to see such a transformation taking place within strictly secular, leftist formations, such as the Kurdish ethnonationalist movement. As stated earlier, the Kurdish movement, which is rooted in strong secularism and Marxism, has been flying ethnoreligious colors, especially since the early 2000s. We do not really see such a systematic effort to accommodate Islam and Islamic actors among other leftist circles in the Turkish polity. We do see some initiatives by other leftist political formations or movements to appeal to conservative or pious voters (e.g., efforts to co-opt conservative politicians from the center-right or having female party members wearing headscarves). However, as the empirical chapters of the book illustrate, such cosmetic or superficial and short-term initiatives are not really comparable with much more systematic, comprehensive, and long-term efforts of the secular Kurdish movement to reinterpret Islamic ideas, values, and principles in line with its ethnonationalist interests and objectives and to co-opt Islamic actors. This difference is probably because of the fact that the constituency of the Kurdish ethnonationalist movement has been relatively more religious (for more on this, see chapter 3).

Despite this striking change, there is a very limited number of works directly dealing with the increasing role of religion in the Kurdish ethnopolitical movement in the Turkish context, for example, works by van Bruinessen (2000a, 2000b), Houston (2001), and Gürbüz (2016). However, in addition to being outdated, the works by van Bruinessen and Houston do not really provide a comprehensive theoretical and explanatory analysis of the secular Kurdish movement's evolving relations with Islam. Gürbüz's study indirectly touches on pro-Kurdish groups' relations with Islam by examining competition or rivalry among social movement organizations in southeastern Turkey (e.g., pro-Islamic groups such as Kurdish Hezbollah and secular pro-Kurdish civil society organizations). In other words, this recent work does not provide a detailed and thorough account of the Kurdish ethnopolitical movement's Islamic opening in the past decades either. In brief, it is surprising that this intriguing development in secular Kurdish ethnopolitics and its theoretical and practical implications still remain an understudied and undertheorized phenomenon in the fast-growing scholarly literature on the Kurdish issue.

Thus, it is worth raising the following research questions: Why do we see the aforementioned, unexpected shift? What does it mean? How can we explain this interesting development in secular Kurdish ethnopolitics? For what reasons (ideational and/or material) do ethnopolitical leaders and entrepreneurs develop new attitudes and discourses toward religion and/or ethnicity or nationalism? Why and how do political elites swing between "religionism" and "nationalism"? What are the general causes and mechanisms of such swings? What might the enabling and/ or constraining factors be in ethnopolitical elites' efforts to mold ethnic categories and movements? Further, how are ethnonational boundaries affected by such elite actions and discourse? What roles do elites play in ethnic boundary-making processes? Why, when, and how do they demarcate, maintain, and transform the symbolic and social boundaries of an ethnic category or movement? What might the implications of the case of the Islamic opening of the secular, leftist Kurdish movement be for the broader theoretical debate on ethnicity and nationalism, particularly for ethnic boundary-making processes?

Methodological Approach

Focusing on the Islamic opening of the secular, left-oriented Kurdish ethnopolitical movement in Turkey in the past decades, this research project conducts a *case study*. Defined as "the intensive study of a single case for the purpose of understanding a larger class of similar units" (Gerring 2007, 20) or, similarly, as an "extensive and in-depth analysis of some social and political phenomenon" (Yin 2009, 4), the case study is quite useful for investigating novel phenomena, analyzing complex causal mechanisms and processes, and assisting with hypothesis generation as well as theory development and refinement (see George and Bennett 2005; Gerring 2007; Levy 2008; Brady and Collier 2010).

With regard to the units of analysis, this study qualifies as a single-case study, and so I focus on within-case variation (i.e., shifts in the Kurdish movement's attitudes toward Islam and Islamic actors). In addition,

I conduct *process tracing*, which is a particular type of within-case analysis. Associated with small-N, case-oriented research, process tracing is advantageous for uncovering causal mechanisms, processes, and sequences underlying observed phenomena or outcomes (see George and Bennett 2005). Process tracing is also quite helpful for analyzing the sequence of events, decisions, and steps over time that links the initial events and conditions to outcomes (i.e., the Islamic opening of the secular Kurdish ethnonationalist movement in Turkey).

To obtain more credible, valid, and persuasive results, and thus a more comprehensive and deeper understanding of the issue, I also use *triangulation* as a research strategy, which simply means "the observation of the research issue from (at least) two different points" (Flick 2004, 178). Triangulation is achieved by using multiple research techniques and a wide range of data sources (Rothbauer 2008; S. Hastings 2010; Stoker 2011). Such a combination (qualitative and quantitative evidence) is expected to increase inferential leverage and confidence in the ensuing results and so generate a more accurate and complete picture of the phenomenon under investigation (Bryman 2004; Cox and Hassard 2010; Tarrow 2010; Stoker 2011). I apply *data triangulation*, which refers to utilizing "data drawn from different sources and at different times, in different places or from different people" (Flick 2004, 178). Thus, this research project utilizes various approaches to and techniques of data collection and data sources, primarily semistructured, in-depth interviews; ethnographic field research; textual analyses (e.g., discourse analysis of key documents); and electoral data.

For this study, I conducted 104 interviews with 88 participants in several provinces in Turkey (primarily Ankara, Diyarbakır, Istanbul, and Tunceli) between 2011 and 2015.[7] Informants were selected from different political circles (e.g., Islamic and secular), professions (e.g., politicians, local administrators, intellectuals, columnists, activists, civil society representatives), and ethnic origins (e.g., Turks and Kurds).[8] I also participated as an observer in the Democratic Islam Congress, organized by the Kurdish movement in Diyarbakır in May 2014, where I had the opportunity to sit in on and make detailed notes of discussions within the Kurdish movement about religious issues. My empirical analyses are enriched with textual analyses that include discourse analyses of the key documents and texts (e.g., publications or political programs of Kurdish organizations) and statements by Kurdish ethnopolitical elites and leading figures of the Kurdistan Workers' Party (Partiya Karkaren Kurdistan, PKK) and electoral data (i.e., electoral performance of pro-Kurdish political parties at local and general elections).

Conceptual Issues

It has been observed that "conceptual wrangles continue to haunt" ethnicity and nationalism studies (Cederman 2002, 422). As such struggles still persist in the literature (see also Hale 2004; Wolff 2006; Chandra 2012b), it is necessary to define the key concepts used throughout this book, that is, ethnicity, ethnonationalism/ethnopolitics, nation, and nationalism. When we look at the existing literature, we see a plethora of definitions and uses of these concepts, some of which are contradictory. Instead of addressing the persisting conceptual challenges or offering the "right" definition, in this volume I simply provide a working definition of these terms. Rather than creating new definitions, I benefited from several definitions of these key terms in the existing literature (e.g., Weber 1968; Schermerhorn 1970; Kasfir 1979; van den Berghe 1981; Gellner 1983; Horowitz 1985; Anderson 1991; Olzak 1992; Cornell 1993; Connor 1994; Hutchinson and Smith 1996; Kellas 1998; Conversi 1999; Cederman 2002; Brubaker, Loveman, and Stamatov 2004; Hale 2004; Chai 2005; Chandra 2006, 2012c; Smith 2006; Cornell and Hartmann 2007; R. Jenkins 2008; Bayar 2009; Brubaker 2009; Wimmer 2013).

The existing definitions tend to treat ethnicity as a type of collective identity and/or category. In addition, we can identify three major dimensions of ethnicity as a collective identity across those definitions: *hereditary/innate* (e.g., common descent or ancestry, language, phenotype, homeland or region of origin); *cultural* (e.g., norms, values, traditions, symbols, beliefs, memories); and *subjective/cognitive* (e.g., self-consciousness, self-identification, imagination, recognition, classification, categorization, interpretation). Thus, borrowing from those definitions, this study considers ethnicity as a subjectively felt belonging to a collectivity or group, distinguished by a claim to a common origin or descent (real or putative),[9] language, and territory (actual or mythical homelands), as well as a somewhat shared distinct culture (e.g., myths, memories, symbols, values, customs, rituals, norms) (see also Wimmer 2013, 7).

Ethnonationalism (or *ethnic nationalism*) refers to a political movement or a form of identity politics (see Rothschild 1981; Breuilly 1993; Lecours 2000; Romano 2006; Wolff 2006; Eriksen 2010). As Rothschild (1981, 6) states, ethnonationalism is "the transformation of ethnicity from a purely personal quest for meaning and belonging into a group demand for respect and power." Another definition suggests that "ethnonationalism is the action of a group that claims some degree of self-government on the grounds that it is united by a special sense of solidarity emanating from one or more shared features and therefore forms a 'nation'" (Lecours 2000, 105). For Romano (2006, 23), ethnonationalist movements "seek to heighten ethnic identification within a target population and then in turn politicize ethnic identity in order to challenge the state." Finally, Eriksen (2010, 10) remarks that "most ethnic groups, even if they ask for recognition and cultural rights, do not demand command over a state. When the political leaders of an ethnic movement make demands to this effect, the ethnic movement therefore by definition becomes a nationalist movement." These definitions and treatments suggest that in the case of ethnonationalist movements and processes, ethnicity is no longer an issue of cultural or social markers but an issue of politics. As a particular type of political movement, ethnonationalist movements might have quite diverse demands, ranging from the legal recognition of their distinct ethnic identities to certain cultural and political rights, such as language rights and power-sharing arrangements such as regional autonomy or total separation.

Many definitions of *nation*, on the other hand, associate the term with notions of self-rule or self-government, political autonomy, independence, territorial self-determination, or sovereignty and statehood (e.g., Kedourie 1960; Gellner 1983; Anderson 1991; Brass 1991; Calhoun 1993; Kellas 1998; van den Berghe 2001; Cederman 2002; Wolff 2006; Cornell and Hartmann 2007; R. Jenkins 2008; Barker 2009; Eriksen 2010; Wimmer 2013; Brubaker 2014). For example, Calhoun (1993, 229) states the following: "Certainly a crucial difference between ethnicities and nations is that the latter are envisioned as intrinsically political communities, as sources of sovereignty, while this is not central to the definition of ethnicities." Barker (2009, 9) concurs: "What separates a nation from an ethnic group or other group identity is political ambition—specifically the goal of self-rule or self-determination. . . . A movement becomes nationalist in nature when its goal becomes self-determination." Similarly, Eriksen (2010, 144) puts forward that "nationalism and ethnicity are kindred concepts, and the majority of nationalisms are ethnic in character. The distinction between nationalism and ethnicity as analytical concepts is a simple one. . . . A nationalist ideology is an ethnic ideology which demands a state on behalf of the ethnic group." Finally, Wimmer (2013, 8) notes that "if members of an ethnic community have developed national aspirations and demand (or already control) a state of their own, we describe such categories and groups as nations" (see also Wolff 2006, 54).

Regarding *nationalism*, the literature treats it as a political ideology/principle/doctrine or as a political/ideological movement. For Kedourie (1960, 9), nationalism is constituted by three propositions: "that humanity is naturally divided into nations, that nations are known by certain characteristics which can be ascertained, and that the only legitimate type of government is national self-government." According to Gellner (1983, 1), nationalism is a political principle, which "holds that the political and national unit should be congruent." Breuilly (1993, 2) treats nationalism as a political movement with three basic assertions: "a) There exists a nation with an explicit and peculiar character, b) The interests and values of this nation take priority over all other interests and values, [and] c) The nation must be as independent as possible, which usually requires at least the attainment of political sovereignty." Considering nationalism as an ideological movement, Smith (2006, 175) suggests that nationalism advocates "the attainment and maintenance of autonomy, unity and identity on behalf of a population, some of whose members deem it to constitute an actual or potential 'nation.'"

Given these definitions or conceptualizations, how should we conceptually treat the case of the Kurdish movement? Following the foregoing definitions and the general orientation in the existing literature on the Kurdish issue (e.g., see Entessar 1992, 2010; van Bruinessen 2000a, 2000b; White 2000; Natali 2005; Romano 2006; Marcus 2007; Watts 2010; Gürbüz 2016), this study treats Kurdishness and the Kurdish movement as typical forms of ethnicity and ethnonationalism, respectively. Although the origin of the Kurds is still disputed, there is a general consensus that they are the descendants of the Medes, an Indo-European tribe (see Entessar 1992, 3; White 2000, 14). The Kurdish language is regarded as a member of the Iranian languages, which stem from the Indo-European family (Entessar 1992, 4; van Bruinessen 2000a; White 2000, 16; Jwaideh 2006, 11). The most widely spoken dialects are Kurmanji, Zaza, Sorani, and Gorani (van Bruinessen 2000a; Romano 2006, 3). Kurds, who inhabit a land divided among Turkey, Iraq, Iran, and Syria, are regarded as one of the largest ethnic communities in the world without an independent state of their own (e.g., Gottlieb 1994; van Bruinessen 2000a; Gunter 2004). In the Turkish setting, Kurds constitute the second-largest ethnic group after Turks. Since the Turkish state has not collected data on ethnicity since 1965, there has since been no clear consensus on the size of the current Kurdish population in Turkey; estimations, however, correspond to 15% to 18% of the total Turkish population (see also Romano 2006, 24; Marcus 2007, 3; Watts 2010, xi; Yeğen, Tol, and Çalışkan 2016, 16).[10] The results of our public opinion surveys (conducted in 2011, 2013, and 2015) are in line with this estimate: on average, 16% of survey respondents identified themselves as Kurdish.[11] Despite massive migration to major western and central cities such as Istanbul, Ankara, and Izmir, at least half of Kurds still live in the eastern and southeastern provinces of Turkey (see Koc, Hancioglu, and Cavlin 2008, 450).[12] Regarding religious characteristics, our survey results suggest that the vast majority (around 90%) of the Kurds in Turkey, similar to their Turkish compatriots, subscribe to the Sunni *mezhep* or *madhab* (a Muslim school of law or *fiqh* [jurisprudence]).[13] The majority of Sunni Kurds (around 70%) adhere to the Shafi school, while 30% practice within the Hanefi school.[14]

The term *Kurdish movement* in this study refers to secular, left-oriented pro-Kurdish groups, which constitute by far the largest, most powerful Kurdish ethnonationalist or ethnopolitical movement in the Turkish setting (Marcus 2007, 267; Watts 2010, 22). Since the mid-1980s, this movement has posed a major challenge to the Turkish state (see Gunter 1997; Özbudun 2000; Kramer 2000; Moustakis and Chaudhuri 2005; Somer 2005; Marcus 2007; Watts 2010; Aydin and Emrence 2015).[15] As a culturally and politically self-aware ethnic group, Kurds have been demanding certain cultural rights such as speaking, publishing, and broadcasting in Kurdish, public education in Kurdish, and political rights such as constitutional recognition of Kurdish ethnic identity, political representation, and power-sharing arrangements such as decentralization, self-rule (*özerklik, öz yönetim*), or regional autonomy.

Regarding the state attitude, a politics of denial, suppression, and assimilation dominated Turkey's Kurdish policy from the mid-1920s until the 1990s (Imset 1996; van Bruinessen 2000a). In this period, the state simply denied the ethnopolitical nature of the problem, defining it instead as an issue of socioeconomic underdevelopment or backwardness (i.e., the prevalence of feudalism, ignorance, and poverty in the southeast) and a security concern (banditry and terrorism incited and sponsored by foreign powers) (see also Yeğen 1996, 2007, 2011; Romano 2006; Marcus 2007; Romano and Gurses 2014; Aydin and Emrence 2015). As a solution, the state primarily relied on military measures to enhance national and regional security and exterminate the PKK (e.g., declaring a state of emergency in the region; updating military technology; increasing the number of troops deployed in the region; recruiting local people as armed village guards; empowering border protection and security; engaging in cross-border operations; depopulating the region through forced village evacuations, mass arrests, extrajudicial executions, etc.) and socioeconomic policies to promote modernization and development in the area (e.g., efforts to raise income and education levels; transferring economic resources; facilitating and encouraging investments and improving infrastructure).

Beginning in the early 2000s, however, the Turkish state moderated its attitude vis-à-vis the Kurdish issue and recognized the ethnopolitical aspect of the problem and so initiated democratization efforts in addition to socioeconomic and security measures. In this new era, Turkish governments have implemented major legal and institutional changes and granted some cultural rights to Kurds, such as legalizing publishing and broadcasting in Kurdish and learning the Kurdish language, allowing parents to give their children Kurdish names, allowing political party campaigns in Kurdish, and introducing elective Kurdish courses. Since 2009, the Turkish and Kurdish sides have also been negotiating for a final peaceful settlement of the three-decade-long armed conflict. Some major initiatives in this new period have been the 2009 Kurdish Opening and the 2009–2011 Oslo Talks with the PKK leadership. In late 2012, the government launched a new initiative to find a peaceful solution to the armed conflict and started direct talks with imprisoned PKK leader Abdullah Öcalan (also known as the Peace Process). In March 2013, Öcalan sent a message from prison on İmralı Island (in the Sea of Marmara) and called for the end of armed struggle against the Turkish state and declared a cease-fire. Following Öcalan's historic message, the PKK leadership in Northern Iraq declared a cease-fire and announced that the PKK would withdraw its militants from Turkey. However, in the aftermath of the June 2015 general elections, the cease-fire and the peace process collapsed, and the severe armed conflict between security forces and the PKK resumed.

Rather than providing a general survey of the Kurdish issue in Tur-key, this study focuses on the dominant wing of the Kurdish movement (i.e., the secular, leftist, ethnonationalist formations) and examines its relations with Islam, which have shown interesting shifts and transforma-tions in the past decades.[16] As I analyze the shifting attitude of the Kurd-ish movement toward Islam, I focus on both the legal and illegal wings of the movement. On the illegal side, we have the PKK as the main actor. As a secular, leftist, and armed movement, the PKK emerged out of the revolutionary left in Turkey in the late 1970s and became the dominant political formation of Turkey's Kurds (see also N. Özcan 1999; Yavuz 2001, 9–10; Taspinar 2005; Romano 2006; Marcus 2007; Tezcür 2009, 2015; Jongerden and Akkaya 2011). Initially, its ultimate goal was to estab-lish a united Kurdistan based on Marxist-Leninist principles. For that purpose, the PKK initiated an armed struggle against the Turkish state in the first half of the 1980s. Since then, the fighting between Turkish security forces and PKK members has resulted in over 35,000 casualties, the destruction of about 3,000 villages, and the internal displacement of at least 3,000,000 people.[17] By the mid-1990s the PKK had started to distance itself from separatist and Marxist ideas. Instead, the PKK-led Kurdish movement proposed a peaceful solution to the Kurdish conflict and appropriated a discourse of democratic rights and freedoms for Kurds (Imset 1996; White 2000; Yavuz 2001; Romano 2006; Gunes 2012b).[18] Especially since the early 2000s, the PKK has rejected claims for national liberation and statehood and instead put increasing emphasis on Kurd-ish rights and demands, such as the constitutional recognition of Kurdish ethnic identity, language rights (e.g., education in one's mother language), and political and administrative decentralization and power-sharing ar-rangements. For instance, rejecting secession, PKK leader Öcalan pro-posed "democratic autonomy" (*demokratik özerklik*) for Turkey and "democratic confederalism" (*demokratik konfederalizm*) for the region.[19]

On the legal side, there were several pro-Kurdish, secular, ethnic po-litical parties that appeared on the Turkish political scene in the early 1990s (Watts 1999, 2006, 2010).[20] These parties operated in a format that could be called *issue parties*: their primary concern was the Kurdish issue. In general, they argued that the Kurdish problem could not be reduced to a security issue; it was instead a complicated problem with ethnic, political, psychological, and socioeconomic dimensions. Hence, they advocated a peaceful and democratic solution to the Kurdish conflict and further democracy in Turkey. As a result, these parties have articulated several demands, such as the constitutional recognition of Kurdish ethnic identity, cultural rights (e.g., publishing, broadcasting, and education in Kurdish), decentralization and empowerment of local government, ending the state of emergency in southeastern Turkey, investigating extrajudicial killings, removing the village guards system, and a general amnesty for PKK members. They also demanded socioeconomic development in the southeast, where Kurds constitute the vast majority of the population (see also Watts 2010). However, these parties were accused of involvement in separatist activities and propaganda against the indivisible integrity of the Turkish territory and nation and of helping the "separatist," "terrorist" PKK. As a result, most of the successive pro-Kurdish political parties were banned by Turkey's Constitutional Court. Currently, the Peoples' Democratic Party (Halkların Demokratik Partisi, HDP), which was formed in 2012 and succeeded the BDP in summer 2014, represents the Kurdish movement in legal party politics in Turkey.

Findings/Arguments

This study analyzes the shifting attitude of the secular, leftist Kurdish movement toward Islam and Islamic actors in the past decades through the lens of the boundary approach, which is primarily concerned with boundary-making or construction processes such as the emergence, reproduction, and transformation of the symbolic and social boundaries of an ethnic group or movement (e.g., see Barth 1969a; Lamont 2000; Lamont and Molnár 2002; Alba 2005; Wimmer 2008a, 2013; Jackson and Molokotos-Liedeman 2015). As the empirical chapters illustrate, Kurdish ethnopolitics since its inception in the late 1970s has involved striking boundary processes (e.g., contesting or challenging the official understanding of national identity and of the state's discourse on the Kurdish issue, as well as making, unmaking, and remaking the boundaries of Kurdishness and of the Kurdish movement itself) and so offers us an excellent laboratory for exploring ethnic boundary-making processes and dynamics.

It is, however, unfortunate that the boundary approach has so far not been employed in a comprehensive way in studying the Kurdish case.[21] One recent study (Aydin and Emrence 2015), which analyzes the organizational, ideological, and strategic aspects of Kurdish insurgency and counterinsurgency, attempts to utilize this approach. However, that study focuses on the territorial zones of armed conflict between the PKK and Turkish security forces. Due to its conscious focus on physical or territorial borders of the conflict between the Kurdish armed groups and the security forces, it neglects boundary-making processes and dynamics at symbolic and social levels. Thus, as one of the initial studies utilizing the boundary approach in the Kurdish context, this work not only will shed light on the recent shifts within the Kurdish movement with respect to its relations with Islam and Islamic actors and so help us gain insights into Kurdish ethnopolitics but also will contribute to our understanding of ethnic boundary processes, particularly boundary-making strategies and boundary contestations.

This study divides the evolving relations between the secular Kurdish movement and Islam into three different stages or periods: (1) an indifferent/apathetic and/or antagonistic/aggressive attitude in the 1970s and 1980s, (2) a sometimes ambivalent but increasingly friendly approach in the 1990s, and (3) an accommodative attitude and the rise of a Kurdish-Islamic synthesis since the early 2000s. Approaching such a trajectory from the perspective of boundary-making theory, this study treats the Kurdish movement's Islamic opening as a major case of boundary work and suggests that each of these periods is associated with a different boundary-making strategy: boundary contraction, boundary expansion, and boundary reinforcement or empowerment, respectively. Thus, with a hostile attitude toward Islam and Islamic actors and movements in the 1970s and 1980s, the Kurdish ethnonationalist movement contracted both symbolic boundaries of Kurdishness in its ethnonational imaginary and the social boundaries of the movement itself. By developing an increasingly friendly approach toward Islam and Islamic circles in the 1990s, secular Kurdish ethnopolitical elites expanded the contracted symbolic and social boundaries of the movement. Since the early 2000s, we have seen even more systematic and comprehensive efforts by secular Kurdish ethnopolitical elites to accommodate Islam and Islamic actors. These efforts might be interpreted as the reinforcement or empowerment of expanded boundaries.

Regarding the causes of the Kurdish movement's boundary expansion (i.e., its Islamic opening), I demonstrate that a group of strategic and ideational factors at global, national, and regional levels encouraged and/or forced Kurdish ethnopolitical leaders to redraw symbolic and social boundaries of the movement. First, the end of the Cold War in the early 1990s undermined support for Marxist ideas in Turkey in general, and as a result, the PKK-led movement began to distance itself from Marxism (for instance, in 1995 it removed the hammer and sickle from its flag). *Ideological shift* (i.e., the declining influence of Marxism) created more favorable conditions for the rise of a more positive approach toward religion within the movement. In other words, the declining influence of Marxism facilitated the Islamic opening of the Kurdish movement in the post-1990 period.

We should also take into account of the role of movement's *need to expand its social basis* and *increase its popularity* in Kurdish society. As is well known, the Kurdish movement, led and dominated by the PKK, emerged as a small-scale armed struggle in the late 1970s. However, the movement's survival and success in its struggle against the central state necessitated expanding its popularity and support among the Kurdish masses. This effort required developing a friendlier approach to the traditions, values, and norms of Kurdish society, such as Islamic beliefs, values, and attachments. Indeed, by the early 1990s, the Kurdish struggle had gained mass character (i.e., turned into a mass movement). Such a transformation prompted the movement to expand its activities into the legal political arena. As a result, the People's Labor Party (Halkın Emek Partisi, HEP), established in June 1990, became the first legal pro-Kurdish party. Kurdish ethnopolitical leadership expected that such lawful formations would give new voice to the movement and so expand its legitimacy and influence among the Kurdish masses. The expansion of the movement's social basis further incited the ethnopolitical leadership to be more accommodative vis-à-vis the values, beliefs, and norms of Kurdish society. In other words, as the PKK-led Kurdish movement diffused into Kurdish society, Islamic ideas, values, and circles gradually made their way into the movement. In brief, the need to expand the group's popular support base forced the secular Kurdish leadership to have more respect for Kurdish culture, which has been characterized by a religious, traditional, and conservative lifestyle.

Another factor that facilitated the adoption of a more positive stance toward Islam and Islamic actors was *electoral pressures* (i.e., the rise in popularity among Kurds of pro-Islamic political parties). In the 1990s, pro-Islamic National Outlook Movement parties (i.e., the Welfare Party, Refah Partisi [RP], and the Virtue Party, Fazilet Partisi [FP]), and in the 2000s, the AKP gained substantial electoral popularity in the Kurdish region. As chapter 3 shows, the main political rivals of the secular Kurdish movement in regional electoral politics have been conservative or Islamic political formations. Electoral competition with Islamic or conservative political actors further urged the Kurdish ethnopolitical leadership to accommodate Islam and Islamic actors.

Related to electoral pressures and dynamics, we should also acknowledge the distinct role of *legitimacy struggles* between Kurdish ethnopolitical elites and their rivals. Both legal and illegal Islamic or conservative groups (e.g., the AKP and Kurdish Hezbollah) and the Turkish state have constantly attempted to delegitimize the secular Kurdish movement in the eyes of the Kurdish masses, particularly among conservative Kurds, by calling Kurdish ethnopolitical actors "Marxist," "atheist," "infidels," "heretical," or "un-Islamic" and therefore "illegitimate." In other words, conservative political circles and the state have attempted to contract religious boundaries with an intention to delegitimize the secular Kurdish movement and marginalize pro-Kurdish parties in the electoral contest. My in-depth analysis of the Kurdish case indicates that such boundary-making efforts and boundary struggles or contestations can become intense and antagonistic especially during electoral periods. Facing such labels and accusations, the Kurdish ethnopolitical leadership felt the need to substantially shift its attitude toward religion. Put differently, such boundary work by Kurdish ethnopolitical leadership was also a counterstrategy against its political opponents' efforts to contract Islamic religious boundaries.

The boundary expansion in the Kurdish case was not without any tension, however. This study shows that the boundary work by Kurdish ethnopolitical elites involved both internal and external tensions and contestations. Internally, Alevi Kurds, who are relatively more liberal and secular than Sunni Kurds, raised some concerns and attempted to contest the rise of the movement's Islam-friendly approach. Alevi Kurds' contestation of the boundary work by the Kurdish ethnopolitical leadership suggests that an ethnic group's internal heterogeneity increases the likelihood of internal boundary contestations. In this case, the Alevi Kurds' contestation of the Islamic opening failed due to the highly centralized and hierarchical structure of the Kurdish movement. As the book's empirical chapters show, one notable feature of the Kurdish movement has been its centralized and hierarchical organizational structure, led and dominated by its unchallenged leader and theoretician, Abdullah Öcalan. This situation suggests that although intragroup heterogeneity increases the likelihood of boundary contestation by coethnics, such internal contestations may have limited impact in hierarchically organized ethnonationalist movements. Externally, conservative, Islamic, and nationalist rival political actors (e.g., the ruling AKP) have tried to delegitimize the movement's efforts by claiming that it still subscribes to Marxist-

Leninist and atheist ideas and understandings. In other words, as a response to the Kurdish movement's boundary expansion, they attempted to shrink religious boundaries. Thus, the Kurdish case provides us a rich laboratory in which to conduct an in-depth analysis of the processes of boundary contestations (internal and external) that are likely to arise when such major boundary work takes place.

This particular case has major theoretical and practical implications for ethnicity and nationalism studies in general and for Kurdish ethnonationalism and Turkish politics in particular. The ramifications of the study will be discussed in detail in the conclusion. Briefly, this study will add to the several theoretical debates within ethnicity and nationalism studies. First, by examining the role of ethnopolitical elites in ethnonationalist processes (e.g., boundary making), this study sheds light on the basic theoretical rivalry between primordialist and circumstantialist/constructionist/instrumentalist perspectives. The in-depth analysis of the case of the Islamic opening of the secular Kurdish ethnonationalist movement suggests that we need to transcend such dichotomous understandings and instead give due attention to both structural and agential and given/durable/fixed and flexible/contingent/constructed aspects of ethnicity and nationalism.

Second, by analyzing the shifting attitude of the secular Kurdish movement toward Islam from the perspective of the boundary approach, this study shows that the theory has much to offer in enhancing our understanding of ethnicity and nationalism phenomena. The book contributes to the research on ethnic boundary making in several ways. By investigating boundary processes in the Kurdish case, the book illuminates how ethnopolitical elites make and remake symbolic and social boundaries of an ethnic movement, what strategies boundary makers follow, and how boundary contestations (internal or external) take place. The Kurdish case particularly helps us generate or extract some specific hypotheses about the processes of boundary contestation. Unfortunately the existing studies of ethnic boundary making offer us little insights about boundary contestation, and so it remains an undertheorized issue in the existing literature. This study suggests that boundary making is inherently a political process, which might involve both internal and external struggles or contestations over symbolic and social boundaries. Regarding when and under what conditions boundary contestation is more likely to take place, this study shows that electoral periods increase the likelihood of external boundary contestation; in relatively more heterogeneous ethnic groups or movements, internal boundary contestation (i.e., struggle over symbolic and social boundaries among coethnics) becomes more likely; and in the case of ethnonationalist movements characterized by a hierarchical organizational structure and unified leadership (i.e., the absence or weakness of elite competition or rivalry), internal boundary contestations is less likely to succeed.

This study also enhances our understanding of the interplay between religion and ethnicity and nationalism in the context of a Muslim society. From that perspective, the study enhances our knowledge and understanding of the role of religion in Kurdish ethnopolitics. For instance, assuming a mutually exclusive relationship between religious and ethnic identifications and attachments, many people within conservative or pro-Islamic circles claim that promoting Islam and Islamic values in society would contain or constrain Kurdish ethnonationalism (also known as the "Islamic peace hypothesis"). Can Islam really serve as an antidote for Kurdish ethnonationalism? This study expands our comprehension of the recent developments and shifts within Kurdish ethnopolitics with respect to religion and shows that it is problematic to expect Islam to contain ethnonationalist orientations or aspirations. In other words, the findings of this study challenge the Islamic peace hypothesis.

This study also discusses the implications of the Islamic opening of the secular, leftist Kurdish movement for Turkish leftist politics and the debates on political Islam. As has been widely acknowledged, most of the Turkish leftist circles have been strongly secular and antireligious. The shift toward religion in the Kurdish case implies that such boundary work may trigger similar debates and possibly transformations in Turkish leftist circles.

Finally, this particular case study also has major ramifications for the debates on political Islam. The empirical analyses show that while Kurdish ethnopolitical elites have expanded the symbolic and social boundaries of the movement to incorporate Islamic ideas and actors, they have also attempted to promote a more liberal, democratic interpretation of Islam. Given that the rise of relentless violence by radical jihadist Islamic groups (e.g., Al-Qaeda, Boko Haram, and the Islamic State of Iraq and Syria—ISIS or Daesh) across several parts of the world in the past decades has revived the conventional debate about whether Islam is really compatible with secular, liberal, democratic values, such an initiative by the secular Kurdish movement becomes quite significant and deserves further scholarly attention.

Organization of the Book

The book is organized as follows: Chapter 1 focuses on theoretical issues. The chapter first presents the main assumptions and arguments of ethnic boundary-making theory. Next, it introduces key terms such as the notions of boundary and symbolic and social boundaries. Then, the chapter discusses main boundary-making strategies and internal and external boundary contestation processes, which are likely to be triggered by major boundary work. Finally, the chapter advances some specific hypotheses about boundary-making processes, particularly about boundary contestation.

Chapter 2 presents the evolving relations between the secular Kurdish movement and Islam since the late 1970s and interprets the movement's shifting attitude toward Islam from the perspective of the boundary approach. This chapter shows that the movement, which initially adopted a secular, Marxist outlook, distanced itself from Islam and Islamic actors and movements during the 1970s and 1980s. In other words, the Kurdish movement showed a strong secular ethnonationalist character in its initial period. To put it in more theoretical terms, by dissociating themselves from Islam, the Kurdish ethnopolitical leaders contracted the symbolic boundaries of Kurdishness and the social boundaries of the movement itself. Then, the chapter documents the rise of an increasingly positive and welcoming attitude toward Islam and Islamic actors within the secular Kurdish movement in the post-1990 period, arguing that Kurdish ethnopolitical leaders were expanding the social and symbolic boundaries of the movement. Finally, the chapter shows that in the 2000s the movement initiated much more systematic and comprehensive steps to accommodate Islam and Islamic actors, reinforcing the expanded boundaries.

Chapter 3 analyzes the causes, mechanisms, and consequences of Kurdish movement's boundary work. The chapter addresses the following questions: Why, how, and with what consequences has the secular Kurdish movement adopted a much more Islam-friendly attitude? How can we theorize the Islamic opening of the secular Kurdish movement? What can we learn about ethnic boundary-making processes from this particular case? The chapter draws attention to the role of four causal factors behind Kurdish boundary expansion: ideological shift (i.e., the declining influence of Marxism); the need to expand the movement's social basis and popularity; electoral politics; and legitimacy struggles. The chapter then scrutinizes internal and external boundary contestations activated by the Kurdish ethnopolitical leadership's boundary work and analyzes whether such contestations had any impact on boundary-making efforts of the Kurdish leadership. The chapter finally engages with some possible alternative considerations.

Finally, the conclusion first summarizes the key arguments of the book and then focuses on the broader theoretical and practical implications of the study, particularly for the boundary approach (e.g., ethnic boundary-making and boundary contestation processes), for ethnicity and nationalism studies (the ramifications for structural, e.g., the primordialism and sociobiological approaches, and agential, e.g. constructionist, instrumentalist, and elite theory, perspectives in the field), for the nexus between religion and nationalism, for the evolution of Kurdish ethnopolitics, and for the debates on secularism and political Islam in the region.

Given such a structure of the book, readers who are not really interested in the theoretical discussion on the processes of ethnic boundary-making and boundary contestation might skip chapter 1 and move to the remaining chapters for the analyses of the Islamic opening of the secular, leftist Kurdish movement in the past decades and the broader implications of the case of Kurdish boundary work.

1

The Boundary Approach to Ethnicity and Nationalism

In analyzing the shifting attitude of the Kurdish movement toward Islam in the past decades, this study utilizes the boundary approach as a main theoretical framework. As many studies also acknowledge, boundary making is an inherent part of ethnic or national group formation and identification, as well as of ethnic and nationalist movements. For instance, Nash (1989, 10) convincingly explains, "Where there is a group [ethnic group or movement], there is some sort of boundary, and where there are boundaries, there are mechanisms to maintain them." Similarly, Wimmer (2013, 3) suggests, "Social and symbolic boundaries emerge when actors distinguish between different ethnic categories and when they treat members of such categories differently." Regarding ethnic or nationalist movements, Conversi (1995) indicates that nationalism entails boundary creation and boundary maintenance processes. In the same way, Eriksen (2010, 10) remarks, "Like ethnic ideologies, nationalism stresses the cultural similarity of its adherents and, by implication, it draws boundaries vis-à-vis others, who thereby become outsiders" (see also Handler 1988; Cornell and Hartmann 2007). Hence, the boundary approach is a highly relevant theoretical tool for ethnicity and nationalism studies. As the current study shows, it is also highly useful in making better sense of the causes, mechanisms, and consequences of the recent shifts and transformations in Kurdish ethnopolitics (i.e., the Islamic opening of the secular, leftist Kurdish movement in the past decades).

This chapter first presents the main assumptions and arguments of the boundary approach and then draws some specific, exploratory hypotheses about ethnic boundary-making processes, particularly about the processes of (internal and external) boundary contestation.

Ethnic Boundary-Making Theory: Assumptions and Arguments

Boundary-making theory, which is primarily concerned with boundary-making or construction processes such as the demarcation, reproduction, and transformation of the boundaries of ethnic or national categories and of ethnonationalist movements, was first presented in the late 1960s in a collection of ethnographic studies edited by Fredrik Barth (1969a).[1] Challenging the idea that stable and shared intrinsic, cultural features constitute ethnicity, this seminal work offers a more subjectivist, relational, processual, and interactionist approach to ethnicity and suggests that the focus of research should be on the dynamics of intergroup interactions, encounters, boundaries, and self-categorization or self-identification processes rather than on the "cultural stuff" that ethnic or national categories contain. For Barth (1969b), groups are the products of boundary production and reproduction during interactions between insiders and outsiders (see also R. Jenkins 2015, 20). As Brubaker (2009, 29) notes, "Barth was reacting against the static objectivism of then prevailing approaches to ethnicity, which sought to ground ethnicity in stable, objectively observable patterns of shared culture." Along the same lines, Cederman (2002, 413) suggests, "Reacting to such reified conceptions of ethnicity, Fredrik Barth (1969) shifted the attention from cultural 'essences' to ethnogenesis through boundary formation. . . . According to this type of constructivist anthropology, groups do not consist of objective cultural traits but need to be viewed through the self-categorization of [their] members." Similarly, R. Jenkins (2015, 14) notes, "[For] Barth, boundaries are produced and reproduced during interaction across them; thus group boundaries are osmotic, in that there is always traffic across them, in each direction. This interaction also produces and reproduces the groups on either side of the boundary. Which means that it is not what is within the boundary—the well-known 'cultural stuff'—but the boundary maintenance processes that constitute and reconstitute the group; they are in many ways the group."

Wimmer, who provides the most advanced version of the boundary-making approach in more recent literature on ethnicity and nationalism, defines its main features as follows:

> [In the boundary-making approach] ethnic distinctions result from marking and maintaining a boundary irrespective of the cultural differences observed from the outside. . . . Researchers would no longer study "the culture" of ethnic group A or B, but rather how the ethnic boundary between A and B [is] inscribed onto a landscape of continuous cultural transitions. Ethnicity [would be] no longer synonymous with objectively defined cultures, but rather [would refer] to the subjective ways in which actors [mark] group boundaries by pointing to the specific diacritics that [distinguish] them from ethnic others. (2013, 22–23)

Thus, focusing on the role of intergroup processes and dynamics in the social construction (production and reproduction) of ethnic boundaries and so in ethnic-group formation, this approach provides a dynamic, practical, processual, and situational understanding of ethnicity and nationhood (Brubaker 2009). Therefore, this perspective treats ethnic or national boundaries as "fluid, policed, crossable, movable" (Lamont 2014, 815; see also Wallman 1978; Lamont 2000; Eriksen 2010). Sharing the Barthian framework, Wallman (quoted in R. Jenkins 1986, 175), for instance, notes that "ethnicity is the process by which 'their' difference is used to enhance the sense of 'us' for purposes of organization or identification. . . . Because it takes two, ethnicity can only happen at the boundary of 'us,' in contact or confrontation or by contract with 'them.' And as the sense of 'us' changes, so the boundary between 'us' and 'them' shifts. Not only does the boundary shift, but the criteria which mark it change" (see also Esman 1994; Terrier 2015).

The Notion of Boundary

Before going further, some discussion on the key term of this approach (i.e., the notion of *boundary*) will be useful. A boundary refers to "simultaneously *where* something stops and something else begins, and something that *indicates* where something stops and something else begins" (R. Jenkins 2015, 13–14). For Conversi (1999, 564), "The point of contact between different others, the domain—imaginary or real—where in-group and out-group meet and face each other is called boundary" (see also Wallman 1978, 206). Quite importantly, Conversi (1999, 564) warns against the interchangeable use of the terms *boundary* and *border* by noting, "the latter may simply refer to a line drawn between two spaces, whereas the former may be used to stress the binding quality of what, and who, is included on this side of the fence."[2]

Boundaries serve key functions in sociopolitical life. As Tilly (2005, 133) suggests, social boundaries "interrupt, divide, circumscribe, or segregate distributions of population or activity within social fields." Likewise, Conversi also lists several functions of social boundaries. A boundary, for Conversi (1999, 565),

> does not simply refer to the outward-looking practice of delimitation, but also to the inward-looking process of self-definition. A boundary can encircle, enclose, contour, and outline, as well as frame, fix, set, assign, and establish. In other words, boundaries are made to bind. . . . And, although a boundary may be an hindrance or a barrier, it is also a tie and a connective liaison, its metaphorical next of kin being the bridge. Boundaries circumscribe separate realms, as well as delimit and mark out distinct values, behaviours, and laws. Their restrictive and exclusive power is compensated by their inclusive character vis-à-vis what and who lies within the boundary. Boundaries are normative insofar as they have the power to restrict, prescribe, and proscribe.

As this quotation also implies, other than separating in-group members from out-group members, boundaries also divide "the meanings that are attached to the identities on either side" (Cornell and Hartmann 2007, 84). In brief, the notion of boundary in this study does not refer to territorial, physical borders but rather to ideational, symbolic, and social structures, which "enclose, mark, and signal" belonging to an ethnic category or movement (Conversi 1999, 553).[3]

Symbolic and Social Boundaries

The boundary approach conceives ethnicity as an intangible, imagined, cognitive boundary with two main aspects or dimensions: symbolic and social (Lamont and Molnár 2002; Alba 2005, 22). Lamont and Molnár (2002, 168) define symbolic boundaries as "*conceptual distinctions* made by social actors to categorize objects, people, practices, and even time and space. They are tools by which individuals and groups struggle over and come to agree upon definitions of reality. . . . Symbolic boundaries also separate people into groups and generate feelings of similarity and group membership" (emphasis added). Social boundaries, on the other hand, are conceptualized as "*objectified* forms of social differences manifested in unequal access to and unequal distribution of resources (material and nonmaterial) and social opportunities" (Lamont and Molnár 2002, 168; emphasis added). The authors suggest that the former operates at the intersubjective level and the latter concerns groupings of individuals.[4] These definitions imply that symbolic boundaries are more about the subjective, ideational components of an ethnic category (the ideas, values, norms, and/ or symbols that constitute a particular ethnicity) because social boundaries are related to relatively more objective social interactions and encounters, such as the inclusion and exclusion of actors (who should belong to an ethnic group or movement, who is an in-group member, who is an out-group member).[5] It is emphasized that both of these aspects are real, substantially shaping sociopolitical processes and outcomes (see also Fuller 2003).

As indicated previously, the earlier version of the boundary approach was more concerned with the impact of interactions and transactions on social boundaries, neglecting symbolic boundaries (i.e., the cultural content of ethnic categories). For instance, separating symbolic and social boundaries from each other, Barth (1969b, 15) suggests that the focus of investigation should be on "the ethnic boundary that defines the group" rather than "the cultural stuff that it encloses."[6] Thus, earlier versions of the boundary approach focused on "what goes on at the boundary" rather than "what is inside the boundary" (R. Jenkins 2015, 15). In other words, for the boundary approach, we should study the boundaries of ethnic groups from "the outside in" rather than "from the inside out" (Conforti 2015, 142). It was believed that developments and social interactions at and across boundaries have determining impacts on internal structures and dynamics (i.e., the cultural content of ethnic identity). Thus, in such an account, the "cultural stuff" becomes "an *effect* and not a *cause* of boundaries" (Eriksen 2010, 46). As R. Jenkins (2008, 13) observes, "Shared culture is, in this model, best understood as generated in and by processes of ethnic boundary maintenance, rather than the other way round: the production and reproduction of difference *vis-à-vis* external others is what creates the image of similarity internally, *vis-à-vis* each other" (see also Wallman 1978).

This orientation (i.e., focusing on social boundaries rather than ethnic substance or cultural contents), however, constitutes a major limitation. It makes sense to treat social boundaries and cultural content as analytically distinct dimensions of ethnic categories or movements; however, it is problematic to assume and focus on only a one-way relationship between them. Since shifts in symbolic boundaries (i.e., the substance and content of ethnicity) also directly affect social boundaries (see also Conversi 1995; R. Jenkins 2008), it is more realistic to assume a constant, mutual interplay between the symbolic and social boundaries. In other words, what goes on within the boundary also affects what goes on at and outside the boundary. As Jackson (2015b, 193) also notes, "The cultural content demarcated by different boundaries is manipulated and politicized in diverse ways and across contexts, in order to maximize, or in some cases reduce, the distinctiveness between different population categories."

Given such a limitation of the earlier versions of the boundary approach (i.e., the tendency to disregard or neglect what exists or happens inside the boundary), more recent studies of ethnic boundary making pay greater attention to the contents of ethnic categories, or the "cultural stuff," and so symbolic boundaries (e.g., see Nagel 1994; Conversi 1995, 1999; Cornell 1996; Cornell and Hartmann 2007; R. Jenkins 2008; Wimmer 2013; Jackson and Molokotos-Liederman 2015). As Jackson (2015a, 3) warns, "Studying ethnicity and nationalism through a boundary approach, while also accepting that the content of social categories informs how boundaries are drawn and vice versa, is vital." Similarly, Conforti (2015, 142) cautions that "we must not downplay the value of the cultural elements as a central factor in defining the boundaries of ethnic groups." The in-depth analysis of the Islamic opening of the secular Kurdish movement confirms that the cultural content of an ethnic identity or category does matter. For instance, empirical analyses show that the degree of ethnic-group heterogeneity and intragroup divisions and cleavages do shape boundary-making processes, such as ethnopolitical leaders' boundary-making strategies and the processes of boundary contestation, particularly internal boundary contestation.

Like social boundaries, the symbolic boundaries of an ethnic category and of an ethnonationalist movement are mutable as well. Regarding shifts in the symbolic boundaries (or the "cultural stuff"), Nagel (1994, 162–163) identifies two types or forms of boundary work: "construction" (i.e., revisions of current culture and innovations such as the creation of new cultural forms) and "reconstruction" (i.e., revivals and restorations of historical cultural practices and institutions). The former occurs "when current cultural elements are changed or when new cultural forms or practices are created"; the latter takes place "when lost or forgotten cultural forms or practices are excavated and reintroduced, or when lapsed or occasional cultural forms or practices are refurbished and reintegrated into contemporary culture" (Nagel 1994, 162–163). Thus, with reconstruction, ethnopolitical actors might incorporate previously ignored or suppressed ideational elements (e.g., religion) into the ethnic category or movement and shift its symbolic boundaries.

The Kurdish case analyzed in this study constitutes a good example of the reconstruction of symbolic boundaries. With the Islamic opening in the post-1990 period, the Kurdish ethnopolitical leaders quit their anti-Islamic attitudes and instead developed an Islam-friendly approach. As a result, they have incorporated previously excluded Islamic ideas, values, and principles into their ethnonationalist discourses, strategies, and programs. By adopting a more religion-friendly notion of Kurdishness, Kurdish ethnopolitical leaders have remade the symbolic boundaries of the Kurdish ethnic category in their ethnonationalist outlook.

The shifts in the symbolic boundaries of an ethnic category or movement might have substantial impact on social boundaries and interactions across ethnic-group boundaries. Again the Kurdish case illustrates this point well. By developing an Islam-friendly attitude in the past decades, Kurdish ethnopolitical leaders have reconciled with Islam, expanding the symbolic boundaries of the movement. We see that such boundary work at the symbolic level resulted in rapprochements with certain groups but tensions with others. For instance, the empirical chapters of this study display that the Islamic opening of the secular Kurdish movement reduced the distance between itself and the conservative Kurdish masses, while it increased the tension with rival political actors with conservative or Islamic leanings, such as the AKP. Thus, this particular case confirms that there is a constant and mutual interaction between the symbolic and social boundaries of an ethnic category or movement.

Boundary-Making Strategies

As Terrier (2015, 47) succinctly states, "boundaries do not operate without human action." Human agents consciously or unconsciously make and remake ethnonational boundaries. Both subjective (e.g., sense of belonging, myths, symbols) and objective (e.g., ancestry, ethnicity, language, territory) elements and features of ethnic and national identities or categories are subject to interpretation and reinterpretation by human agents. As Calhoun (1993, 223) notes, "ethnic identity is constituted, maintained, and invoked in social processes that involve diverse intentions, constructions of meaning, and conflicts. Not only are there claims from competing possible collective allegiances, there are competing claims as to just what any particular ethnic or other identity means." Similarly, Segal and Handler (2006, 59) observe that "even when the existence of a nation is least contested, neither outside observers nor the nation's most patriotic proponents are ever able to reach closure in their attempts to identify what trait, or trait-bundle, defines the shared national identity, or character, of the nation. Nationalist movements are instead engaged in a ceaseless politics of culture—an ongoing effort to identify, create, and maintain the purported common denominator of their national identity." Such efforts to identify the constitutive elements of an ethnic or national identity should be interpreted as boundary making or boundary construction because determining what a particular ethnic category entails also means setting or demarcating its boundaries. As Conversi (1995, 77) also notes, all processes of identity construction (including nationalism) are simultaneously boundary generating and boundary deriving. Similarly, Jackson (2015a, 1) asserts that distinguishing the national or ethnic self from the nonnational or nonethnic other should be understood as a form of boundary making.

Cultural, intellectual, and political elites are the key actors in boundary-making processes. Operating like political entrepreneurs, ethnopolitical leaders not only identify what symbols, beliefs, ideas, values, principles, and traditions are associated with a particular ethnicity or nationhood but also play a substantial role in determining who belongs to an ethnic category and/or movement and who does not (see also Kasfir 1979; Conversi 1999, 564; Lecours 2000; Cederman 2002; Wolff 2006; Terrier 2015). In other words, beyond identifying group members and policing social boundaries, ethnic entrepreneurs define, maintain, or transform the symbolic boundaries of an ethnic category or movement as well. Such boundary works might involve tacit, unconscious and/ or deliberate, strategic processes (Fuller 2003).

In boundary-making processes (e.g., demarcating, maintaining, or demolishing symbolic and social boundaries of an ethnic category or movement), boundary makers might be motivated by diverse interests such as material (e.g., political or economic power and resources) and ideational (e.g., honor, prestige, recognition, dignity, belonging, legitimacy) expectations. In order to achieve those interests, ethnopolitical elites utilize a variety of strategies (see Fuller 2003; Wimmer 2013). Wimmer (2013, 44–79) presents a comprehensive list of boundary-making strategies. "Expansion," as one form of boundary shift, refers to moving an existing boundary to incorporate certain other ethnic categories or groups. The second form of boundary shifting, "contraction," means shrinking or narrowing ethnic boundaries, excluding certain groups.[7] These definitions suggest that 'boundary expansion' and 'contraction' are more related to changing the topography or location of existing boundaries (Wimmer 2013, 49–56). And these two common strategies can take place at both social and symbolic levels. In other words, both symbolic and social boundaries might be expanded or contracted. As noted earlier, ethnopolitical elites and leaders might modify the "cultural stuff" of ethnic categories or movements (i.e., remaking symbolic boundaries) as well as redefining insiders and outsiders (i.e., remaking social boundaries). This study interprets the Islamic opening of the secular Kurdish movement in the past decades as a typical case of boundary expansion, taking place at both symbolic and social levels.

"Transvaluation" involves changing the meaning of an existing ethnic boundary to challenge the hierarchical ordering of ethnic categories. Wimmer identifies two subtypes of transvaluation: "normative inversion," in which the members of an excluded or despised ethnic category challenge the symbolic ethnic category and claim moral and cultural superiority vis-à-vis the dominant group; and "equalization," which refers to establishing moral and political equality (rather than superiority) with respect to the dominant ethnic category (see also Fuller 2003). Another strategy is "positional move" (boundary crossing and repositioning in the ethnic hierarchy), which might take place at either the individual or group level. Wimmer (2013, 58) states, "When transvaluation does not represent a valuable option, moving one's own position within a hierarchical system of ethnic categories might represent a more appropriate strategy. One can either change one's individual ethnic membership or reposition one's entire ethnic category. As in transvaluation, the boundaries of ethnic categories are not contested. Unlike [in] transvaluation . . . the hierarchy is accepted, but not one's own position in that system" (see also Zolberg and Woon 1999; Eriksen 2010). As noted earlier, boundary shifting (in the form of either contraction or expansion) involves changes in the topography of ethnic or national boundaries (i.e., boundary relocation). However, in the case of boundary crossing, actors move from one side of a boundary to another, without any major alteration in the definition of the boundary itself. As Loveman and Muniz (2007, 923) also state, "boundary crossing implies that categorical membership changes with the acquisition of new traits; the symbolic boundary presumably remains fixed, and reclassification reflects individual or intergenerational mobility across it."

Finally, "blurring" refers to putting emphasis on shared or crosscutting, nonethnic social cleavages to decrease the significance of ethnicity as the foundation of categorization and social organization (see also Jackson 2015b, 209–210). Actors attempt to decrease the salience of ethnic categories by promoting nonethnic principles, ideas, values, and symbols.[8] For instance, many conservative or Islamic circles in Turkey emphasize the notion of the "Islamic brotherhood" between ethnic Turks and Kurds in response to Kurdish ethnonationalist claims. By stressing Islam as a shared value between these two groups, Islamist circles attempt to deemphasize ethnic attachments and so blur ethnic boundaries (more on this in the conclusion).

Wimmer (2013) also lists several tools employed by boundary makers as they follow the foregoing boundary-making strategies: discursive and symbolic means (e.g., categorization and identification practices such as public ceremonies, rituals, and speeches; usage of visible cues such as somatic diacritics and dress patterns inscribing ethnic boundaries); discrimination against out-group members (formal discrimination through legal and institutional mechanisms and informal / de facto discrimination); peaceful or violent political mobilization (increasing the salience and relevance of ethnic divisions or reproducing and re-inforcing group boundaries); and finally coercive and violent policies (e.g., assimilation, ethnic cleansing, resettlement laws). The case of the Islamic opening of the Kurdish movement, discussed in detail in the following chapters, displays that Kurdish ethnopolitical elites particularly utilize discursive and symbolic means (e.g., employing Islam-friendly discourse and increasing references to Islamic ideas, principles, and practices such as certain verses of the Koran and the Charter of Medina) and mobilization tools (e.g., organizing civilian Friday prayers, the Democratic Islam Congress, and commemoration ceremonies) as they try to reconcile with Islam and Islamic actors.

The Bounded Nature of Boundary Making

Do ethnopolitical elites make, remake, or unmake ethnic boundaries ad libitum? Definitely not. Agents are not that free in their boundary-making efforts, simply because boundary-making processes are nested within existing social, political, economic, and historical structures and conditions. Wimmer (2013) also acknowledges the constraining impact of structural factors on agency and pays particular attention to the influence of institutional structures (e.g., nation-state, legal structure), power hierarchies (i.e., distribution of political, economic, and symbolic power), and networks of alliances on boundary-making efforts and processes (e.g., the choice of boundary-making strategies and the kind of emerging boundaries). Wimmer (2013, 89) notes that "actors are constrained, enabled, and enticed, first, by the institutional environment that makes it appear more plausible and attractive to draw certain types of boundaries—ethnic, class, regional, gender, tribal, or others. Second, the distribution of power defines an individual's interests and thus which level of ethnic differentiation will be considered most meaningful. Third, the network of political alliances will influence who will and who will not be counted as 'one of us'" (see also Cornell 1996). Similarly,

Lecours (2000, 121) warns against methodological individualism and states, "Social and economic structures provide the larger context for the behaviour of political actors. . . . The cultural make-up of a society presents specific options, and limitations, to political elites." Likewise, Conversi (1995, 81) emphasizes structural constraints and draws attention to internal constraints on boundary-making efforts: "It is highly unlikely that nationalist leaders can manipulate their constituencies at their own discretion, as extreme instrumentalists insist."

Drawing attention to the situational nature of boundary-making processes, Jackson (2015b, 193) also asserts that actors' boundary work is "dependent on the social context in which it takes place, limited by the cultural repertoires and available categories that have been institutionalized as social boundaries over time." In a similar vein, Lamont (2000, 7) suggests that boundary work is shaped by "the cultural resources that people have access to and the structural conditions in which they are placed." Additionally, she remarks that "some patterns of self-identification and boundaries are more likely in one context than in another. This is not to deny the importance of individual agency but to stress the fact that it is bounded by the *differentially structured* context in which people live" (2000, 244). Cornell and Hartmann (2007, 208) also draw attention to the role of contextual factors in boundary processes by introducing the notion of "construction sites," which refer to "arenas in which processes of identity construction occur." They suggest that politics, labor markets, residential space, social institutions, culture, and daily experience constitute some critical construction sites, molding boundary processes.

Thus, since ethnopolitical actors are embedded in social and political systems, both historical contexts (legacies, traditions) and the larger social, political, and economic environments of ethnic categories and movements encircle boundary-making processes such as boundary-making strategies and styles. In addition, as the Kurdish case also indicates, the internal structures and dynamics of ethnic groups also fashion ethnopolitical leaders' boundary-making efforts. Briefly, boundary-making processes are conditioned or bound by both internal (e.g., the structures of ethnic categories and movements) and external factors and dynamics.

External and Internal Boundary Contestations

Another important aspect of boundary-making processes is boundary contestation. Since boundary processes involve actors with different levels of power and authority and divergent views, interests, and strategies, boundary making is an inherently political process. As a result, as some of the existing studies also acknowledge, boundary-making processes might be highly contentious or conflictual (e.g., see Fuller 2003; Wimmer 2008a, 2008b, and 2013; R. Jenkins 2015, 14). For instance, Fuller (2003, 4) notes the following: "Because particular boundaries suit some purposes more than others, their meaning, placement, and structure may be highly contested, and boundaries are often a key site for struggles over social relations generally. Even the most institutionalized cultural boundaries can be (and are) plausibly redrawn as people struggle to enact, change, or dissolve distinctions in ways consonant with their wider purposes."

Wimmer (2013, 25) concurs, stating that "ethnic categories might be contested rather than universally agreed upon. Such contestation is part of a broader politico-symbolic struggle over power and prestige, the legitimacy of certain forms of exclusion over others, and the merits of discriminating for or against certain types of people."

Boundary contestations or struggles, however, remain undertheorized in the existing literature.[9] Further in-depth analysis of boundary contestation would be invaluable for boundary approaches. In particular, we need to spend more time thinking about questions such as, how, when, and under what conditions do boundary contestations take place? And when are boundary contestations more likely to succeed? In this section, we attempt to provide some preliminary answers to such questions.

Boundary-making processes might involve external and/or internal struggles over ethnic boundaries. External boundary contestation

simply refers to struggles and competition between insiders and outsiders over where symbolic and social boundaries should be drawn.
Boundary workers' efforts (e.g., expansion or contraction of symbolic
and social boundaries of an ethnic group or movement) might threaten
the ideational and/or material interests of out-group members. Being
challenged by such efforts, outsiders (e.g., ruling state elites, political
opponents, or members of other ethnic groups or movements) might
try to prevent or delegitimize boundary workers' efforts or initiatives.
To achieve such goals, outsiders might employ various strategies such
as expanding and/or contracting ethnic, religious, and ideological
boundaries. Under the presence of ethnic competition and conflict
(e.g., interethnic rivalry over scarce political, economic, and symbolic
resources), such boundary struggles between insiders and outsiders
might get quite intense.

External contestation might in turn have substantial impact on the
boundaries of ethnic categories and of movements. To illustrate how
external contestation might shape ethnic boundaries, we can utilize
Richard Jenkins's (2008) analytical distinction between "internal" and
"external" ethnic identification, which are two mutually interdependent
but analytically distinct processes. In the case of internal identification
(also called "group identification"), "members of a group signal to fel-
low group members or others a self-definition of who they are, their
identity" (R. Jenkins 2008, 55). Jenkins (55) explains that the internal
definition of identity is necessarily interactional and social because such
processes "presuppose an audience, without whom they make no sense,
and a shared framework of meaning." External identification (also called
"social categorization" because it involves the identification of *others* as a
collectivity), on the other hand, refers to "other-directed processes, during which one person or set of persons defines the other(s) as 'X,' 'Y,' or
whatever" (55). Jenkins suggests that external identification might take
a consensual or conflictual form. In the case of the consensual form,
others validate or endorse internal definition(s) of themselves. Regarding the conflictual form, "there is the imposition, by one set of actors on

another, of a name and/or characterization that the categorized do not recognize" (55).

Regarding the nexus between internal and external definitions (or between group identification and social categorization), Jenkins claims that these two processes are analytically distinct but not isolated from each other. As he notes, "each is chronically implicated in the other in an ongoing dialectic of identification. The categorization of 'them' is too useful a foil in the identification of 'us' for this not to be the case, and the definition of 'us' too much the product of a history of relationships with a range of significant others. . . . Ethnicity—the production, reproduction and transformation of the 'group-ness' of culturally differentiated collectivities—is a two-way process that takes place across the boundary between 'us' and 'them'" (2008, 55). Similarly, Eriksen (2010, 77) asserts that "the Barthian view of ethnicity as a system of mutually exclusive self-ascriptions must be slightly modified: the ascription attributed by *others* also contributes to creating ethnicity, and may be of paramount importance." Cornell and Hartmann (2007, 83) also acknowledge the impact of both internal and external construction processes and dynamics on group identity and boundaries:

> Construction involves both the passive experience of being "made" by external forces, including not only material circumstances but also the claims that other persons or groups make about the group in question, and the active process by which the group "makes" itself. The world around us may "tell" us we are racially distinct, or our experience at the hands of circumstances may "tell" us that we constitute a group, but our identity is also a product of the claims we make. These claims may build on the messages we receive from the world around us or may depart from them rejecting them, adding to them, or refining them.

Returning to the impact of external boundary contestation on ethnic boundaries, we should acknowledge that it almost always involves processes of "external definition" or "social categorization." As outsiders contest ethnic boundaries, they usually attempt to impose alternative categories or labels (usually disparaging ones in the case of conflictual situations) on the ethnic group or movement that they challenge. As the empirical chapters of this study illustrate, rival political movements with conservative or Islamic orientations constantly label the secular, leftist Kurdish movement as "infidels," "heretical," or "un-Islamic."

Such attempts of external definition, however, might have major consequences for boundary processes. Facing challenge or threat by outsiders, group members are likely to become much more defensive about their ethnic identity. As a result, they are likely to put internal divisions or conflicts aside and be more assertive with respect to issues related to their group identities and boundaries. As R. Jenkins (2008, 59) suggests, "the experience of categorization may strengthen existing group identity through a process of resistance and reaction. Thus, the experience of being categorized as 'A' may, only apparently paradoxically, contribute to the reinforcement, or even perhaps the formation, of [the] group identity as 'B.'" Likewise, Cornell and Hartmann (2007, 64) note, "Competition . . . often leads, via social closure, to an emphasis on ethnic or racial boundaries. It is thereby likely to reinforce and reproduce [these boundaries]." In the same way, Eriksen (2010, 81) remarks, "Conspicuous forms of boundary maintenance become important when the boundaries are under pressure." Thus, contestation of group boundaries by outsiders is likely to solidify internal identification, group attachments, and cohesiveness (see also Hale 2004). In other words, rather than weakening or undermining ethnic boundaries, external contestation might empower or thicken them. In brief, given the dialectical relationship between external and internal identifications, external boundary contestation might lead to major consequences for ethnic identification. It might result in either boundary reinforcement or boundary shift.

The preceding explanations suggest that contestations of ethnic boundaries by out-group members should also be regarded as one form of ethnic boundary work. As indicated earlier, the notion of boundary by definition presumes two separate spheres (i.e., inside and outside). Since contestations stemming from outside the boundary are likely to affect (directly or indirectly) what goes on within the boundary, these should qualify as one type of boundary work by outsiders. To put it differently, external boundary contestation can also be interpreted as boundary work, which might lead to the construction or reconstruction of the boundaries of ethnic groups and of movements. As the empirical chapters discuss in detail, Islamic or conservative political actors have been trying to delegitimize the secular, leftist Kurdish movement in the eyes of the conservative Kurdish masses by externally defining or categorizing the movement as "Marxist," "atheist," "Satanic evil," and "un-Islamic." Such an external identification or social categorization by competing conservative or Islamic political actors was one of the triggering factors behind the Islamic opening of the secular Kurdish movement in the past decades.

Internal boundary contestation, on the other hand, encompasses conflicts over ethnic boundaries among insiders (i.e., in-group members or coethnics) and may be relatively more destabilizing. Although several conceptualizations assume or treat ethnic groups as unitary actors or highly homogeneous entities with a shared culture and identity,[10] we should not exaggerate the internal homogeneity and cohesion of ethnic groups. Several studies even openly reject the idea that an ethnic group is constituted by a unique, common culture and shared identity. For instance, claiming that a common culture cannot be regarded as a defining feature of ethnic groups, Chandra (2012c) suggests that it is not realistic to expect all ethnic-group members to share all the same values, symbols, codes, and norms. Chandra (2012c, 88) suggests that instead of associating ethnic groups with a common culture by definition, we should take a common culture to be a variable: "Ethnic groups can vary in the degree to which they share a common 'content'—of which culture can be one component." Similarly, Brubaker (2009, 30) claims that "the strength, salience, content, and consequences of ethnic, racial, and national identifications are variable across time, contexts and persons." In the same way, Wimmer (2008b, 981) also draws attention to ethnic-group heterogeneity: "[Several authors] *assume*, rather than demonstrate, that an ethnic category represents an actor with a single purpose and shared outlook. Such ontological collectivism overlooks, however, that ethnic categories may shift contextually and that there might be substantial disagreement among individuals over which ones are the most appropriate and relevant ethnic labels" (emphasis in original; see also Wimmer 2009, 245–246).

Ethnic-group heterogeneity might originate from several sources. For instance, group members might attribute quite different meanings to the cultural markers delineating ethnic boundaries, including relatively more objective markers or diacritics, such as shared ancestry, language, or region (see also Eriksen 2010). In addition, it is quite often the case that an ethnic category or movement might be divided along other dimensions, such as religion (e.g., Alevi Kurds vs. Sunni Kurds), class, ideology, and region. Hence, borrowing from Wallman (1978), an ethnic category or movement might involve "sub-boundaries" due to nonethnic divisions and cleavages. As a result, one can find quite diverse views and opinions within an ethnic group or movement about how and where symbolic and/or social boundaries should be drawn (see also Cornell and Hartmann 2007; Conforti 2015). Internal diversity or heterogeneity, in turn, creates a favorable environment for internal boundary contestation. The following section presents hypothetical expectations regarding internal and external boundary contestations.

Hypotheses

When and under what conditions do boundary contestations (internal and external) take place? This section proposes some exploratory hypotheses about the processes of boundary contestation. To begin with external boundary contestation, we note that electoral periods in polities allowing competitive politics increase the likelihood of boundary work and boundary struggles. External boundary contestation in particular becomes much more common during such periods. As Wallman

(1978) suggests, the need for group definition facilitates the proliferation of boundary messages. During electoral periods especially, political elites feel the need to distinguish themselves (e.g., (re)iterating their own mission, programs, and policies) from those of competing groups. Such actions and statements occur because electoral politics involves intense elite competition for legitimacy and popularity in the eyes of potential voters. Political elites not only try to increase their appeal but also attempt to discredit or delegitimize their opponents.

A common strategy pursued by competing political actors is *othering*, which refers to identifying, categorizing, or treating certain actors as different from oneself or the mainstream. As one form of external identification or social categorization (see earlier), othering serves two main purposes: (1) marking and naming those who are thought to be different from oneself and (2) (re)constructing one's identity in reference to others (Weis 1995; Jensen 2011). Actors involved in othering practices tend to declare or treat certain actors as different, marginal, unorthodox, inferior, incompetent, or illegitimate. Obviously, such discourses, attitudes, and actions constitute one form of identity formation and so boundary making (see also Lamont 2000; R. Jenkins 2008; Jackson 2015a).

Since political elites frequently resort to such discourses and actions during electoral periods, electoral competition involves the constant making, remaking, and unmaking of boundaries (ideological, ethnic, religious, moral, etc.). Hence, electoral periods provide great opportunity for researchers to investigate boundary processes (ethnic or nonethnic). Unfortunately, the study of elections tends to focus on political or economic issues. Such an orientation, however, is "unable to incorporate electoral politics based on identities, in which the competition is often over how politicians and voters define the identity categories to which they belong rather than their issue-positions" (Chandra 2012b, 44). Thus, we can put forth the following:

Hypothesis 1: Electoral periods increase the likelihood of boundary work in general and external boundary contestation in particular.

The Kurdish case appears to be quite useful to illustrate the plausibility of this hypothesis. As this book's empirical chapters show, boundary work by competing elite groups (e.g., the secular Kurdish ethnopolitical elites and Islamist or conservative elites) gets rather intense during electoral periods. For instance, during the visits of conservative political elites to Kurdish areas while campaigning, they frequently label the secular Kurdish movement as "atheist" or "un-Islamic." In other words, they attempt to contract religious boundaries to undermine the societal popularity and legitimacy of the secular Kurdish movement in the eyes of conservative Kurdish voters. Not surprisingly, such efforts trigger counter boundary work by Kurdish ethnopolitical leadership. As Watts (2010, 130) also observes, electoral periods provide "important means by which pro-Kurdish politician-activists could legally challenge official discourse, promote a pro-Kurdish political platform, publicize the parties, and appeal to different constituencies."

Regarding internal boundary contestation, in the case of ethnic groups with a high degree of internal diversity or heterogeneity, boundary makers' efforts might trigger reactions or resentments among coethnics (intraethnic dissension), paving the way for internal competition and tensions. For instance, as boundary makers attempt to expand symbolic or social boundaries to include new ideational elements or groups, some insiders might try to restore previous boundaries or even shrink them. Thus, as an exploratory proposition, we might put forward the following:

Hypothesis 2: In relatively more heterogeneous ethnic groups or movements, internal boundary contestation (struggle over boundaries among coethnics) becomes more likely.

This hypothesis appears to be quite relevant to the Kurdish case. A widely acknowledged feature of Kurdish society is its high degree of internal heterogeneity. Besides tribal differences, Kurds are divided into various linguistic (e.g., Kurmanji, Sorani, and Gorani), sectarian (e.g., Sunni-Shafi, Sunni-Hanefi, and Alevi) and ideological (e.g., nationalist, secular, Islamist) groups. Given such a heterogeneous group structure, it becomes highly likely that the ethnopolitical leadership's boundary work would be contested by certain groups within the Kurdish ethnic category.

It is not surprising that power differentials might also condition internal boundary contestation. As Wimmer (2009, 258) also suggests, "the distribution of power between various participants in these struggles influences their capacity to shape the outcome." For instance, in hierarchically organized ethnic groups, internal boundary contestations take place within the shadow of power hierarchies. This situation implies that opposition by subordinate coethnics to the boundary-making efforts of ethnopolitical leaders would more likely be suppressed in hierarchically organized ethnic groups or movements characterized by clear leadership and power relations. In other words, in hierarchical ethnic categories, boundary makers (i.e., superordinates, located at the top echelons of the power hierarchy) would face fewer overt internal challenges. Therefore, in the case of such ethnic groups and movements, boundary work would be relatively smoother. Thus, another hypothesis about boundary work could be the following:

Hypothesis 3: In hierarchically organized ethnic groups or movements, internal boundary contestation is less likely to succeed.

Again, the Kurdish case provides a quite useful context for investigating this hypothesis. As discussed in the following chapters, the Kurdish ethnonationalist movement is characterized by a highly centralized, hierarchical organizational structure. Thus, we might expect that coethnics' contention of the boundary work initiated by the Kurdish ethnopolitical leadership would have limited impact on the leadership.

However, internal boundary contestation might be potentially more destabilizing in the case of strong divisions or cleavages at the elite level. Differences might emerge in the ruling cadre or among superordinates regarding where ethnic boundaries should be drawn. This situation would facilitate the efforts of boundary contesters or challengers. In the case of strong elite divisions, subordinate coethnics might find some allies at the elite level and so challenge more effectively the existing or redrawn boundaries defended by another elite faction. In other words, elite competition or rivalry would favor internal boundary contestation by opposing subordinate coethnics, increasing the likelihood of successful boundary contestation. Thus, we might postulate the following:

Hypothesis 4: In case of highly unified ethnopolitical leadership (i.e., absence or weakness of elite competition or rivalry), internal boundary contestation would be less likely to succeed.

This hypothesis should also hold in the Kurdish case because another defining feature of the Kurdish movement in the Turkish setting is a high degree of elite unity. Given the strong leadership cult and the tendency to associate any internal opposition with treason or betrayal to the leadership and the Kurdish cause, it would be quite difficult or highly costly to challenge the position of the leadership. Hence, the movement has not allowed any counterelites to emerge and gain power vis-à-vis the leadership. Such an organizational structure and culture would limit the chances of coethnics' contesting ethnic boundaries successfully.

Conclusion

Since almost all ethnic and nationalist identifications and movements involve boundary processes (e.g., the creation, maintenance, and transformation of ethnic or national identities and boundaries), ethnic boundary-making theory emerges as a highly relevant and valuable theoretical device in ethnicity and nationalism studies. As Wimmer (2013, 3) also claims, "Focusing on social and categorical [symbolic] boundaries allows us to study the formation and dissolution of ethnic groups with more precision than standard sociological approaches that take the existence and continuity of such groups and categories for granted."

In addition to being highly relevant to ethnicity and nationalism studies, the ethnic boundary-making perspective is a powerful theoretical tool also because it takes into account the role of both agential and structural factors and dynamics in boundary processes. Most earlier studies drawing on the boundary approach have a tendency to view ethnic boundaries as persistent and static social structures and so focus on boundary maintenance rather than boundary shifts. Thus, they provide consciously or unconsciously structuralist accounts of ethnic boundaries. Updated versions of the boundary approach, however, provide more dynamic accounts of boundary processes and focus on making and unmaking boundaries by collective or individual actors and movements (Wimmer 2013, 45). In other words, we see greater room for human agency in newer versions of the boundary approach to ethnicity and nationalism. Thus, paying due attention to both agential and structural factors and dynamics and having special focus on interaction and relationality, the ethnic boundary-making approach provides us a rich theoretical repertoire and so enables us to capture both the enduring or fixed and the contingent, fluid, or flexible aspects of ethnicity and nationalism phenomena. In other words, the ethnic boundary-making perspective helps us acquire a richer understanding of the complex and multifaceted nature of ethnicity and nationalism. Given all these advantages, it is not surprising that the boundary approach, which was introduced in the late 1960s, has become increasingly popular in ethnicity and nationalism studies in the past decades (e.g., Lamont 1992, 2000; Conversi 1995, 1999; Zolberg and Woon 1999; Fuller 2003; Alba 2005; Bail 2008; R. Jenkins 2008; Wimmer 2008a, 2008b, 2009, 2013; Jackson and Molokotos-Liederman 2015).

That being said, developing specific hypotheses about boundary processes and illustrating them through small-N designs (e.g., single or comparative case study) or testing them through large-N research (e.g., regression analysis) would be highly valuable for developing and refining this theory further. Thus, by examining the Islamic opening of the secular Kurdish movement from the perspective of the boundary approach, the ensuing empirical chapters will conduct a plausibility probe of the hypotheses about the processes of boundary contestation given earlier. Plausibility probes are regarded as a type of case study that "allows the researcher to sharpen a hypothesis or theory, to refine the operationalization or measurement of key variables, or to explore the suitability of a particular case as a vehicle for testing a theory before engaging in a costly and time-consuming research effort" (Levy 2008, 6). The researcher conducting this type of study "probes the details of a particular case in order to shed light on a broader theoretical argument" (Levy 2008, 6). Levy (2008, 6–7) expands that description by explaining that plausibility probes help analysts "demonstrate the empirical relevance of a theoretical proposition by identifying at least one relevant case" (see also Eckstein 1975). Thus, the Islamic opening of the secular Kurdish movement analyzed in this study also serves as a particular case to probe or investigate the empirical plausibility, strength, and validity of the hypotheses presented earlier. Such an endeavor in turn would help us improve or refine ethnic-boundary-making theory.

2

The Islamic Opening of the Kurdish Movement

In this chapter, we trace the evolving relations between the Kurdish movement and Islam since the late 1970s. Rather than reviewing the entire history of the Kurdish issue in the Turkish setting, this chapter focuses on the Kurdish movement's attitude and approach toward Islam and Islamic actors to set the stage for a causal analysis of the recent Islamic opening within the Kurdish movement, provided in chapter 3.

Chapter 2 is structured as follows: The first part provides a brief discussion on the nexus between religion and nationalism in general. Then, we move to the Turkish setting for a concise look at the competing nationalisms and their interactions with religion. This brief discussion helps us better contextualize the transformation within the Kurdish movement. Next, the chapter presents the rise of the leftist, secular Kurdish ethnonationalist movement on the Turkish political scene in the late 1970s. The remaining sections first focus on the Kurdish movement's indifferent, apathetic, and sometimes highly antagonistic attitude toward Islam in the 1970s and 1980s and then turn to the rise of the Islam-friendly attitude within the movement in the past decades. Lastly, the chapter interprets those changes (i.e., the Islamic opening of the Kurdish movement) from the perspective of the boundary approach, presented in chapter 1.

Religion and Nationalism: A Typology

For a better sense of the changing relations between the Kurdish ethnonationalist movement and Islam, it is useful to begin with some discussion on the nexus between religion and nationalism in general. On that topic, this study uses a basic typology to help us compare different positionings of political movements vis-à-vis religion and nationalism.

Hypothetically speaking, political actors and movements might have either positive (inclusionary) or negative (exclusionary) attitudes toward religious and nationalist ideas. These two dimensions generate a fourfold typology (i.e., four ideal-typical attitudes toward religious and nationalist orientations), shown in figure 2.1.[1]

Political actors in the first quadrant strongly embrace religious and nationalist ideas, hence I call them *religious nationalists*. Religious nationalism simply refers to the "fusion of nationalism and religion such that they are inseparable" (Rieffer 2003, 225). Thus, religion becomes "central to national identity and to the conception of what it means to belong to the given nation" (Barker 2009, 13). Several contemporary nations and nationalisms involve sacred meanings, rituals, myths, and symbols, and religious nationalisms have been on the rise in the Western and non-Western world (see Rieffer 2003; Smith 2008; Barker 2009; Gorski and Türkmen-Dervişoğlu 2013). Some illustrative cases include Jewish far-right nationalist groups such as the Kach Party (1971–1994) and the National Religious Party (1956–2008) in Israel; Catholic nationalists in Northern Ireland; and Muslim nationalist formations such as Hamas in

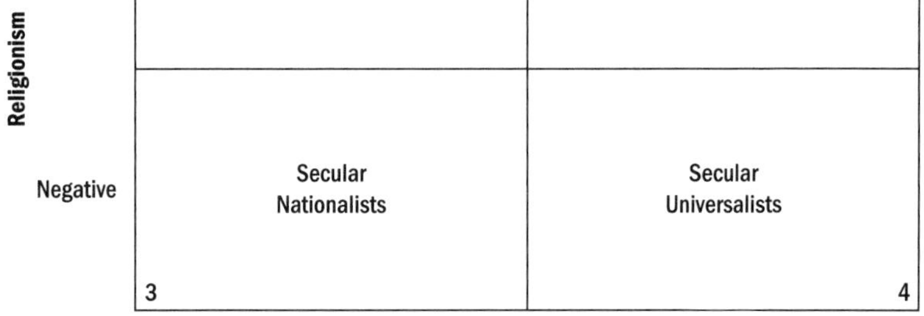

| | **Nationalism** | |
	Positive	Negative
Positive	1 Religious Nationalists	Religious Universalists 2
Negative	3 Secular Nationalists	Secular Universalists 4

(left axis label: **Religionism**)

FIGURE 2.1. A typology of attitudes vis-à-vis religion and nationalism.

Palestine, the Justice and Development Party (Adalet ve Kalkınma Partisi, AKP) in Turkey, and Chechens in Russia.

In the second quadrant, we have a positive attitude toward religion but a negative stance toward nationalism. I label actors in this cell as *religious universalists*. Several moderate or radical Islamist movements emphasize the notion of *ummah* (the worldwide community of Muslim believers) and *Islamic brotherhood* instead of specific ethnic or national identities and constitute exemplary cases of this type (e.g., jihadist groups or movements, which prioritize and promote a universalizing Islamic identity).

The third configuration is constituted by a positive attitude toward nationalism but a negative posture toward religion and the clergy. Actors in this quadrant are *secular nationalists*. Secular nationalism, which tends to reject the role of religion and religious institutions and actors in political realm, emerged in eighteenth-century Europe and America and became quite widespread in the modern world in the mid-twentieth century (e.g., French nationalism, Kemalist nationalism in Turkey, Nasserism in Egypt, and Nehruism in India) (Juergensmeyer 2006, 182).

Finally, in the fourth quadrant, we have political actors who are distant from both religious and nationalist ideologies. I call actors in this category *secular universalists*. Several Marxist socialist circles, which expected that nationalist and religious identities and attachments would be replaced with supranational socialism led by the working class, constitute illustrative examples in this category. Although these ideal-typical categories may be more or less static, the positions of the political actors within them are not. Political actors can change their attitudes and/or discourses toward religion or nationalism and so occasionally move from one configuration to another (e.g., for an analysis of a transition from Islamism to secular nationalism in the Acehnese context, see Aspinall 2007, 2009).

If we apply the foregoing typology to the Kurdish case in the Turkish setting, we can determine that the Kurdish ethnonationalist movement emerged as a strictly secular nationalist movement in the 1970s (i.e., the third cell in figure 2.1). However, as presented shortly, as of the early 1990s, we have seen an increasingly positive attitude vis-à-vis religion within the movement. To better contextualize the Kurdish case, it is imperative to take into account the larger political atmosphere in the Turkish setting. Especially since the early 1990s, Turkish politics has involved two competing nationalisms: Turkish and Kurdish. In addition to these forces, Islamist ideas and movements have played an increasing role in the Turkish polity in this period. Thus, in the past decades, we have seen an interesting interplay among Turkish nationalism, Kurdish nationalism, and Islam in the Turkish polity.[2]

We might roughly sketch the three domains and the interactions among them as a Venn diagram, as shown in figure 2.2. In area x of figure 2.2, we have secular nationalists (e.g., the Republican People's Party, Cumhuriyet Halk Partisi, CHP). Area xy includes Turkish-Islamist groups such as the Great Unity Party (Büyük Birlik Partisi, BBP), the Nationalist Action Party (Milliyetçi Hareket Partisi, MHP), and the currently-in-power AKP.[3] Relatively more Islamist political actors should be located in area y. The closest, if not ideal, example of this type would be the National Outlook Movement (NOM), currently represented by the Felicity Party (Saadet Partisi, SP). Although this movement has had strong nationalist orientations, it has sometimes attributed primary importance to Islam and the Muslim community (*ummah*) (see Bora 2003). In area zy, we see conservative or Islamist pro-Kurdish circles such as the Kurdish Hezbollah (currently represented by the Free Cause Party, Hür Dava Partisi or Hüda-Par), the Zehra Group (Zehra Vakfı and Zehra-Der), and the Azadi Movement/Initiative (Hareketa Azadi). Area z has been conventionally occupied by the secular, leftist Kurdish movement, currently represented by the legally operating Peoples' Democratic Party (Halkların Demokratik Partisi, HDP) and the outlawed Kurdistan Workers' Party (Partiya Karkaren Kurdistan, PKK). Finally, certain secular leftist circles, which are skeptical of both nationalist and religious ideologies, position themselves in area t.

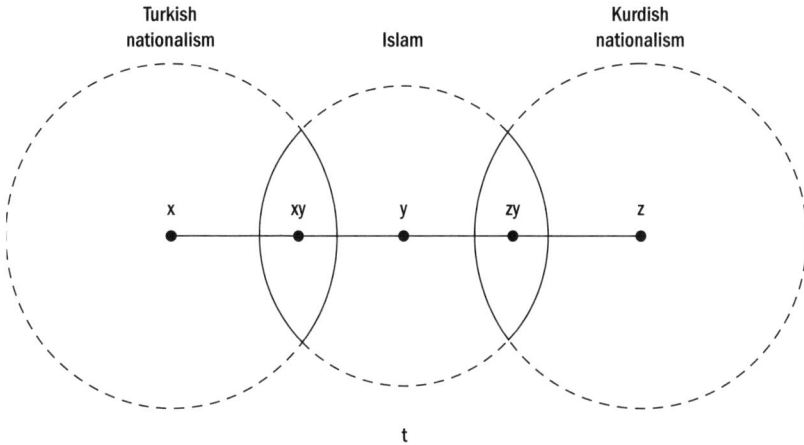

FIGURE 2.2. Three major political forces (Turkish and Kurdish nationalisms and Islam) in the Turkish polity.

As in figure 2.1, while the areas or domains might be more or less static, the positions of political actors are not. In other words, political actors might change their attitudes and discourses toward religion and/ or nationalism and so occasionally move from one configuration to another one. For instance, in the 1970s, the MHP, a then-proponent of pan-Turkist nationalism, determined that because Islam is an integral part of Turkish national identity, the party would develop a more pro-Islamic discourse and attitude (see Bora 2003). To depict this change in ideology via figure 2.2, the party would move from area x toward area xy.

A much more striking case of such changes is the relatively recent Islamic opening of the secular, leftist Kurdish movement, which constitutes the focus of this study.[4] It is intriguing that the Kurdish ethnonationalist movement, which is rooted in secularism and Marxism, has adopted a much more lenient approach toward Islam in the past decades. As van Bruinessen (2000b, 56) also observes, "The PKK ... [has] adopted a more respectful attitude towards Islam. It had initially, like all left-wing movements in Turkey, been not only secularist but distinctly anti-religious. Having discovered how strongly attached to Islam many Kurdish villagers are, it renounced its earlier irreligiosity and founded two Muslim affiliates, the Union of Religious Persons and the Union of Patriotic Imams." Thus, recognizing Islam as an important social and political force, the Kurdish movement has co-opted actors, symbols, principles, and values from the Islamic domain (getting closer to area zy in figure 2.2).

In the following, we first trace the rise of the secular Kurdish movement in Turkey. Then we examine the initial period in the Kurdish movement's relations with Islam, which was characterized by indifference or apathy and sometimes hostility and aggression. Finally, we turn to the development of a more Islam-friendly approach within the Kurdish movement in the past decades (i.e., the Islamic opening of the movement).

The Rise of the Secular, Leftist Kurdish Movement in Turkey

Before focusing on the Kurdish movement's evolving relations with Islam, it is useful to have a brief look at the trajectory of the secular Kurdish movement in Turkey.

Kurdish nationalist activism in Turkey emerged in the initial years of the Republic. In the 1920s and 1930s, the young Republic was challenged by several rural Kurdish revolts. According to one study, between 1924 and 1938, there were 18 uprisings in Republican Turkey, 17 of which took place in eastern Anatolia and 16 of which involved Kurds (Kirişçi and Winrow 1997). These revolts, however, were severely suppressed by the Turkish state.

The Kurdish revolts in that period reacted primarily to the Turkification, centralization, and secularization attempts of the young Republic. In addition to nationalist sentiments and demands, these revolts involved strong tribal and religious divisions and dynamics (van Bruinessen 1992; Romano 2006, 27–33). For instance, several of them were led by influential large landowners (i.e., *aghas*) and tribal or religious leaders (e.g., the Sheikh Said Revolt, 1925, and the Dersim Revolt, 1936–1938). It is argued that the lack of unity was one of the main reasons behind the failure of the Kurdish revolts during the early Republic. As Romano (2006, 32–33) observes,

Part of the problem lay in the nature of Kurdish elites at the time—they were almost exclusively tribal leaders, religious sheikhs, or large landowners. There were few "modern" elites, meaning non-religious or tribally affiliated members of the bourgeoisie, intellectuals or the professional classes. When tribal leaders took the helm of a revolt, members of traditionally competing tribes would likely either not participate or they would assist the government in putting down the revolt. If the uprising[s] were led by a religious figure, then Kurds belonging to other religious denominations or orders were unlikely to participate. (See also Nagel 1978)

After relative silence in the 1940s and 1950s, Kurdish ethnopolitical activism reappeared in the 1960s and 1970s (White 2000; McDowall 2004; Romano 2006). In that period, Turkish society and politics experienced fundamental changes. First, we saw major socioeconomic transformations such as urbanization and increasing levels of education and income. During the early Republican period, the vast majority of Turkish society lived in rural areas; until the 1950s, only one-fourth of the population lived in urban areas. Since then, however, we have seen a steady increase in the urban population.[5] Kurds, most of whom used to live in remote, rural areas, have constituted one of the major groups in this human flow into urban centers in eastern and western Turkey (particularly into Istanbul, Izmir, and Ankara) (see also van Bruinessen 2000a; McDowall 2004, 403–404; Romano 2006, 42, 112; Watts 2010, 34–35). This migration led to an increase in the size of urban, educated Kurdish population (Marcus 2007, 19; Gunes 2012b; S. Aslan 2015, 120–125).

In addition to such socioeconomic changes, major political developments occurred in that period. In mid-1940s, Turkey experienced a transition to multiparty politics. In 1950, the opposition Democrat Party (Demokrat Parti, DP) won the elections against the CHP and ended the 27-year single party rule. The DP's increasing authoritarianism, however, resulted in a coup, led by junior military officers, in May 1960, which removed the DP government from power. This intervention led to a new constitution, which was approved in a referendum in July 1961. The main motivations of those who drafted the new document were to introduce stronger checks and balances on governmental power and enhance individual rights and freedoms, for example, freedom of association, thought expression, press, and publication. The 1961 constitution also granted greater autonomy to universities, allowed organizing trade unions and calling for strikes, and created a more independent judiciary, all of which led to a relatively more liberal political environment in Turkey. Such a political and legal setting facilitated the growth of the left (Romano 2006, 44). The 1960s and 1970s thus experienced the rise of ideology politics. Increasing ideological competition, polarization, and violence between the socialist left and the nationalist conservative right led to a major political upheaval in Turkey's urban settings during this period (see Ahmad 1993; Çarkoğlu 1998).

The Kurdish movement reemerged in such a social and political environment, which certainly shaped its characteristics in the modern period. For instance, compared to the Kurdish revolts during the early Republic, which were led by traditional local elites such as landowners, tribal leaders, and sheikhs, the leading figures of the Kurdish movement in the 1960s and 1970s were more educated, secular, and urban (e.g., intellectuals, writers, unionists, lawyers, teachers, and university youth) (see also van Bruinessen 2000b; McDowall 2004; Natali 2005; Romano 2006; Watts 2010; Jongerden and Akkaya 2011; Gunes 2012a; S. Aslan 2015). In other words, the traditional feudal, tribal, religious leadership was replaced with more modern, urban elites. On this point, it is worth quoting Romano (2006, 62):

> Elites available to support Kurdish nationalist movements in the 1920s and 1930s tended to be aghas, tribal leaders, and religious sheikhs. Consequently, the movements that arose during this time period were conservative, melding religion, tribal politics, and Kurdish nationalism together, but not seeking to transform Kurdish society or modes of economic production. By the 1960s and 1970s, however, the majority of

the old elites were either gone (killed, exiled, or reduced to insignificance and poverty) or co-opted by the state. In their place, leftist union leaders, intellectuals, media figures, and members of the professional classes emerged as the allies available to both leftist and Kurdish nationalist projects.

White (2000, 205) makes a similar observation: "The [Kurdish] movement matured from its initial form as a combined religious-political, tribal-dominated movement, towards a less parochial, 'purer' nationalism, led centrally by urban Kurds—including some intellectuals—formed in the Turkish Left."

Much more importantly, the Kurdish movement in this era got involved in the socialist movement and so showed much more secular and leftist features (Birand 1992; van Bruinessen 2000a, 2000b; Entessar 2010; White 2000; Natali 2005; Romano 2006; Marcus 2007; Watts 2010; Jongerden and Akkaya 2011; Yanarocak 2014; Tezcür 2015). Again, quoting Romano (2006, 62), "Most of the Kurdish movements (such as the PKK) that arose at this time in turn espoused a socialist and revolutionary brand of Kurdish nationalism." As a result, Marxist, socialist ideas, concepts, and frames such as economic redistribution, class struggle, and anti-imperialism shaped pro-Kurdish groups' discourse on the Kurdish issue (Watts 2010).

The Turkish Worker's Party (Türkiye İşçi Partisi, TİP), established in 1961 by several trade-union leaders as a legal socialist party, became the first leftist legal political party to draw attention to Kurds' economic and political problems (e.g., inequality, discrimination, oppression, and socioeconomic underdevelopment) (van Bruinessen 2000a; Romano 2006). The party's emphasis on social and economic equality and justice and its criticisms of landlords' (*aghas*) tight grip over the Kurdish masses were highly appealing for Kurdish intellectuals and activists. As a result, many Kurdish activists (e.g., Tarık Ziya Ekinci, Musa Anter, Kemal Burkay, Naci Kutlay, and Mehdi Zana) took sides with the TİP and participated in its activities as deputies or party officials (McDowall

2004, 409; Marcus 2007, 19; Watts 2010, 38–41; Gunes 2012b, 59; S. Aslan 2015, 125–126).[6]

Another prominent leftist pro-Kurdish organization was the Revolutionary Eastern Cultural Hearts (Devrimci Doğu Kültür Ocakları, DDKO).[7] Formed by Kurdish students and intellectuals in Ankara in 1969 as an umbrella organization, the DDKO had several branches in Kurdish-populated provinces and emerged as the main organization highlighting Kurds' problems and demands (Aydin and Emrence 2015, 19; Gunes 2012b; Tezcür 2015). Similar to the TİP, the DDKO approached the Kurdish issue from a Marxist perspective and drew attention to problems such as the oppression of Kurdish villagers by landlords and tribal leaders and the suppression of Kurds and Kurdish ethnic identity by the military. As Marcus (2007, 21) observes, this organization "wanted to address social and cultural issues of concern to Kurds. The group blended the Marxism so popular at the time with a Kurdishness, thus marking a new step in development of a Kurdish political identity in Turkey" (see also Yanarocak 2014).[8]

Believing that other Turkish leftist groups (e.g., Revolutionary Youth [Dev Genç] and labor unions such as the Confederation of Progressive Trade Unions [Devrimci İşçi Sendikaları Konfedarasyonu, DİSK]) were not very much interested in Kurds' problems (e.g., the suppression of Kurdish ethnic identity, the socioeconomic backwardness of Kurdish regions), an increasing number of Kurdish nationalists broke away from the Turkish left and established their own left-wing organizations, particularly in the second half of the 1970s (van Bruinessen 2000a, 231; McDowall 2004, 414; Natali 2005, 106; Entessar 2010, 117–126; Watts 2010, 42–43; Gunes 2012b, 65–80; S. Aslan 2015, 114–164). Some of them were as follows: Beş Parçacılar (1976); Şivancılar (1972); Revolutionary Democratic Culture Association (Devrimci Demokratik Kültür Dernekleri, DDKD; 1974); Socialist Party of Turkish Kurdistan (Turkiye Kurdistanı Sosyalist Partisi, TKSP);[9] Kawa (1976); Denge Kawa (1978); Rizgari (Liberation; 1977); Ala Rizgari (the Flag of Liberation; 1978); Kurdistan National Liberationists (Kürdistan Ulusal Kurtuluşçuları,

KUK; 1977); TEKOSIN (Struggle; 1978); YEKBUN (Unity; 1979); Kurdistan Socialist Movement (TSK; 1980); and the PKK (1978) (see van Bruinessen 2000a, 232; Romano 2006, 47; Entessar 2010, 120–123; Jongeden
and Akkaya 2011, 125; Gunes 2012b). Thus, by the second half of the
1970s, several independent legal and illegal Kurdish organizations had
emerged on the Turkish political scene, protesting state policies toward
Kurds on the one hand and competing against each other on the other
(see also Aydin and Emrence 2015, 19–20).[10]

Those leftist Kurdish formations, however, failed to garner widespread
support among Kurds. The only exception was the PKK, led by Abdullah Öcalan.[11] As Tezcür (2015, 249) notes, "When Abdullah Öcalan and
his friends established the PKK in November 1978, there were already
close to a dozen Kurdish nationalist organizations. These organizations
published journals and newspapers, established youth associations, were
influential in unions and professional associations, organized peasants
to occupy land, fielded candidates in local and national elections, and
even planned to initiate an armed struggle. However, the PKK eclipsed
all these more established organizations even before the 1980 coup and
became the hegemonic Kurdish nationalist group by 1984."

There are several reasons for the rise of the PKK as the dominant
Kurdish ethnonationalist group among Kurds. One argument draws
attention to the role of the PKK's initial campaigns against landowners
(petty notables locally known as *aghas*) and tribal leaders in Kurdish
regions to win the sympathy of Kurdish peasants, who suffered under
feudal subordination.[12] For instance, Romano (2006, 74) asserts, "The
PKK, with only a few hundred cadres, was able to increase the Kurdish population's sympathy and support by coordinating actions that
mattered to the local people, [the] most important of which was opposition to the landlords and exploitative tribal chiefs." Similarly, van
Bruinessen (2000a, 241) states that "tribal or landed elites never gained
much influence in it [the PKK], distinguishing [it] from most other
Kurdish organizations, whose leadership usually included at least a
few such persons. Much of the PKK's violence was directed against the

haves [i.e., powerful landlords] in the name of the have-nots [landless peasants]" (see also Birand 1992; Imset 1996; White 2000; McDowall 2004). It is claimed that such unprecedented attacks against oppressive tribal leaders and landlords increased the PKK's popularity among Kurdish peasants in the region (see also Birand 1992, 94; White 2000, 156; Tezcür 2015).

Another factor facilitating the PKK's ascendance to the dominant or hegemonic position among Kurds was that in accusing other groups of being "collaborators," "revisionists," "pro-imperialists," and/or "agent provocateurs," the PKK did not hesitate to use violence toward rival Kurdish groups active in the region and in Europe (van Bruinessen 2000a, 233; White 2000, 135–153; Romano 2006, 136; Gunes 2012b). On the PKK's use of violence for nationalist mobilization, Tezcür (2015, 256) notes that "PKK violence was a strategic decision on the part of its leadership to compete effectively against other Kurdish organizations. Being a late comer, the PKK employed violence to develop a niche. The PKK deliberately decided not to establish a regular publication like other organizations until 1982. Instead, it sought to achieve influence primarily through violent means. Consequently, in less than two years, the PKK emerged as the leading Kurdish nationalist organization in Turkey." Thus, strategic use of violence against political rivals and the Kurdish peasantry[13] also helped the PKK emerge as the dominant revolutionary group within the Kurdish movement (see also Birand 1992, 76–103; Aydin and Emrence 2015, 20–21).

Finally, the 1980 military intervention, which had quite a destructive impact on leftist groups, as it weakened or eliminated the bulk of the PKK's competitors, such as the KUK, also facilitated the PKK's ascendance to a hegemonic position (Romano 2006, 85; Gunes 2012b; Tezcür 2015). Foreseeing the coup, most senior PKK leaders escaped to Lebanon and Syria before the intervention (Birand 1992; van Bruinessen 2000a; Imset 1996; Gunes 2012b).[14] By fleeing abroad before the coup, the PKK leadership avoided the wrath of the military regime. Hence, the PKK is the only major Kurdish organization that survived the military intervention (van Bruinessen 2000a, 251).

As a result of these factors, the PKK emerged as the dominant political voice of Turkey's Kurds in the 1980s and became "the largest, most enduring Kurdish nationalist challenge ever to threaten Turkey" (Romano 2006, 92; see also Marcus 2007, 34–42, 305; Jongerden and Akkaya 2011; Gunes 2012b; Aydin and Emrence 2015, 20; Tezcür 2015). It was the PKK that successfully drew international and domestic attention to the Kurdish issue. As Romano (2006, 159) notes, "If there is one thing that every observer of the conflict, be they Turkish generals, Kurdish peasants, or western academics, generally agree on, it is that the PKK succeeded in bringing the Kurdish issue back into the limelight of public discourse in Turkey."

Like several other Kurdish nationalist groups in the 1970s and 1980s, the PKK was also under the influence of socialist ideas. Abdullah Öcalan, founder and unchallenged leader of the PKK, in his youth was involved in the socialist movement, particularly the DDKO and Dev Genç (Birand 1992; van Bruinessen 2000a, 233; McDowall 2004, 420; Romano 2006, 70; Jongerden and Akkaya 2011, 126). For instance, when he was a student at Ankara University, Öcalan participated in a protest of the killing of the leftist, revolutionary militants (i.e., Mahir Çayan and his friends) in Kızıldere in 1972. For joining this demonstration, he was arrested and spent seven months in prison. After this experience, Öcalan concluded that revolutionary methods and strategies were necessary to advance the Kurdish cause in Turkey. In 1974, Öcalan became a member of the Ankara Democratic Higher Education Association (Ankara Demokratik Yüksek Öğretim Derneği, ADYÖD), which embraced socialist ideas and developed close relations with Dev-Genç.[15] After ADYÖD was banned in 1975, Öcalan and some of his friends from the group (e.g., Haki Karer, Kemal Pir, Ali Haydar Kaytan, Duran Kalkan, and Cemil Bayık) decided to set up a Marxist-Leninist organization with a goal of fighting for an independent Kurdish state (Marcus 2007, 23–29). They also decided to move their activities from Ankara to Turkey's eastern and southeastern regions. In 1977, Öcalan organized a meeting in Diyarbakır, after which they concluded that the Kurdish-populated areas of Turkey were a colony.

They claimed that Kurdish feudal groups (e.g., tribal leaders, landowners [*aghas*]), religious leaders, and the bourgeoisie had cooperated with the Turkish state and ruling classes to exploit the Kurdish peasantry and the working class. Furthermore, they maintained that in addition to exploiting regional resources, the Turkish state also suppressed Kurdish ethnic identity. Imperialism and capitalism were identified as other major problems, undermining Kurdish national ideals and interests. Öcalan and his group felt that the solution to all these problems was to establish an independent, Marxist-Leninist Kurdistan, where feudal and capitalist classes would be destroyed and the peasantry and proletariat would be liberated. This document constituted the aims of the PKK, which was established a year later in November 1978 in a village of Diyarbakır.

Thus, influenced by the revolutionary left in Turkey in the late 1970s, the PKK was motivated by a general goal of establishing a united, independent Kurdistan based on Marxist-Leninist principles. For instance, in one of the PKK's founding documents, Öcalan declares that "scientific socialism" constitutes the group's main guide in its struggle for Kurdish national liberation and for a classless society (Öcalan 1994; see also PKK 1984). Similarly, in his later writings, Öcalan presents the PKK as the vanguard of the Kurdish nationalist and revolutionary movement and states that "when they initiated the PKK movement in the late 1970s, they considered socialist ideology and utopia as their sacred guides and followed them strictly as they fought for Kurdish national freedom" (Öcalan 2001, 64, 86; see also Criss 1995; Imset 1996; N. Özcan 1999; White 2000; Yavuz 2001; Marcus 2007; Taspinar 2005; Romano 2006; Jongerden and Akkaya 2011; Gunes 2012b; Aydin and Emrence 2015).

As the main instrument of achieving an "independent, socialist Kurdistan," the PKK adopted the strategy of a "protracted people's war" (see Öcalan 1994, 122–125; see also PKK Program, in Özcan 1999, 350–369). As Jongerden and Akkaya (2011, 124) also note, "The PKK is widely known for its strategic employment of violence, the party name being commonly used as a synonym for its guerilla army. Although the PKK uses violence to obtain its goals, however, it would be wrong to characterize it as a military organization. The PKK is a political organization using violence to reach its objectives . . . and might best, therefore, be considered a 'militant political organization'" (see also Gunes 2012b, 91–92). Determining that violence was the only road to national liberation, the PKK initiated its armed attacks in the aftermath of Turkey's transition from a military regime to a civilian regime in 1983. The first major armed attack by the PKK took place on August 15, 1984. The PKK attacked the security units and public buildings in Eruh (Siirt) and Şemdinli (Hakkari) towns, close to the Iraqi border.

The Secular Kurdish Movement and Islam

After this brief overview of the emergence of the secular Kurdish movement, led and dominated by the PKK, we now move to its relations with Islam and Islamic actors. It would be appropriate to divide the PKK-led Kurdish movement's association with Islam into three consecutive periods: (1) indifference and/or hostility (the 1970s and 1980s), (2) a sometimes-ambivalent but generally friendly approach (the 1990s), and (3) an accommodative attitude and the rise of Kurdish-Islamic synthesis (2000 onward). In the following sections, we analyze each stage.

The First Stage (1970s and 1980s): Indifference and/or Hostility

It is widely accepted that, having strong secular, leftist, Marxist orientations, the Kurdish movement initially distanced itself from religious issues and movements. Several observers even argue that the PKK had an *anti*religious attitude in this period (van Bruinessen 2000b; Romano 2006; Aydin and Emrence 2015; Jacoby and Tabak 2015; Gürbüz 2016; Dag 2017). For instance, Romano (2006, 134) states, "True to Marxist doctrine, the PKK attacked religion as a veil of conservatism and ignorance, which helps keep Kurds in their backward and oppressed condition." Van Bruinessen (2000b, 13) also observes that most of secular Kurdish nationalists "considered Islam as one of the major forces oppressing their people." Similarly, Aydin and Emrence (2015, 11) note that the PKK "rejected religious-based programs, which had informed previous Kurdish revolts in the region. Accordingly, insurgent ideology allowed no room for hyphenated identities in the Kurdish community. It fiercely competed against Kurdish Islam, ignored Alevi identity, and hardly mentioned Zazas, the last two being distinct ethno-confessional groups within the Kurdish community." Jacoby and Tabak (2015, 350) also observe that the PKK's traditional discourse regarded Islam as "being responsible for spreading linguistic and cultural subordination." They observe that PKK leader Öcalan believed that religion had an anesthetic effect on Kurdish people in the region. Finally, Gürbüz (2016, 114) shares similar observations: "The [PKK] guerillas regarded the traditional culture [Islamic beliefs, norms, and values] as a pacifying social force that made Kurds obedient to the Turkish authorities. Öcalan long emphasized that Sunni Islam played a strong role in maintaining the enslavement of Kurds."

Indeed, in the PKK's key documents, we see an indifferent, apathetic, and sometimes highly hostile attitude toward religion and religious groups and movements. For example, the 1978 "Path of Kurdistan Revolution: A Manifesto" (Kürdistan Devriminin Yolu: Manifesto), one of the group's founding documents and one that was republished several times, lays out the movement's views and understandings on various issues. In this key text, we see a highly skeptical and antagonistic attitude toward religion and religious actors. Öcalan (1994, 24), for instance, states, "the anesthetic effect of Islamism on the masses is one thousand times greater than that of bourgeois ideologies." Öcalan claims that the dominant powers used religion as the Trojan horse to conquer and control Kurds from the inside. For Öcalan, Islamist ideologies and movements have had a negative impact on Kurdish national identity, retarding the evolution of a national consciousness among Kurds. In other words, in this key document, Öcalan views religion as a barrier to the development of national awareness and unity among Kurds and states, "All of those powers or groups who occupied or controlled Kurdistan have instrumentalized religion to conceal their exploitation of the local people and to weaken or suppress Kurdish national values by promoting understandings based on *ummah*. Since the medieval period, religion has been the major instrument [of dominant powers] to exterminate the spirit of national resistance among Kurds" (1994, 25). For Öcalan, religious actors (e.g., religious orders and sheikhs) constitute another Trojan horse in Kurdistan. Believing that they work to advance the interests of dominant powers rather than Kurdish national interests, Öcalan calls them traitors.

In another important PKK document (*The Founding Declaration*, *Kuruluş Bildirgesi*, first published in 1979), we see the same hostile attitude toward religion. For instance, it states,

> With the rise of Islam, Arabs established a strong empire and emerged as one of the expansionist powers during the medieval period. They established a colonial regime based on feudalism and imposed it on Kurdish people in the region. This regime, which lasted for almost a century, weakened our people in all spheres. . . . And the tribal leaders and landlords, who embraced Islamic and Arabic values and culture, acted as traitors. Cooperating with occupying powers, they opened severe wounds in the Kurdish body. As carriers of Arabic and Persian language and culture, they constituted the biggest internal obstacle in front of our people's national progress and development. (PKK 1984, 22)

In brief, Öcalan treats religion and religious actors and sectarianism as leftovers or artifacts of the medieval period and asserts that they serve the interests of the feudal-comprador system. We see the same negative attitude toward religion in the original party program, drafted in 1977 and approved in 1978 (see N. Özcan 1999, 355–356).

Later, Öcalan continued to express similar inimical views about the role of religion in sociopolitical life. For instance, during one of his addresses to PKK members (probably in Bekaa Valley, Lebanon, or in Damascus, Syria), Öcalan asserts that throughout history, religion has been abused by the dominant, hegemonic classes and powers to control, suppress, and exploit the subordinate, disadvantaged classes (Öcalan 2001, 31–38). Put differently, for Öcalan, religion serves the interests of dominant classes or groups by masking political and economic domination and exploitation. Having such a negative view of religion and religious actors, Öcalan (1994, 107) identifies them as one of the major obstacles of "the Kurdish national liberation movement."

Altan Tan, a prominent pro-Islamic Kurdish political figure recruited by the Kurdish movement (see later in this chapter), also claims that the Kurdish movement had an anti-Islamic attitude during its initial phase.[16] Dag (2014) similarly draws attention to the movement's antireligious outlook during the 1970s and 1980s: "In the 1980s, the PKK launched an armed organisation to fight against imperialism. It had a leftist orientation, in particular a Marxist-Leninist perspective, which usually considers religion one of the main obstacles to opening people's minds up for freedom. As a result, until the late 1980s, the religious stance was dramatically rigid, and religious figures and symbols were all targets for attack."

Most of my interviewees also emphasized the Kurdish movement's indifferent, apathetic, and sometimes highly hostile or antagonistic attitude toward Islam before the 1990s.[17] For instance, Ruşen Çakır, a writer, journalist, and expert on Islamist and Kurdish movements and actors, stated to the author, "During the 1970s, I was in Istanbul and took part in the leftist movement. The leftist movements in Turkey in that period embraced strong materialist perspectives. The leadership cadre of the Kurdish movement also adopted the same materialist understandings. As a result, they were indifferent toward religion, sometimes even belittling or mocking religion and religious formations. They viewed religion as a kind of obstacle in front of their movement."[18] Mücahit Bilici, an associate professor of sociology at John Jay College, City University of New York, who also closely follows Islamist and Kurdish movements, made similar observations. He remarked, "It is a well-known fact that the Kurdish movement emerged as a socialist, Marxist movement. Regarding its relations with Islam, it certainly had an exclusionary attitude. [One could even say] it was against Islam."[19] As another example, Selahattin Çoban, a lawyer, human rights activist, and former chairperson of the Diyarbakır branch of the Association for Human Rights and Solidarity for the Oppressed (İnsan Hakları ve Mazlumlar İçin Dayanışma Derneği, or Mazlumder), maintained that "in its early period, the Kurdish movement believed that religion was an obstacle for progress. For instance, the Kurdish leadership claimed that one reason for the socioeconomic backwardness in the region was religion. As a result, the movement distanced itself from religion and religious circles. They sometimes even had a hostile attitude toward religion."[20] Finally, Martin van Bruinessen, a prominent name in Kurdish studies, concurred: "Both in Iraq and in Turkey, the Kurdish movement emerging in the 1960s–1970s was secular in character, although many of the actors, especially in Iraq, were personally pious people. In Turkey, the movement emerged within or beside the left and was secular or even antireligious."[21]

In brief, the strongly secular, leftist Kurdish ethnonationalist movement initially regarded religious loyalties and attachments as an obstacle to the emergence of a national consciousness and progress among Kurds. Kurdish ethnopolitical elites simply treated Islam as an alien, unnatural, and disruptive factor in Kurdish society. As a result, the movement distanced itself from religious issues and groups, sometimes adopting highly hostile and aggressive discourse and attitude toward them.

The Second Stage (1990s): A Friendly Approach toward Religion

Beginning in the early 1990s, we see growing interest in religious issues within the PKK-led Kurdish movement. The movement gradually amended its indifferent or antagonistic attitude toward Islam and adopted a much more Islam-friendly position. For instance, Öcalan's 1990 book *A Revolutionary Approach to Religion* (*Din Sorununa Devrimci Yaklaşım*) should be interpreted as an effort by the movement to develop a new attitude toward religion. In the book, Öcalan admits that the classic Marxist approach and the leftist circles in Turkey had a negative, rejectionist attitude toward religion. Distinguishing the PKK from those circles, Öcalan emphasizes that the group now values all religions and beliefs and so rejects radical secularist understandings, which do not respect people's beliefs and traditions. Treating religion as a basic human need, Öcalan argues that religion plays a vital role in social life. He also praises the Prophet Muhammad and Islam by presenting the former as an important revolutionary and the rise of the latter in the seventh century as a great revolution. Öcalan adds that the values and ideals pursued by the PKK are compatible with the essence of Islam, which is, for him, progressive, revolutionary, egalitarian, just, and anti-imperialist. He also claims that the PKK fights against oppression and injustice, as does Islam.

Öcalan, however, complains that throughout history Islam has been corrupted and turned into an instrument of domination and exploitation by power holders. He declares that the PKK will fight against any individuals (e.g., imams, sheikhs), groups, or institutions (e.g., religious orders, Islamist political parties, and the state) that have been abusing religion to advance their particular political and economic interests. In the book's conclusion, he also calls on the PKK to revise its approach toward religion. Öcalan (2008, 75–76) notes, "Islam has been used as an instrument of subjugation and exploitation by fascist and imperialist groups. . . . They also attempt to use Islam to suppress and weaken our national liberation movement. . . . We should show that they have nothing do to with Islam, and they just deceive people with religion. . . . As revolutionaries, we should turn the gun of religion against these fascist and imperialist groups. . . . We should [also] respect and value people's religious beliefs and emphasize and promote the progressive, revolutionary, anti-imperialist aspects of Islam."

In line with this new approach toward religion, the PKK also encouraged and supported the formation of pro-PKK conservative religious institutions, groups, and movements, such as the Union of Alevis of Kurdistan (Kürdistan Aleviler Birliği, 1992), the Union of Yezidis of

Kurdistan (Kürdistan Yezidiler Birliği), the Union of Kurdistan Patriotic Imams (Kürdìstan Yurtsever İmamlar Birliği, 1991), and the Islamic Movement of Kurdistan (Kürdistan İslami Hareketi, 1993) (Barkey and Fuller 1998, 70; White 2000; McDowall 2004, 434–435; Natali 2005, 115; Marcus 2007, 244; Gunes 2012b, 110; Jacoby and Tabak 2015, 351). As Marcus (2007, 244) observes, "The PKK had never shown an interest in linking up with religious Islamic movements—which downplayed Kurdish identity in favor of Islamic identity—and it seemed the PKK hoped to undercut other Islamic groups by forming its own. The difference was this new group was openly nationalist, asserting that different Islamic nations have the right to live independently and develop their own culture, a reference to the Kurds."

In 1994, addressing a group of Kurdish students attending Al-Azhar University, Öcalan (quoted in N. Özcan 1999, 219) argued that the PKK movement was not in contradiction with Islam and claimed that he used to be a devout Muslim:

> The PKK movement represents a mixture of revolutionary socialism and revolutionary Islam in Kurdistan. Some people such as fake leftists and fake Islamists claim that socialism and Islam are contradictory. I disagree with them. Islam is compatible with socialism. . . . We should realize our own Islamic revolution. . . . Then we can have more time for praying and performing *namaz*. I am not against *namaz* or fasting, but currently *jihad* [meaning Kurdish national struggle] comes first. Actually, I used to perform *namaz* and pray constantly. Why, do you think, did I quit performing *namaz*? I had to quit it because I became involved in this struggle.

During an interview he gave to Özgür Gündem in 1994, Öcalan (1995, 94) praised Islam, as follows: "Prophet Muhammad says that 'an Arabic person is not superior to a Persian.' . . . Thus, there is no room for racism in Islam. It is based on universalism. We see understandings such as brotherhood and *ummah* within Islam. Islam does not discriminate against any group because of their linguistic or cultural differences. . . . True Islam does not reject or deny any language or culture."

Furthermore, at the PKK's fifth congress, which took place in January 1995, the PKK leadership made highly conciliatory statements about religion, arguing that Islam was actually compatible with Kurdish nationalist goals and desires:

> With their culture and belief, Kurds constitute one of the most important components of the Islamic community. Till now, Turks, Arabs, and Persians have used Islam against Kurds. However, Islam does not belong to one nation. . . . Like other Islamic nations, Kurds should have the right to live independently and develop their culture autonomously. Embracing Islam should not mean being a slave to other Islamic countries. Rather, fighting against slavery and domination is compatible with Islam. Hence, fighting against Turkish, Arabic, and Persian colonialism and exploitation is a duty for our people, who believe in Islam. (PKK 1995, 98–99; see also Marcus 2007, 244)

The congress also hailed and endorsed pro-PKK conservative formations (listed earlier) and declared that the PKK would continue to encourage and support their activities (see PKK 1995, 95–98).

Thus, beginning in the early 1990s, we see growing interest in religious matters and a softening attitude vis-à-vis religion and religious actors and movements within the secular Kurdish movement (see also van Bruinessen 2000b; Houston 2001; Gürbüz 2016; Dag 2017). This was the initial phase of the Islamic opening of the secular Kurdish movement.

The Third Stage (2000 Onward): Toward Kurdish-Islamic Synthesis

In the 2000s, we have seen an even friendlier attitude toward Islam within the secular Kurdish movement. Islamic ideas, principles, references, and actors have become much more visible within the movement, and they mark the rise of an accommodative attitude toward Islam. In this section, I present several examples of such a shift in Kurdish movement's discourses and actions.

CIVILIAN FRIDAY PRAYERS

To begin with, in March 2011, as part of larger civil disobedience campaigns (*sivil itaatsizlik*), the pro-Kurdish BDP organized "civilian Friday prayers" (*sivil Cuma*) outside mosques in civic squares in several cities in eastern and southeastern Turkey (e.g., Batman, Diyarbakır, Hakkari, Şanlıurfa, Şırnak, Mardin, Muş, and Van). The Kurdish movement initiated these prayers to boycott usual Friday prayers at state-controlled mosques. Thousands of people attended these alternative Friday prayers, led by pro-BDP Kurdish *meles*, who volunteered to deliver them.[22]

In mosques, all of which are controlled by the state, imams are required to deliver *khutbahs* (sermons in mosques during Friday prayers) in Turkish, and the texts are centrally prepared by Diyanet (the Directorate of Religious Affairs)[23] in Ankara and then sent to all mosques around the country. However, in the case of civilian Friday prayers, Kurdish *meles* prepared their own *khutbahs* and delivered them in Kurdish. The *meles* argued that one purpose of these civilian Friday prayers was to draw attention to the right to pray in one's mother language (i.e., Kurdish, in this case). For instance, *Mele* Zahit Çiftkuran, chairperson of the pro-Kurdish DIAYDER (see the following subsection) argued, "Islam necessitates sermons in one's mother language. In the region, the majority of people adhere to the Sunni-Shafi school [of Islam], and according to the Shafi teachings, *khutbahs* must be understood by the people who attend the Friday prayers. Thus, people in the region demand Kurdish *khutbahs*. That is why we initiated a signature campaign. Once we gather enough signatures, we will submit our petition to Diyanet."[24] Meeting in Diyarbakır in May 2013, Kurdish *meles* concluded that the civilian Friday prayers had achieved their goals to a certain extent (e.g., Diyanet gave permission for Kurdish sermons to occur in certain mosques in the region) and decided to end them in July 2013.[25] This initiative by the Kurdish movement drew much national attention and sparked heated debates in political and religious circles at the time (see also Sarigil and Fazlioglu 2013). As Çiçek (2013, 161) also observes,

> The Kurdish movement's efforts to build a new policy with respect to Islam at the level of discourse, practice, and representation have made it difficult for the AK Party to manage the Kurdish issue with an Islamist discourse. Civilian Friday prayers have played a crucial role in this regard. The Kurdish movement's support [for] the prayers, active involvement of Kurdish *meles* committed to the Kurdish movement, and their criticisms of statist Islam in their sermons have broken the influence of [the] AK Party's claims regarding [the] anti-Islamic character of the Kurdish movement. [Due to the] AK Party's refusal to allow sermons in [the] Kurdish language, the central demand of civilian Friday prayers has once again disclosed the nationalist limits of [the] AK Party's politics of Islamic brotherhood.

FIGURE 2.3. A view from civilian Friday prayers (*sivil Cuma*), held on March 4, 2016, in Sümerpark, Diyarbakır. Courtesy of Mahmut Bozarslan, a journalist based in Diyarbakır.

CO-OPTING CONSERVATIVE FIGURES AND FORMATIONS

In line with the Kurdish movement's new approach toward religion, it has taken many conservative individuals into its ranks. For instance, in recent local and general elections, pro-Kurdish political parties have nominated an increasing number of *meles* and activists, columnists, academics, and politicians with a conservative or Islamist background. For example, during the 2011 general elections, the BDP supported popular candidates from conservative Kurdish circles, such as Altan Tan and Şerafettin Elçi. Similarly, during the March 2014 local elections, the party nominated female candidates (wearing headscarves), three of whom were elected as mayors (in Hazro-Diyarbakır, Kocaköy-Diyarbakır, and Erciş-Van). The policy of including conservative figures into the movement was maintained during the 2015 general elections. The HDP, which has represented the Kurdish movement in party politics since summer 2014, nominated other popular conservative figures such as Hüda Kaya, Nesrin Hilal Şanlı, Seher Akçınar Bayar, Ayhan Bilgen, Adem Özcaner (from the Azadi Movement), and Kadri Yıldırım (a professor of divinity). The candidate list also included some men of religion (e.g., retired state imams such as the former Diyarbakir mufti Nimetullah Erdoğmuş).[26]

The movement also included several conservative figures as decision makers. For instance, Altan Tan, Ayhan Bilgen, and Hüda Kaya were also members of the HDP's Central Executive Committee. These changes suggest that the Kurdish ethnopolitical movement, in addition to expanding its symbolic boundaries, has also expanded its social boundaries.

As part of the Kurdish ethnopolitical movement's co-option strategy, it has also encouraged the formation of conservative civil society organizations sympathetic to the Kurdish cause. For instance, in July 2007, pro-Kurdish men of religion (e.g., active and retired *meles*, *seydas*—more senior, authoritative Islamic scholars—and some retired state imams) established the Association for the Solidarity of Imams and Religious Scholars (Din Alimleri Yardımlaşma Derneği, DIAYDER), which is based in Diyarbakır. Subsequently, DIAYDER opened several branches in eastern (e.g., Hakkari, Şırnak, and Van) and western provinces having a substantial number of Kurds (e.g., Adana, Istanbul, Izmir, and Mersin). As an association supportive of the Kurdish movement, DIAYDER cooperates with other pro-Kurdish organizations and political parties. For instance, as seen in figure 2.4, the Istanbul branch of DIAYDER hosted Selahattin Demirtaş, coleader of the pro-Kurdish HDP, before the June 2015 general elections. Pro-Kurdish *meles* affiliated with DIAYDER also appear at the electoral rallies and meetings of pro-Kurdish political parties, giving speeches to mobilize mass support for these parties in local and general elections. In addition, by attending condolence (*taziye*) and commemoration (*anma*) events, leading *mawlids* (see the later subsection), getting involved in dispute-resolution processes as mediators, and participating in several other communal activities such as wedding ceremonies, these pro-Kurdish men of religion encourage ties between the Kurdish ethnopolitical movement and

FIGURE 2.4. Before the June 2015 general elections, the Istanbul branch of DIAYDER hosted Selahattin Demirtaş, coleader of the pro-Kurdish HDP, April 29, 2015. *Photo source*: Facebook page of Democratic Islam Congress (Demokratik İslam Kongresi, DİK) (accessed September 15, 2016).

the Kurdish masses. In DIAYDER's efforts to promote Kurdish rights and freedoms, it frequently employs Islamic ideas and references. The Kurdish movement has also put together several commissions to deal with religious matters. For instance, the Commission of Peoples and Beliefs (Halklar ve İnançlar Komisyonu) was formed within the Democratic Society Congress (Demokratik Toplum Kongresi, DTK), established in 2007 as an umbrella organization of pro-Kurdish associations and groups. Including several religious figures such as nonstate imams (*meles* and *seydas*) and religious leaders of minority groups, the commission was expected to represent various religious communities (e.g., Muslims such as Sunnis and Alevis, and non-Muslims such as Syriacs, Armenians, and Yezidis) within the DTK and to organize religion-related activities. We have seen similar commissions formed within pro-Kurdish parties such as the BDP and the HDP.

DEMOCRATIC ISLAM CONGRESS

Another quite intriguing initiative has been the Democratic Islam Congress, called for by imprisoned PKK leader Öcalan and organized in May 2014 by the BDP and the DTK. Around 350 delegates (composed of men of religion [*meles* and *seydas*], politicians, activists, writers, journalists, academics, and intellectuals from Europe, Turkey, Iraq, Iran, and Syria, most of whom were sympathetic to the Kurdish movement) met in Diyarbakır. Over two days, they discussed issues such as notions of justice, freedom, and peace in Islam and women and Islam.[27]

The congress opened with a reading of the Koran. This was followed by a message from Öcalan sent from İmralı prison. In it, Öcalan greeted participants by calling them his "Muslim brothers." Citing several verses from the Koran, Öcalan rejected both an authoritarian secularist approach and radical Islamic understandings and argued that the movement's notion of Islam is based on pluralism, democracy, equality, justice, and freedom. He also suggested that a more democratic Islam should be promoted in "Kurdistan" against radical Islamic groups and movements (e.g., Kurdish Hezbollah, Al-Qaeda, and ISIS).

The congress's concluding statements, which included several references to Islamic ideas and principles and verses from the Koran, reiterated that "the true essence" of Islam is constituted by values and norms such as peace, justice, equality, freedom, and democracy. Speakers argued that Islam, as a religion of peace and justice, can substantially contribute to finding a peaceful solution to the Kurdish issue. The concluding statements also included strong references to the Charter of Medina (aka the Constitution of Medina or the Medina Contract), which was drafted by the Prophet Muhammad in the aftermath of his Hijra (departure) from Mecca to Medina in 622. The charter involved an agreement between Muslims (e.g., Muhajirun, the emigrants, and Ansar, Medina residents who helped the Prophet Muhammad) and non-Muslims (e.g., Jewish, Christian, pagan groups, and non-Muslim Arabs) living in Medina. The charter aimed to define the rights and freedoms of the different ethnic and religious communities residing in Medina and to ensure peace and cooperation among all those groups, putting forward a notion of *ummah* composed of multiple, equally legitimate ethnicities, languages, and beliefs (see Denny 1977). The participants of the 2014 Democratic Islam Congress agreed that this charter can and should serve as a model for a possible peaceful solution to the Kurdish conflict in Turkey.

After the Congress, Kurdish ethnopolitical elites continued to draw attention to the charter as an ideal model of a social contract. For instance, during meetings with local religious leaders in Güroymak (Bitlis) as part of campaigns before the November 2015 general elections, HDP coleader Selahattin Demirtaş stated, "The Charter of Medina, drafted by our Prophet Muhammad, constitutes one of our key references. It is a highly significant document. If we wish to build a society based on equality and brotherhood, we cannot ignore this document."[28]

The second general meeting of the congress was held in Istanbul in mid-December 2015. Around 400 delegates from 30 provinces and 300 guests from Turkey, Europe, the Middle East, and Africa met in Istanbul and discussed for three days various themes such as the Kurdish issue,

FIGURE 2.5. A scene from the Democratic Islam Congress, May 10–11, 2014, Diyarbakır. Courtesy of Mahmut Bozarslan.

democracy, peace, social justice, just war, women's rights, workers' rights, youth, and environmental protection. Like the first congress, the second was opened by reading verses from the Koran. The concluding statements, which also included several references to the Koran, reiterated that Islam is a religion based on peace, democracy, tolerance, freedom, equality, social justice, and an ecologist understanding. It was reiterated that the Charter of Medina offers an ideal model of the peaceful coexistence of different religious and ethnic groups and of regional autonomy. Hence, the congress continued to suggest that the charter should be taken as a reference point for the peaceful settlement of the Kurdish issue.[29]

EFFORTS TO PROMOTE RELIGIOUS FREEDOMS

The Kurdish movement has also become more outspoken and active about religious rights and demands. As a case in point, after the June 2011 elections, BDP deputies proposed a bill suggesting that female deputies should be allowed to wear headscarves during parliamentary sessions.[30]

This initiative surprised many circles because in Turkish politics it has been conservative parties rather than secular ones fighting the headscarf ban. Likewise, supporting civilian Friday prayers, the BDP leadership demanded Kurdish sermons in state-controlled mosques. In April 2011, BDP leader Selahattin Demirtaş stated, "Everyone listens to sermons in Kurdish in the mass prayers held in city squares in the Southeast [civilian Friday prayers]. Mosques are not the homes of the state but of Allah. The rules in the mosques should be set by the people attending that mosque, not by the state. If the state is deciding which language is going to be spoken in mosques, this has nothing to do with religion. Let people pray in the way they want."[31] In January 2016, the pro-Kurdish HDP leadership also supported the government's initiative to reschedule the official noon break on Fridays to allow public officials or employees to attend Friday prayers. Considering the regulation incompatible with the secular nature of the Republic, several leftist circles publicly criticized such an initiative by the conservative AKP government.[32] However, the secular Kurdish movement openly welcomed it.[33]

MAWLIDS

Likewise, in April 2014, pro-Kurdish groups (e.g., the BDP, DIAY-DER, and the DTK) organized for the first time a mass meeting to celebrate the anniversary of the Prophet Muhammad's birthday (also known as *mawlid*)[34] in Diyarbakır and Van.[35] Such meetings can also be interpreted as a response to *mawlid* gatherings thought to have been spearheaded by Kurdish Hezbollah in April 2011 and 2012 in Diyarbakır, attended by hundreds of thousands.[36] In other words, given the fact that rival Kurdish groups (e.g., Islamic Hezbollah) have been mobilizing the Kurdish masses by organizing religious activities such as *mawlid* gatherings, the secular Kurdish movement felt the need to respond to such initiatives by organizing its own *mawlid* meetings.[37] The movement also started to organize *mawlid*-type gatherings to commemorate PKK members killed during armed conflict with security forces (see also Jacoby and Tabak 2015).

IFTAR DINNERS, PRAYING ROOMS

Municipalities controlled by pro-Kurdish parties in the region (e.g., the BDP and the HDP) started to organize public *iftar* dinners during Ramadan. Furthermore, praying rooms (*masjid*) have been arranged in party buildings for those who would like to perform *namaz* during their visits.

COMMEMORATING RELIGIOUS KURDISH FIGURES

Pro-Kurdish parties also began to organize commemoration ceremonies for religious figures with an important place in Kurdish history. For instance, the BDP organized a commemoration ceremony for Sheikh Said on June 29, 2011, the anniversary of his execution. Sheikh Said was a Kurdish cleric from the Naqshbandi religious order and led the first major Kurdish rebellion against the newly established, secular Turkish Republic in early 1925.

The commemoration ceremony for Sheikh Said constitutes an interesting development within the secular Kurdish movement. As van Bruinessen (2000b, 144) notes, many Kurdish nationalists during the 1970s and 1980s viewed the Sheikh Said rebellion, which involved both religious and nationalist motivations (Olson 1989), as a religious reactionary revolt and so were reluctant to embrace his legacy. However, participants of the commemoration ceremony referred to Said not only as an Islamist but also as a nationalist Kurdish leader. It was claimed during the commemoration ceremony that by sacrificing his life for the Kurdish cause, Sheikh Said had sowed the seeds of Kurdish nationalism in Turkey.[38]

During the ceremony, other prominent Kurdish figures—such as Said Nursi (1877–1960), a Kurdish Sunni Muslim theologian regarded as the founder of the Nur movement (Nurculuk) in Turkey;[39] Melaye Ciziri (1570–1640), a Kurdish writer, poet, and mystic; Feqiye Teyran (1590–1660), a Kurdish poet and writer; and Ehmede Xani (1650–1707), a Kurdish writer, poet, and philosopher—were also commemorated. The ceremony also involved reading several verses from the Koran and praying.

ISLAMICIZED DISCOURSE

In addition to the preceding actions and initiatives, Kurdish ethnopolitical actors have been increasingly utilizing Islamic ideas and principles
in their discourses to express their grievances and to legitimize ethnic
diversity, their demands, and the Kurdish movement. For instance, we
see frequent references to certain verses from the Koran, such as the 13th
verse of Surah 49 (*Al-Hujraat*) and the 22nd verse of Surah 30 (*Rum*).[40]
The former reads, "O mankind! We have created you from a male and a
female and have made you into nations and tribes that you may know
each other. Surely the noblest among you in the sight of Allah is the
most godfearing of you. Allah is All-knowing, All-aware." The latter
states, "And of His signs is the creation of the heavens and earth and the
variety of your tongues and hues. Surely in that are signs for all living
beings."[41] Kurdish *meles* close to the movement refer to those verses constantly. Citing them, they argue that if all languages and races are created
equally by Allah, the denial and suppression of the Kurdish language and
rights means direct violation of Allah's verses. For instance, referring
to *Al-Hujraat*, Mele Zahit Çiftkuran, chairperson of DIAYDER, stated,
"[State and government officials] tell us that we are religious brothers,
but they use the Islamic brotherhood to suppress and silence Kurdish
demands. . . . When we look at the Koran, we see that Allah created
different races and languages equally. One is definitely not superior to
another. . . . We are, however, [in reality], unequal brothers. Diyanet, for
instance, does not really represent all religious sects. It takes side with
the Sunni-Hanefi school" (quoted in Sarigil and Fazlioglu 2013, 558).[42]
During a speech at the BDP's second congress in October 2012, party
chairperson Selahattin Demirtaş also cited the Koran in condemning the
state's monolithic understanding of national identity, which is based on
the Turkish language and Turkish nationhood: "It is no longer meaningful to promote monolithic understandings based on a single language
and nationhood in this country. Those who consider themselves as Muslims should not impose such understandings upon Kurds. If you look
at the *Maide surah* of the Koran, for instance, there Allah says that 'had

Allah willed, he would have made you one nation.' . . . You do not see such 'one language, one nation' understandings around the world except in fascist regimes."[43]

Kadri Yıldırım, a former scholar of Islamic theology at Mardin Artuklu University and elected as a deputy from the HDP list in the November 2015 general elections, also utilizes an Islamic discourse to justify Kurdish demands. For instance, he stated to the author, "Islamists in Turkey have distorted Islam. Their discourses and actions are not really compatible with the essence of true Islam as defined by the Koran. . . . If we look at the Koran, we see that it recognizes multiple languages, races, cultures, and identities. It is clearly stated that different languages and races are created by Allah. This means that if you suppress or discriminate against any language, nation, or culture [including Kurdish], you also violate the verses of the Koran."[44]

During public meetings and rallies organized by pro-Kurdish groups, we also have seen ethnonationalist and religious slogans intermingled. A striking example of such an ethnoreligious discourse was that during a public rally organized by the pro-Kurdish DTP in Suruç, Urfa, in September 2009, pro-Kurdish participants chanted, "Ya Allah Bismillah, Seroke me Abdullah [Öcalan]!" (O Allah, in the name of Allah, our president is Abdullah).[45]

Another interesting case was Öcalan's 2013 Nowruz (New Day, the New Year) message. On March 21 of that year, Öcalan's communication from İmralı Island was read by BDP deputies (Sırrı Süreyya Önder and Pervin Buldan) to a large crowd (around 1,000,000 Kurds), gathered in Diyarbakir Square to celebrate the Nowruz festival. With this historic message, Öcalan called for an end to secessionist demands and the 30-year armed struggle and asked for Kurds' support for the unity and peaceful coexistence of Turks and Kurds under "democratic confederation." Another highly striking aspect of the message was his reference to Islam. Öcalan emphasized the unity and brotherhood of Turks and Kurds under the flag of Islam by stating, "Turkish people should be aware of the fact that they have been living with Kurds under the flag of Islam for almost 1,000 years and their coexistence with Kurds is based on frater-nity and solidarity."[46]

In Öcalan's writings from the İmralı prison, given to his lawyers and relatives and published later, he maintains Islam-friendly views and atti-tudes. He exalts Islam by arguing that it was originally a progressive move-ment and that the Prophet Muhammad had a revolutionary personality. Öcalan (2007, 141) claims, however, that Islam degenerated: "Muhammad would have exclaimed . . . 'I am not a Muslim!' if he could have seen the contradiction between the present modern times and his *ummah* [the Muslim community that lived during the Prophet's lifetime]. . . . What happens today in the name of Muhammad amounts to an insult of his person. In himself he concentrated on contemporary religion, philosophy and science at the highest level to establish an optimum order of state, society and productivity. In his own lifetime he shook the world. How can the present Islamic societies be called Muhammadan?"

Leaked minutes of meetings between Öcalan and officials and depu-ties from pro-Kurdish political parties (i.e., the BDP and the HDP) at İmralı prison from February 2013 to March 2015 also show Öcalan's positive stance toward Islam. According to these documents, which were published as a book in November 2015, Öcalan (2015, 20) states,

> Justice, rule of law, and Sufism constitute the essence of Islam. However, Islam was corrupted. You should prevent that corruption. . . . Kurds are religious people. When I was young, I was also a religious person. For instance, I used to perform *namaz*. I had memorized 33 *suras* from the Koran. The imam in our village used to praise me. . . . In 1969, I attended a secret meeting of Kısakürek [Necip Fazıl Kısakürek, an Islamic poet, novelist, and playwright]. . . . I do not want to offend anyone, but I do not approach Islam from the perspective of a classic [antireligious] leftist jargon. . . . Kurdish people have strong religious beliefs.[47]

Almost all of my interviewees also acknowledged the rise of the Islam-friendly attitude and approach within the secular Kurdish movement in the past decades.[48] For instance, Mehmet Yüksel, an HDP representative in Washington, DC, accepted the rise of the new approach toward Islam within the Kurdish movement and stated, "with this shift, the Kurdish movement opened itself to different sections of Kurdish society [e.g., conservative Kurds] and has turned into a much more mature movement, representing a wide range of interests and differences within Kurdish society."[49] Similarly, Fazıl Hüsnü Erdem, of Dicle University, pointed out, "Beginning in the early 1990s, the Kurdish movement has moderated its exclusionary, hostile attitude toward Islam. With this shift, the distance between the secular, leftist Kurdish leadership and conservative Kurdish masses has been gradually shrinking. In other words, the Kurdish movement has adopted a political position and discourse that takes into account social reality [Islam's influence]. The Kurdish movement has opened the door to Islam. As a result, Islamic and conservative groups have gradually diffused into the secular movement."[50] Finally, Zahit Çiftkuran, chairperson of DIAYDER, stated the following: "I agree that the Kurdish political movement initially remained aloof from Islam and Islamic circles. But recently this movement has been paying much more attention to Islam. Now they embrace Islam and Islamic circles. If I may give you an example, when men of religion such as *meles* and *seydas* attend Osman Baydemir's [then-mayor of Diyarbakir metropolitan municipality and a member of the pro-Kurdish BDP] meetings in local communities in districts or villages, [Osman] never walks in front of the *meles*; he follows them."[51]

Interpreting the Kurdish Movement's Islamic Opening

How can we interpret this intriguing transformation within Kurdish ethnopolitics? What do all these discourses and actions mean? First of all, the examples provided in this chapter are sufficient to conclude that since the 1990s, Islam has become part of the political discourses and actions of Kurdish ethnopolitical elites. The secular Kurdish ethnonationalist movement, which ignored or neglected religion before the

1990s, has adopted an increasingly friendly approach to Islam in the past decades. In other words, the movement has simply made peace with Islam and Islamic actors. Conceptually speaking, this study defines the secular Kurdish movement's reconciliation with Islam and Islamic actors as the Islamic opening of the movement. To put it in more theoretical terms, with the antagonistic or hostile attitude of secular Kurdish ethnopolitical elites toward religion and religious actors prior to the 1990s, they had closed themselves off from religion and religious formations (i.e., boundary contraction). In their ethnonational imaginary, they had coupled Kurdish ethnic identity with secular, leftist, and nationalist ideas and values. And such an understanding did not regard Islam as a constitutive element of Kurdish ethnic identity and culture. As stated earlier, religion was treated as something alien and unnatural, with a subversive impact on Kurdish national identity and culture.

However, beginning in the 1990s, the same movement gradually opened the initial boundaries by developing a religion-friendly approach (i.e., boundary expansion). In the 2000s, we have seen much more systematic and comprehensive efforts by the Kurdish ethnopolitical leadership to accommodate Islam and Islamic actors in the movement. Such a reconciliatory attitude has led to the rise of a Kurdish-Islamic synthesis within the Kurdish movement in the recent period (i.e., boundary reinforcement) (see table 2.1 for a summary).

It is important to indicate that the Islamic opening of the secular Kurdish movement involves two related but distinct boundary-making

TABLE 2.1. The Secular Kurdish Movement's Boundary Work with Respect to Islam

	Attitude toward Islam	Islamic closure or opening	Boundary-making strategy
The first stage (1970s–1980s)	Indifferent and/or hostile/aggressive	Closure	Boundary contraction
The second stage (1990s)	Sometimes ambivalent but increasingly friendly	Initial phase of opening	Boundary expansion
The third stage (2000 onward)	Accommodative	Higher level of opening	Boundary reinforcement

processes: (a) Kurdish ethnopolitical leaders have remade the symbolic boundaries of an ethnic category (i.e., Kurdishness) in their ethnonationalist outlook; (b) they have also redrawn the social boundaries of the ethnonationalist movement. Regarding the former, as widely acknowledged, Kurdish ethnonationalism has been an elite-based movement, and Kurdish ethnopolitical elites have played a substantial role in defining Kurdish ethnic identity as well as Kurdish interests and demands. It is widely accepted that Kurdish ethnopolitical actors have played a key role in promoting politicized ethnic awareness and identity among the Kurdish masses in Turkey in the past decades (e.g., see Birand 1992, 280; van Bruinessen 2000a, 20; White 2000, 174; Romano 2006; Tezcür 2009; Watts 2010; Aydin and Emrence 2015). This implies that Kurdish ethnopolitical actors have been the key ethnic and/or national identity builders. From the perspective of the boundary approach, they should be regarded as main ethnic boundary makers. Thus, by incorporating previously excluded Islamic ideas, values, and principles into their policies, strategies, and discourses in the past decades, Kurdish ethnopolitical elites redrew the symbolic boundaries of "Kurdishness" in their ethnonational imaginary. As a result, we see a shift from strongly antireligious, secular notion or understanding of Kurdishness to moderately secular, religion-friendly one within the movement.

With regard to the remaking of the social boundaries of the movement, the shift in the "cultural stuff" (Barth 1969b, 15) or contents of the Kurdish ethnic category then led to a shift in social boundaries. That is, the Kurdish ethnopolitical leaders also expanded the social boundaries of the movement by co-opting pro-Islamic circles. Hence, the increasing visibility of actors with Islamic backgrounds in the Kurdish ethnopolitical movement in the past decades is not a random development but a result of redrawing the symbolic boundaries of Kurdishness. Thus, the Islamic opening of the secular, leftist Kurdish movement has been taking place at both symbolic and social levels.

Having said that, co-opting Islam and Islamic actors does not replace or undermine the ethnic dimension of the Kurdish movement;

ethnonationalist orientations still constitute the dominant color in the Kurdish movement. In other words, by labeling such a transformation within the Kurdish movement as an Islamic opening, this study does not claim that the movement is turning into an Islamic movement. Rather, Islamic elements (i.e., religious ideas, principles, and practices and conservative figures/leaders) are incorporated into, but not taking over, the still-secular ethnopolitical movement. In other words, reconciliation with Islam does not represent a clear break with the movement's secular approach to religion.

It is also important to indicate at this stage that Kurdish ethnopolitical leaders have been careful to distinguish their interpretation of Islam from that of radical Islamic circles (e.g., Kurdish Hezbollah, the Muslim Brotherhood, Salafism, Wahhabism, Al-Qaeda, and ISIS). For instance, in the concluding remarks of the Diyarbakır Democratic Islam Congress, it was claimed that the essence of Islam is libertarian, egalitarian, pluralist, and peaceful. In other words, the Kurdish movement attempts to promote its own understanding of "true Islam" and presents the actions and discourses of radical formations as incompatible with Islam. Kurdish ethnopolitical leaders claim that groups such as Al-Qaeda, Al-Nusra, and ISIS represent "wrong Islam," betraying "true Islam."

This understanding has several implications. First, as Kurdish ethnopolitical leaders expand the ethnic boundaries, they also attempt to contract them. That is, while expanding the symbolic and social boundaries by co-opting Islamic ideas, symbols, and actors into the movement, they also try to limit the boundaries by rejecting radical Islamic interpretations and groups. One reason for such a boundary-making strategy (i.e., the simultaneous adoption of boundary expansion and contraction) is the fear or concern that accommodating all Islam and Islamic actors might alienate certain in-group members with strong secularist orientations, such as Alevi Kurds. This aspect of Kurdish boundary making suggests that not only larger social and political context but also intragroup dynamics and divisions shape the boundary-making strategies and styles of ethnopolitical leaders.

This particular case of boundary work further suggests that as boundary workers (i.e., ethnopolitical leaders) make and remake ethnic boundaries, they act selectively and creatively. In the Kurdish case, we notice that as Kurdish ethnopolitical elites develop a friendlier attitude toward Islam, they borrow the Islamic ideas, principles, and practices that are thought to be compatible with the goals and mission of the Kurdish movement. In other words, the Kurdish ethnopolitical movement has an à la carte approach to Islam. For instance, the recent emphasis on the Charter of Medina by the secular Kurdish movement is not an accidental, random development. The pluralist, inclusionary spirit of the charter provides an opportunity for the Kurdish movement to challenge the monolithic, exclusionary, and suppressive nature of the official understanding of national identity, which is based on Turkishness, as well as the radical interpretations of Islam exhibited by militant Islamic groups. In addition, it is argued that the sociopolitical order that the charter brought for the people living in Medina was based on the principles of local autonomy (*yerel özerklik*) and of self-rule (*öz yönetim*). Again, these are the ideas that have been heavily emphasized by the Kurdish movement in the past few years. The charter, which holds an important place in early Islamic history, has been reclaimed by the secular Kurdish movement in the recent period as a model or framework to be imitated in solving the Kurdish conflict.

Related to this development, as Kurdish ethnopolitical elites incorporate Islam into their political actions and discourses, they also try to promote a particular interpretation of Islam, which is expected to contribute to the Kurdish ethnopolitical cause. For instance, Kurdish ethnopolitical elites increasingly emphasize that Islam is a religion based on values and norms such as justice, equality, freedom, and democracy. These core values and ideas have held an important place in Kurdish movement's discourse for decades. In addition, the Kurdish movement also reinterprets the notion of *ummah*. In conventional Islamic discourse, the notion of *ummah* tends to disregard or suppress ethnic and cultural particularities or differences for the sake of the unity of Muslim believers (see

Houston 2001). In other words, Islamists tend to limit *ummah* to Muslim believers. The Kurdish ethnopolitical movement, however, offers a much more pluralist and inclusive understanding of *ummah*, which includes non-Muslims (e.g., Jews, Christians, Yezidis, Assyrians [Syriacs]) and nonbelievers as well.[52]

Some scholars treat the Kurdish ethnonationalist movement's efforts to reinterpret Islam as the Kurdification of Islam. Gurses (2015, 137), for instance, notes that "years of [Kurdish] conflict have transformed traditional Islamic values and created an Islam that is by and large in line with secular ethnonationalist demands" (see also Dag 2014; Gürbüz 2015, 2016). Thus, the Islamic opening of the secular Kurdish movement is accompanied by another process: the Kurdification of Islam. We can think of these two processes as two sides of the same coin. The diversity of Kurdish society is one major factor that has generated such an outcome. Ethnic-group heterogeneity (i.e., the presence of highly secular groups within Kurdish society, such as Alevi Kurds) shapes the way the ethnopolitical leadership interprets Islam. That is, the heterogeneous structure of the Kurdish ethnic group forces the leadership to promote a more pluralistic and inclusive interpretation of Islam vis-à-vis "the official state Islam," represented by Diyanet, and "the radical jihadist Islam." Kurdish activists openly criticize such versions of Islam. For instance, they argue that the state Islam, which is based on Sunni-Hanefi teachings and understandings, exalts Turkish nationalism and the state and ignores the rights and freedoms of disadvantaged groups such as Kurds and Alevis. Thus, believing that state Islam is not really pluralist and democratic, Kurdish activists claim that it represents a distorted version of "true Islam." As a case in point, pro-Kurdish HDP leader Demirtaş criticized "state Islam" during his visit to the Istanbul branch of DIAYDER as part of his electoral campaign before the June 2015 elections. At DIAYDER, Demirtaş noted, "Yes, we are critical of Diyanet. We believe that the state should be at an equal distance from all religions and beliefs within society and serve them equally. However, that is not the case. Diyanet . . . serves one religion [Islam] and one *madhab*

[Sunni-Hanefi jurisprudence]. What is worse is that Diyanet distorts Islam. This organization puts Islam at the state's service. However, Islam is not a religion to be owned by any state. It belongs to the people."[53]

Conclusion

The strongly secular and left-oriented Kurdish ethnonationalist movement in its initial period distanced itself from religion and religious circles. Denying or rejecting the basic fact that Islam has played an important role in Kurdish society and culture, Kurdish ethnopolitical leaders did not consider Islam as a primary national identifier or a major ethnic marker. In other words, they did not include religious beliefs and values in the set of core values they associated with Kurdish ethnic identity in their ethnonational imaginary. The movement's ethnopolitical leaders sometimes even expressed quite antagonistic views about religion and religious circles. One reason for this indifferent or antagonistic attitude toward Islam was the movement's ideological orientations. As is evident in Öcalan's writings and PKK official documents, until the 1990s the Kurdish ethnonationalist movement adopted an openly leftist, Marxist ideology with a strong secularist orientation. As a result, in the movement's social and political understanding, Kurdish ethnic identity was associated with secular, leftist, nationalist, and revolutionary values and ideas. To put it in more theoretical terms, in the 1970s and 1980s Kurdish ethnopolitical leaders, aloof from religion and religious issues, contracted symbolic and social boundaries by keeping Islamic ideas and actors out of the movement.

In the post-1990 period, however, we have seen a substantial change in the movement's attitude toward Islam and Islamic actors: switching from avowed antireligiosity to an Islam-friendly approach. Especially since the early 2000s, religion and ethnonationalism have been intermingling within the Kurdish movement. Thus, the Kurdish movement has ideationally, socially, and organizationally opened itself to Islam and Islamic circles. Conceptually speaking, such a shift corresponds to two related but distinct forms of boundary work: remaking the symbolic boundaries of an ethnic category (i.e., Kurdishness) and redrawing the social boundaries of the ethnonationalist movement itself. Conceding the significance of Islam in Kurdish society, Kurdish ethnopolitical elites have incorporated Islam into their discourses and political programs. As a result, they redefined the boundaries of Kurdish ethnicity in their ethnopolitical imaginary. In other words, by adding new cultural diacritics (i.e., Islam) to their understanding of "Kurdishness," Kurdish ethnopolitical elites have expanded its symbolic boundaries, at least in their ethnonationalist understandings. This implies that, having made such a shift (i.e., the Islamic opening), the Kurdish ethnonationalist movement has enriched its ideological toolbox. As one would expect, this shift in symbolic boundaries also led to a shift in social boundaries in the sense that the Kurdish movement has also opened itself to certain Islamic actors, especially since the early 2000s. As a result, we have seen a transition from an ethnonationalist struggle *against* (or at least *without*) religion to an ethnonationalist movement *with* religion.

Such a transformation in Kurdish ethnopolitics means that religion has been transferred from the social domain to the political realm. In other words, a sociocultural force has been turned into a political force by the Kurdish movement. Thus, the Islamic opening of secular Kurdish ethnopolitics has been accompanied by the politicization of Islam within the Kurdish context in the past decades. Chapter 3 analyzes the causal factors and mechanisms of this major case of boundary making in Kurdish ethnopolitics in the Turkish setting in recent decades.

3

Explaining the Kurdish Movement's Boundary Making

How can we explain the boundary expansion by the Kurdish ethnopolitical leadership (i.e., its Islamic opening), presented in chapter 2? What were the causal factors and mechanisms of the boundary work? What factors triggered such a boundary shift within the Kurdish movement? What were the immediate consequences of such boundary work? How did such a transformation within the Kurdish movement affect the internal dynamics and the Kurdish movement's interactions with political rivals in local and national politics?

In this chapter, we first discuss the role of several strategic and ideational factors that encouraged and/or forced Kurdish ethnopolitical agents to redraw the symbolic and social boundaries of the movement. Then we move to the internal and external boundary contestations or struggles that were triggered by the boundary work. The chapter closes with addressing some possible alternative considerations about such boundary work in Kurdish ethnopolitics.

The Triggering Factors and Mechanisms of Kurdish Boundary Work
The Declining Influence of Marxism

The collapse of the Soviet Union and the communist bloc in the early 1990s undermined support for Marxist ideas among leftist groups in Turkey. As a result, the PKK gradually distanced itself from Marxism during this period. For instance, during the PKK's fifth congress in January 1995, it removed the hammer and sickle from its flag and emblem (Imset 1996, 95; Romano 2006, 142; Marcus 2007, 244). Quite strikingly, in July 1995, PKK leader Öcalan denounced such ideologies by stating that "the PKK movement has never based itself on Marxist-Leninist ideas and principles."[1]

Instead, the PKK began to emphasize ideas such as democracy, human rights and freedoms, and Kurdish demands (e.g., cultural rights such as linguistic rights, and political rights such as regional autonomy). Both domestic and international concerns played a role in this shift. As Romano (2006, 142) claims, "The organization was aware of the fact that its Marxist-Leninist ideology held little appeal beyond its most active militants. Additionally, the need to attract European support and avoid too much American attention, especially after the fall of the Soviet Union, led the PKK to stress its Kurdish nationalist and human rights grievance frames more than its socialist side." Thus, responding to changes in the larger structural context, the Kurdish ethnopolitical leadership refashioned the movement's ideological orientations. Such a shift created a favorable environment for the rise of a more positive approach toward Islam within the movement. Van Bruinessen (2000b, 54, 56) makes a similar observation: "It was only with the demise of Marxism as a political force that Islam returned to Kurdish politics as a significant factor and Kurdish identity politics to Islamism. . . . The PKK adopted a more respectful attitude towards Islam. It had initially, like all left-wing movements in Turkey, been not only secularist but distinctly anti-religious." Romano (2006, 142) also argues that this ideological shift preceded the rise of a more Islam-friendly approach: "The movement's Marxist ideological attacks on religion had failed to strike a receptive chord in the Kurdish masses, for whom Islam was an important value. Thus the movement began occasionally incorporating an Islamic discourse into its propaganda."

Several interviewees also drew attention to the role that the declining influence of Marxism played in moderating Kurdish movement's attitude toward Islam. For instance, Mithat Sancar of Ankara University stated,

In the 1980s, the PKK operated as a classic Marxist organization. In the early 1990s, the collapse of the Soviet bloc led to a new world order. These major changes in the world also influenced the PKK and triggered a transformation within the Kurdish movement. For instance, beginning in the early 1990s, the PKK gradually distanced itself from classic Marxism. In the same period, we also see a search within the movement for developing a new relationship with Islam. For instance, Öcalan started to write about religious issues. As a result, Islam became part of the political program and activities of the Kurdish movement.[2]

The Need to Expand the Movement's Social Basis and Popularity

Another major factor behind such boundary work was that the secular Kurdish movement needed to expand its social basis and popularity. As presented in chapter 2, the Kurdish movement, led by the PKK, emerged as a small-scale armed struggle in the late 1970s. However, the fledgling group's survival and ability to wage an effective struggle against the Turkish state required the leadership to expand the movement's appeal and popularity among the Kurdish masses in Turkey, the Middle East, and Europe. Such a necessity forced the leadership to reconcile with the values and traditions of Kurdish society (e.g., Islam). Put differently, it was almost impossible for the Kurdish movement to turn into a popular, mass movement (*kitle hareketi*) or people's movement (*halk hareketi*) without changing its antagonistic attitude toward Islam, which occupies a central place in Kurdish social life.

As the existing literature on the Kurdish movement also acknowledges, the PKK-led struggle garnered increasing popular support among Kurds in Turkey and Europe and gained mass character by the 1990s. In other words, a crusade initiated by a small militant group evolved into a strong, transnational mass movement, with multiple legal and illegal branches, structures, and formations in Turkey, in the region, and in Europe (see Birand 1992; Imset 1996; van Bruinessen 2000a; White 2000; McDowall 2004; Romano 2006; Marcus 2007; Watts 2010; Gunes 2012b; S. Aslan 2015; Aydin and Emrence 2015; Tezcür 2015). For instance, White (2000, 2) remarks, "the Kurdish national movement, which originated as a primitive rebellion, is today closer than ever to its popular roots [the Kurdish masses]." McDowall (2004, 439) also draws attention to the PKK's success in creating a strong and coherent national mass movement:

> By 1993 the PKK had been waging its guerilla war for almost a decade. It had every reason to be satisfied with its progress. Since 1984 it had successfully expanded its field of operations, and had become the most serious challenge ever posed against the Republic. . . . It had driven from the field any serious competitors for the Kurdish national mantle. The PKK happily shouted down any other Kurdish voices. . . . It had also galvanized a great swath of Kurds. This was most discernible at Nawruz, when thousands took to the streets, both in Kurdistan and in the cities of migration.

Similarly, Watts (2010, 55) points out the following: "The late 1980s and first years of the 1990s also saw dramatic expansion, diversification, and 'thickening' of the Kurdish national movement inside and outside of Turkey. Conceptualized another way, it is possible to sketch the outlines of an expanding field of Kurdish resistance that consisted of three intertwined tendencies: first, grassroots, social-level politicization and mobilization in the southeastern part of the country; second, the dramatic growth and strength of the PKK; and third, a rise in the number and activities of Kurdish cultural and political organizations, both domestic and transnational."[3]

As the PKK expanded, the movement's activities stretched further into the political, social and economic spheres. As Marcus (2007, 217) notes, "In the early 1990s, the PKK grew from a guerilla force into a real political force, complete with associated publications, cultural institutions, and a political party. Its backers were not only villagers but also teachers, trade unionists, and lawyers. It had a strong presence in the urban centers in western Turkey."[4]

Thus, the PKK-led Kurdish movement, expanding its social basis, became much more organized in the city centers, enhancing its number of *milis* in the region (i.e., eastern and southwestern provinces), recruit-

ing an increasing number of militants, and receiving growing support
from Kurds in eastern Turkey, in western Turkish cities, and in Europe (Romano 2006). The PKK also increased its economic activities
(e.g., "taxing" businesses in urban centers, receiving donations, smug-
gling and partaking in the drug trade, and racketeering) (Aydin and
Emrence 2015, 26). The movement also became much more visible in
the media. For instance, it initiated several pro-Kurdish publications
(magazines and daily newspapers such as *Serxwebun* [Independence],
Berxwedan [Resistance], *Azadiya Welat* [The freedom of homeland],
Gündem, Özgür Gündem, Özgür Ülke, Yeni Politika, Özgür Politika),
satellite television stations (e.g., Med-TV, 1994–1999, which was the
first Kurdish satellite television channel and was based in the UK and
Belgium; MEDYA TV, 1999–2004, based in France and Belgium; and
Roj-TV, 2004 onward, based in Belgium and Denmark), and websites
in various languages. Similarly, the PKK-led movement established
several publishing houses, institutes, associations, and cultural centers,
promoting the Kurdish cause through various activities such as conferences, protests, meetings, demonstrations, cultural festivals, concerts, and
Nowruz celebrations in both Turkey and Europe (Gunes 2012b). The PKK
also enlarged its reach and social basis within the Kurdish diaspora in
Europe:

> The PKK's network in Europe had grown tremendously since the early
> 1980s, when a handful of supporters considered themselves fortunate if
> they could raise a few thousand dollars or get a few hundred people to a
> rally. Just a decade later [i.e., the 1990s], the PKK operated an extensive
> network of cultural clubs, political offices and publishing ventures, spread
> out over half-a-dozen countries. Its annual fund drive raised about $30
> million a year, and the group collected another $20 million or so from its
> festivals, which drew tens of thousands of people, from magazine sub-
> scriptions, which sympathizers bought as a show of support, and all the
> concerts, coffees, and plays that PKK activists staged. (Marcus 2007, 230;
> see also White 2000, 175–177; Gunes 2012b, 101–123)

In enhancing its popularity and respect among Kurds, the PKK has evolved into a kind of parallel government in Turkey's eastern and southeastern regions. As Imset (1996, 83–84) notes, "The PKK, which was already strengthening, had then also the opportunity to establish local authority in various areas, filling the gap of state authority. Secret Kurdish schools started functioning in the darkness of the night. The number of court cases heard at Turkish civil courts declined rapidly as [the] so-called PKK peoples' tribunal came to being. In several provinces the PKK even set up . . . local police and intelligence units."

Growing support for the PKK among Kurds incited the movement then to organize itself in the legal political arena. In addition to the Kurdish movement's armed struggle, it started to operate in legal politics to further expand its legitimacy and popularity in both the international and domestic spheres (Marcus 2007). As Marcus (2007, 160) observes,

> Thousands of . . . young Kurdish men and women began to throw their support behind the group, helping turn the PKK into a mass organization. One reason for the shift was the PKK's relentless guerrilla war, which finally did win it mass trust and respect. The other reason was the group's decision to move into legal, nonviolent activities, giving the rebel group a reach far beyond the war. Over the next three years, the PKK solidified its hold over legal Kurdish politics, Kurdish publishing, and cultural events. This created a new and more varied support base for the PKK and helped it establish full dominance over Turkey's Kurdish national movement.

As a result, the People's Labor Party (Halkın Emek Partisi, HEP) was established in June 1990 as the first legal pro-Kurdish party.[5] The rise of pro-Kurdish political parties as peaceful and legitimate entities in formal, legal party politics further helped PKK's growth. Marcus (2007, 163) notes that "Öcalan's decision to moderate his approach to legal activities—without abandoning the armed struggle—also was good for the PKK. It helped the PKK grow into a mass movement. It gave the rebel group a legal way to promote its views, allowing it to reach more people. Simultaneously, it helped the PKK attract a new group of supporters—people who either could not or did not want to go to the mountains and fight but who were willing to work for a legal political party." As legitimate political channels, pro-Kurdish political parties strengthened the ties between the movement and the Kurdish masses. Strikingly, since the mid-1990s, these parties have gradually enhanced their electoral popularity among Kurds. As table 3.1 and figure 3.1 present, pro-Kurdish parties have received increasing mass support, gaining the majority of Kurdish votes in the 2011 and 2015 general elections. During the latter, for the first time, a pro-Kurdish party (i.e., the HDP) passed the 10% national electoral threshold, securing 80 seats in parliament. During the snap elections held in November 2015, the HDP repeated the same success, this time gaining 59 seats.

As table 3.2 displays, pro-Kurdish parties expanded their popularity in local elections as well. For instance, during the April 1999 local elections, the HADEP gained control of 37 municipalities in the region, including major cities such as Diyarbakir and Van. This victory was an

TABLE 3.1. Support for Pro-Kurdish Political Parties in General Elections (1991–2015)

Elections	Party	National vote (%)	Average regional vote (%)[c]	Seats
1991	HEP/SHP[a]	—	—	22
1995	HADEP	4.2	28.06	—
1999	HADEP	4.8	30.47	—
2002	DEHAP	6.2	40.19	—
2007	DTP/Indep.[b]	5.2	39.30	20
2011	BDP/Indep.[b]	6.6	52.97	36
2015 (J)	HDP	13.1	69.40	80
2015 (N)	HDP	10.76	64.20	59

[a] During the October 1991 general elections, the pro-Kurdish HEP and the social-democratic SHP entered into an electoral alliance with the HEP candidates included on the SHP's list. In 1992, those candidates resigned from the SHP and rejoined the HEP.

[b] The DTP and the BDP supported independent candidates in the general elections to avoid the required 10% national electoral threshold.

[c] The following provinces, which are mostly inhabited by Kurds, are included: Batman, Bitlis, Diyarbakır, Hakkari, Mardin, Muş, Siirt, Şanlıurfa, Şırnak, and Van.

Source: TUIK (www.tuik.gov.tr); YSK (www.ysk.gov.tr).

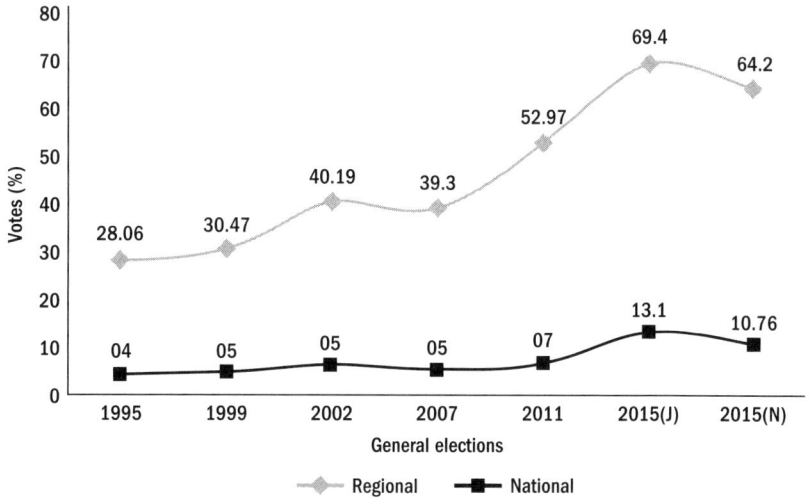

FIGURE 3.1. The national and regional popularity of pro-Kurdish political parties in general elections, 1995–2015 (%).

unprecedented development in the history of Kurdish ethnopolitics. Again, table 3.2 shows that since then, Kurdish parties have gained in popularity and controlled an increasing number of municipalities.

The rise of pro-Kurdish parties in legal party politics (both at the national and local levels) further promoted the movement within Kurdish society. In an analysis of Kurdish party politics, Watts (2010, 13) reaches similar conclusions: "By working within electoral politics, Kurdish challengers gained access to state-allocated material, legal, and political resources that were unavailable to those using armed contention. . . . Entering governmental institutions and participating in formal political arenas created a durable platform for activism that helped the movement withstand failing fortunes on other fronts, created new social and political facts on the ground in Kurdish-majority provinces of the southeast, and helped legitimize the movement through votes. In sum, it furthered the movement in ways that armed struggle could not."

Working through the legal, formal political system and institutions (e.g., parliament, municipal governments, and civil society organizations

TABLE 3.2. Electoral Popularity of Pro-Kurdish Political Parties in Local Elections (1994–2014)

Local elections	Party	National vote (%)	Number of municipalities
1994	DEP[a]	—	—
1999	HADEP	3.82	37
2004	DEHAP/SHP[b]	5.15	54
2009	DTP	5.7	99
2014	BDP/HDP[c]	6.4	102

[a] Due to attacks on DEP party centers and armed assaults on its candidates, the DEP decided not to compete in the local elections of March 1994.
[b] The DEHAP entered into an electoral coalition with the SHP.
[c] The BDP competed in the eastern and the HDP in the western provinces, but the latter failed to win in any municipality.
Source: TUIK (www.tuik.gov.tr); YSK (www.ysk.gov.tr).

such as associations and foundations) in turn magnified the transformative impact of the Kurdish movement on the Kurdish masses. Growing mass support for Kurdish ethnonational political parties suggests that ethnic consciousness and attachments among Kurds have increased in the past decades. Thus, we can confidently suggest that the PKK-led Kurdish movement contributed substantially to the rise of a politicized ethnic consciousness and identity among the Kurdish masses (see also Birand 1992, 280; van Bruinessen 2000a, 20; White 2000, 174; Romano 2006; Tezcür 2009; Watts 2010; Aydin and Emrence 2015). As Romano (2006, 169) points out,

By the 1980s and 1990s, Kurdish nationalist framings enjoyed widespread dissemination through advanced technologies such as desktop publishing, radio, Internet, and satellite television, as well as from diaspora communities well plugged-in to such technology and free to pursue it. The cultural impact of the PKK's contest with the Turkish state polarized society in Turkey. While the bulk of the ethnic Turkish population remained implacably hostile to Kurdish nationalists (as opposed to largely incognizant of the Kurds in the 1950s), within the Kurdish population

Kurdish nationalist sentiment experienced an awakening. This awakening of politicized ethnicity amongst the Kurds is unlikely to be undone by the Turkish state in today's context of easy communication and globalization. (See also Watts 2010, 11)

McDowall (2004, 429) also observes the rise of ethnic consciousness among the Kurdish masses in the early 1990s: "[In March 1990,] the PKK offensive was eclipsed by the burgeoning civil resistance to the security forces. For the first time, families of PKK martyrs dared collect the corpses for burial from the authorities and arranged public funerals which rapidly became opportunities for mass protest." Statements by Necdet Atalay, who was elected mayor of Batman in 2009, constitute a striking instance of the transformative impact of the PKK movement on the Kurdish masses. During a public speech in Lice in August 2008, Atalay stated the following: "We were ashamed of our Kurdishness 30 years ago. How happy for these people [PKK militants], they have taught us how to live with pride. Now, no Kurd is ashamed of her Kurdishness. To the contrary, every Kurd is proud of her identity. This struggle entailed tremendous sacrifices. I hail these honorable individuals in your presence" (quoted in Tezcür 2009, 6).

The results of public opinion surveys conducted as part of a larger research project on the Kurdish issue in Turkey also show that the majority of Kurds embrace the PKK and its leader, Öcalan. For instance, as figure 3.2 displays, although the vast majority of Turks (around 92%) would prefer severely punitive measures taken against Öcalan (e.g., life imprisonment or the death penalty), the majority of Kurds (76%) opt for more forgiving measures (e.g., house arrest or release).[6] This gap between Turks and Kurds also shows itself in their respective attitudes toward the PKK. For instance, only around 6% of Turks support general amnesty for PKK members, while the majority of Kurds (around 70%) endorse it. These figures and the electoral outcomes presented earlier indicate a substantial degree of mass support for the Kurdish ethnopolitical movement.

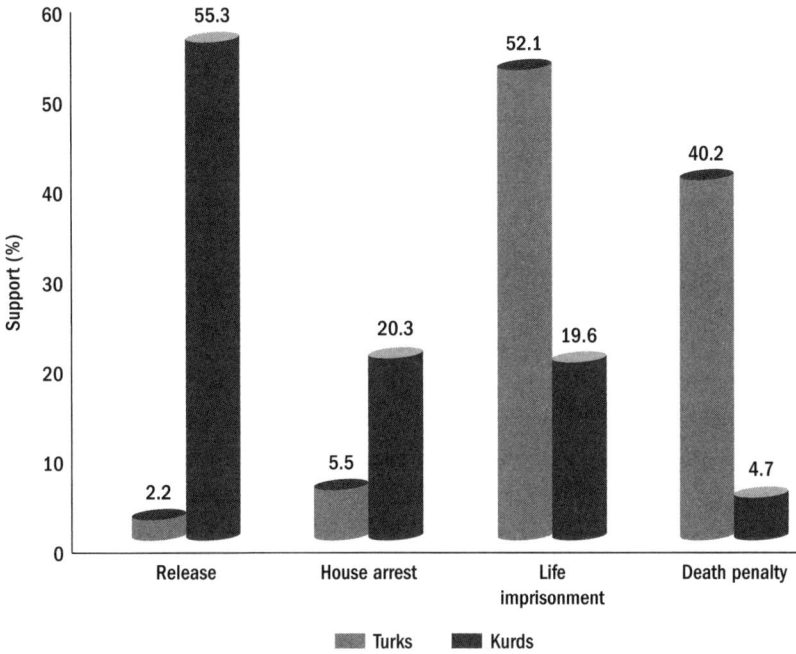

FIGURE 3.2. The distribution of Turkish and Kurdish preferences regarding the status of PKK leader Öcalan, April 2015.

In brief, there have been two different but simultaneous processes at play in the movement's development. On the one hand, the PKK, which has been waging an armed struggle against the Turkish state since the early 1980s, has promoted the rise of a politicized ethnic consciousness and identity among Kurds in Turkey (in Benedict Anderson's [1991] lexicon, a Kurdish "imagined community"; Romano 2006; White 2000; Watts 2010; Gunes 2012b; Aydin and Emrence 2015). By awakening a strong national consciousness among the majority of Kurds through both peaceful and violent means and mechanisms, the ethnopolitical movement has successfully transformed the Kurdish masses and mobilized a substantial number of Kurds to support the movement. As Aydin and Emrence (2015, 130) also conclude, "Insurgencies do not necessarily fight for identities that already exist. Instead, they spend most of their time building new ones. In that respect, civil wars can be viewed as incomplete group-making projects."

On the other hand, as the PKK-led Kurdish movement has gained mass character over time, it has had to adjust its ideological orientations, developing a more positive attitude toward Kurdish cultural values such as Islam, which plays an important role in Kurdish society.[7] In other words, the diffusion of the movement into Kurdish society has led to the moderation of the movement's stance toward Islam. Öcalan also openly admits in his writings in the early 1990s that developing a more welcoming attitude toward the values, beliefs, and traditions of Kurdish society would help the movement strengthen its ties with the people and turn into a truly mass movement. As an example of this continued mindset, in February 2015 during his meeting with HDP officials at İmralı prison, Öcalan (2015, 424) stated, "Leftist socialism should redefine itself. It should internalize Islamic culture. If the left does not accommodate Islam, it will not be successful in this region" (see also Öcalan 2008, 49).

Hence, in order to expand the PKK-led armed struggle and turn it into a mass movement, Kurdish ethnopolitical elites had to develop a more Islam-friendly attitude and approach. This need constituted another motivation behind the expansion of symbolic and social boundaries of the Kurdish ethnopolitical movement. To sum up, as the PKK-led Kurdish movement diffused into Kurdish society, Islamic ideas, values, and circles also gradually dispersed into the secular ethnopolitical movement (i.e., a process of mutual infusion).

Electoral Competition

Another triggering factor behind the boundary work by Kurdish ethnopolitical leadership was electoral rivalry. Figure 3.3 shows that in the 1990s, pro-Kurdish, pro-Islamic, and center-right formations enjoyed a substantial degree of electoral popularity among Kurds in the region. In the early 2000s, however, the electoral popularity of pro-Islamic and conservative political parties (e.g., AKP) among Kurds increased,

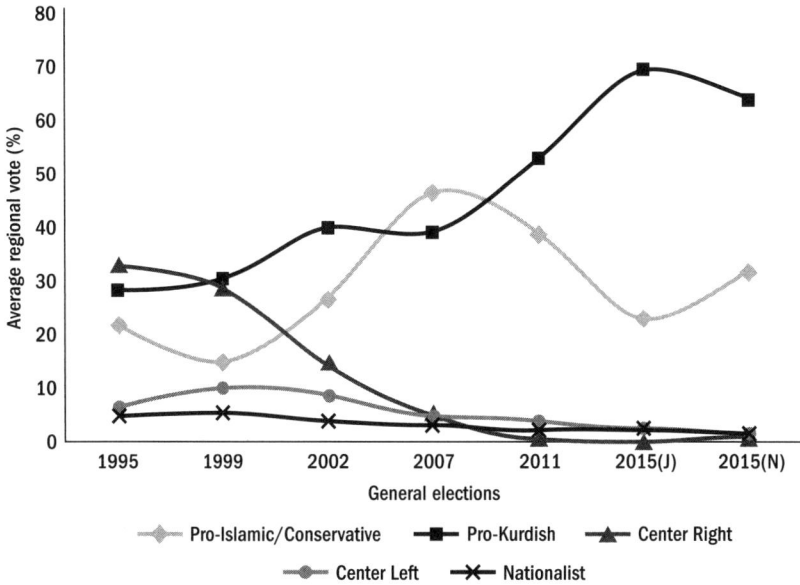

FIGURE 3.3. Electoral popularity of major political orientations in Kurdish provinces, 1995–2015. *Notes: Pro-Islamic/conservative*: RP/FP/SP, AKP; *pro-Kurdish*: HADEP/DEHAP/DTP/BDP/HDP/Indep.; *center-right*: ANAP, DYP, DP; *center-left*: CHP, DSP; *Turkish nationalist*: MHP. The following Kurdish-majority provinces are included in the calculation of average regional vote: Batman, Bitlis, Diyarbakır, Hakkari, Mardin, Muş, Siirt, Şanlıurfa, Şırnak, Van. *Source*: TÜİK (http://www.tuik .gov.tr/) and YSK (http://www.ysk.gov.tr/).

while the electoral popularity of center-right political parties substantially declined. As a result, beginning in the early 2000s, the Kurdish electorate became polarized between pro-Kurdish ethnic parties and pro-Islamic, conservative parties. As the figure displays, the evolution of the electoral popularity of one party is almost the reverse of the other party's, suggesting that the Kurdish party's loss became the conservative party's gain. To put it differently, since the early 2000s, the main rivals of pro-Kurdish parties in the region have been religiously oriented political parties. Even during the 2007 general elections, the most popular party among Kurds was the ruling, conservative AKP. Thus, electoral pressures and competition for votes have forced the secular Kurdish leadership to be much more attentive vis-à-vis religious issues, which has also accelerated the rise of a more accommodative attitude toward Islam and Islamic actors within the secular Kurdish movement.

Legitimacy Struggles

We should also take into account the legitimacy concerns of Kurdish ethnopolitical elites. Both legal (political parties such as the AKP) and illegal (Kurdish Hezbollah, the Party of God) Islamist and conservative formations attempted to delegitimize the Kurdish movement in the eyes of the Kurdish masses, particularly among conservative Kurds, by labeling the Kurdish movement as "Marxist," "atheist," "Satanic evil," "un-Islamic," and therefore "illegitimate." For instance, Kurdish Hezbollah, a radical, militant Kurdish-Islamist organization that emerged in the 1980s with the goal of overthrowing the secular regime and establishing an Islamic Kurdish state, has constantly labeled the PKK as infidel, atheist, and un-Islamic (*mürted*) (Kurt 2015).[8] In the first half of the 1990s, Kurdish Hezbollah constituted a major challenge to the PKK's dominance in the region (see also McDowall 2004; Aydin and Emrence 2015; Kurt 2015). Hezbollah was especially active and strong in Diyarbakir, Batman, and Mardin provinces, where it and the secular, leftist PKK waged a bloody armed conflict in the first half of the 1990s. It is widely believed that in the fierce Hezbollah-PKK clashes, the state sided with the former as part of its counterinsurgency policies and strategies (e.g., see van Bruinessen 2000b, 55; van Bruinessen 2000a, 269; McDowall 1996, 433; Sakallıoğlu 1998, 78; Yavuz 2001, 14; Yavuz and Özcan 2006; G. Jenkins 2008; Gunes 2012b, 129; Elitsoy 2013).[9] For instance, Aydin and Emrence (2015, 121–122) observe that "the state turned a blind eye to the violent competition between the PKK and its Islamic-oriented rival, Hezbollah. In Batman, local officials were instrumental in promoting Hezbollah as a means of preventing nationalists from monopolizing Kurdish political space." In this period, Hezbollah militants were involved in hundreds of political murders, many of which took place in public spaces during the day (Aydin and Emrence 2015, 66). Calling the PKK the "Partiya Kafirin Kurdistan" (meaning the Kurdistan Infidels' Party), Hezbollah presented its armed conflict with the PKK as a holy fight against Marxists, atheists, and infidels (see Elitsoy 2013, 88; Gürbüz 2016, 37).[10]

In addition to Kurdish Hezbollah's name-calling, ruling, conservative AKP officials have also accused the Kurdish movement of being Marxist, Godless, infidel (kafir), atheists, and un-Islamic. To put it in theoretical terms, in order to reduce the support and popularity of the Kurdish ethnonationalist movement among Kurds, AKP officials attempted to shrink or contract religious boundaries by accusing Kurdish ethnonationalists of being against religion. One can find numerous examples of such a boundary-making strategy. Erdoğan, the unchallenged leader of the AKP, has frequently used rather derogatory discourse about the PKK and labeled the Kurdish movement as un-Islamic and therefore illegitimate. For instance, speaking in Elazığ in October 2012, Erdoğan stated the following: "My dear Kurdish brother! Be aware that they [the BDP and the PKK] do not have anything to do with Allah. . . . They believe in and practice Zoroastrianism."[11] In December 2012, Erdoğan repeated similar claims in Ankara:

We made history together. Selahaddin Eyyubi [a Muslim Kurd, who was the first Sultan of Egypt and Syria and the founder of the Ayyubid dynasty] is our common hero. . . . Those who perform namaz [salah] and those who say "La ilahe illallah" [believing in and praying to only Allah] and those who have the love of Allah in their hearts cannot take sides with the terrorist organization [the PKK]. This land has a history shaped by the Koran, ezan [adhan, the call to prayer], and namaz. My religious, Muslim, Kurdish brother! When will you be aware of this conspiracy? You are the grandsons of Selahaddin Eyyubi, and it is time for you to say "Enough!" to this conspiracy. There cannot be any connection or relationship between you and the terrorist organization that does not pray to Allah or turn to the same qibla [the Caaba in Mecca, the holiest place in Islam] as you.[12]

Deputy Prime Minister Cemil Çiçek has made parallel comments: "There were close relations between the Armenian terrorist organization [ASALA] and the PKK. They were like brothers. External actors, who once supported Armenian terrorism to prevent Turkey's progress and development, now support the PKK terrorism. We know that some killed PKK terrorists were not circumcised. This tells us a lot about the nature of this movement."[13]

Such legitimacy struggles and attack speeches become quite fierce in electoral periods. During almost all electoral campaigns, the leadership of the ruling, pro-Islamic AKP declares the secular Kurdish movement as un-Islamic and thus illicit. For instance, during Erdoğan's electoral campaign in Diyarbakır before the June 2011 general elections, he made several references to Islam and the Islamic brotherhood and Diyarbakır's place in Islamic history. He maintained that Diyarbakır is a holy city, hosting the graves of several companions and disciples (*sahaba*) of the Islamic Prophet Muhammad. Erdoğan also insisted that the BDP and the PKK have nothing to do with Islam.[14] He repeated the same claims in front of Kurds attending his party's election meeting in Bingöl. It is worth quoting Erdoğan at length:

> These days, the BDP officials talk about religion. . . . Actually they just abuse your religious beliefs. Since when have the BDP and the terrorist organization [the PKK] attached importance to this nation's religious values and beliefs? These circles have been insulting the nation's religious values. Because we have the upcoming elections, all of a sudden they remembered religion and Islam. . . . Till yesterday, they were claiming that Kurds used to believe in and practice Zoroastrianism, and they say that Kurds were forced by sword to accept Islam. . . . I would also like to draw your attention to the following nonsense statements by their terrorist leader. May God forgive me but he made the following statements: "If God had existed, God would direct me to a wrong path. God is not for Kurds as well. God confuses and misdirects them. That is why I am my own God." Do you know who made these statements?

Apo [Abdullah Öcalan] used these words in his books. . . . BDP officials consider him a prophet. Apo is not that modest. He sees himself as a god. There is even more. He also insults *namaz* by claiming that *namaz* is a theater play. These are all in his books. . . . They are not really religious. Be aware that they just try to abuse religion to gain your votes. You should know that they also martyred a state imam in Hakkari. . . . They also attacked Imam-Hatip schools [imam and preacher education institutions] and their dormitories. . . . As you see, although they talk about religion, they continue to support terrorism.[15]

Another emblematic case was President Erdoğan's electoral campaign before the June 2015 general elections.[16] During his visits to the southeastern provinces, Erdoğan repeated his previous claims that the Kurdish movement was un-Islamic. In Diyarbakır, for instance, he professed that "[the HDP leadership and the PKK] burn schools, libraries and mosques. . . . These days, the HDP leader [Selahattin Demirtaş] says that if they get elected, they would abolish Diyanet. . . . But I know that my Kurdish and Zaza brothers are religious people!"[17] During the election rally in Batman, brandishing a copy of the Kurdish-language Koran published by Diyanet (see figure 3.4), Erdoğan addressed the Kurdish crowd as follows: "They say that they would like to abolish Diyanet. Yes they can say that because they do not have anything to do with Islam. Look at this Koran! Diyanet, which they want to abolish, prepared and published this Kurdish-language Koran. If they were really religious, they would not intend to abolish Diyanet. . . . We seized documents of the PKK, showing that they teach Zoroastrianism in the camps on the mountains."[18]

Similarly, state officials have attempted in their official discourses to discredit or delegitimize the PKK-led Kurdish movement using derogatory terms. For instance, PKK members are usually presented as bandits, terrorists, child kidnappers, and drug dealers (White 2000, 191–200; Watts 2010, 124). A similar strategy employed by the state has been to shrink religious boundaries. Although the Turkish Republic was established in the early 1920s as a nation-state based on strong

FIGURE 3.4. Recep T. Erdoğan waving a Kurdish-language Koran during an electoral rally in Batman, May 2, 2015. Courtesy of Felat Bozarslan, a journalist based in Diyarbakır.

secularist and Turkish nationalist understandings and values, by the 1980s, the state had adopted and promoted Turkish-Islamic synthesis as a kind of official state ideology (see Sakallioğlu 1996; Cetinsaya 1999; Yavuz 2003, 69; Natali 2005; Çarkoğlu and Kalaycioğlu 2009; S. Aslan 2015; Dag 2017). Initially formulated and advocated by a group of right-oriented academics, intellectuals, writers, and politicians known as the Heart of the Enlightened (Aydınlar Ocağı) in the early 1970s, this approach asserts that "Turkishness" is based on two main pillars: (1) Turkish culture, originating from central Asia, and (2) Islam. The adoption of such an approach by the state meant that an Islamic element was added to the official understanding of Turkish national identity. As a result, through various channels and mechanisms such as introducing obligatory religious courses, accelerating the building of new mosques, increasing the number of Imam-Hatip schools and Koran courses, increasing Diyanet's budget and personnel, and promoting university professors with Islamic and nationalist leanings, the state has attempted to promote Turkish nationalist and Sunni Islamic understandings and values in society.[19]

Embracing such an ideology, the Turkish state has attempted to use Islam as an antidote against socialist, leftist groups and movements, including the Kurdish ethnonationalist movement (van Bruinessen 2000b, 33; Dag 2017, 101–102). For instance, as Aydin and Emrence (2015, 93) also observe, as state officials "repeatedly claimed, [Kurdish] rebels were in fact 'Armenians,' 'godless heretics,' and/or 'communists' who threatened the Kurdish community at its core." In addition to using such derogatory terminology, state officials have also attempted to promote Islamic identity in eastern Turkey to contain Kurdish ethnonationalism and separatism. For instance, by distributing leaflets that included certain verses from the Koran, security officers aimed at exalting state authority and delegitimizing Kurdish rebels. As G. Jenkins (2008, 191) observes,

> Starting in the mid-1980s, the Turkish state condoned and even encouraged radical Islamist sentiments in southeast Turkey; both as an ideological bulwark against the Marxist PKK and in the hope that feelings of Muslim solidarity would override any tendency towards ethnic separatism. In March 1986, soldiers began distributing leaflets calling on local people to fulfill their "holy duty" by fighting against the PKK and quoting from the Qur'an. Posters were hung in village cafes and town squares in which the Turkish flag and a picture of a mosque were set side by side with a warning that those who failed to cooperate with the security forces would "become accomplices in the eyes of God in the crimes perpetrated by the separatists."[20]

The writings and statements of the Kurdish ethnopolitical leadership suggest that the Kurdish movement has been highly disturbed by such actions and discourses. For instance, Öcalan complains in his texts that several government-affiliated groups and other formations (e.g., the state, the national intelligence organization, and Islamic groups and movements such as religious orders and the then-Erbakan-led National Outlook Movement) use Islam to promote their particular interests, to exploit and control Kurdish society, and to prevent the rise of a Kurdish national consciousness (e.g., see Öcalan 1995, 122–123; Öcalan 2008, 68–74; see also McDowall 2004, 435).

However, partly in response to such efforts of religious boundary contraction by Turkish conservative and Islamic circles and the state, the Kurdish ethnopolitical leadership softened its attitude toward religion.[21] Öcalan interestingly states that unlike several other leftist movements that have a negative stance toward religion, the Kurdish movement is not against Islam. Rather, he now claims that Islam has a revolutionary essence that is compatible with the Kurdish movement's objectives (see also Dag 2014). In brief, the boundary-making efforts of secular Kurdish ethnopolitical elites were partly triggered by the boundary work of competing or opponent groups (e.g., radical Islamists, conservative political elites, and the state).

Such a counterstrategy by the Kurdish ethnopolitical leadership connotes that external definition or social categorization by outsiders might have a substantial impact on internal definition (or group identity) and group boundaries. The Kurdish case suggests that responding to the ascription attributed by others, ethnopolitical leadership might modify ethnic identification, which would result in redrawing the boundaries of an ethnic category and/or movement.

Boundary Contestations

As indicated in chapter 1, ethnic boundary-making processes can involve major tensions or conflicts. As Wimmer (2013, 10) notes, "the ethnic boundary system can be characterized by conflict and contestation such that no basic consensus emerges over who is what and who should get what—undermining the idea that ethnic communities are held together by [a] 'shared identity.'" Wimmer (2013, 97) further notes that "if different actors pursue different strategies of boundary making, depending on their position in the hierarchies of power and the structure of their political networks, the social field will be characterized by competition and contestation between various modes of classification and various claims to moral superiority, rightful entitlement, and political solidarity associated with them."

Wimmer's (2013) account of ethnic boundary making draws heavily on Pierre Bourdieu's analysis of classification struggles (conflict over "who is what and who should get what") (e.g., see Bourdieu 1984). Agreeing with Bourdieu, Wimmer suggests that such struggles play a major role in modern societies. Wimmer (2013, 205) notes, "First, ethnic categorizations— defining who is what—are an intrinsic part of the struggle over power and prestige that lies at the heart of the process of social closure. Second, individual and collective actors behave strategically—not necessarily rationally in the narrow sense of the term—in these struggles." Thus, boundary work by ethnopolitical leaders (e.g., boundary expansion) might trigger reactions among outsiders *and* insiders (i.e., coethnics), who might have different ideas or preferences about where symbolic and social boundaries should lie and how they should be shifted.

We see both internal and external boundary contestations in the Kurdish case as well. To begin with, it is important to acknowledge that Kurds do not constitute a homogeneous ethnic group but a highly diverse one. In addition to divisive tribal differences, the Kurdish ethnic category involves major class, ideological (left vs. right), linguistic (Kurmanji, Zaza/ Zazaki, Sorani, Gorani), and religious divisions, such as the Alevi-Sunni division and Shafi-Hanefi division among Sunni Kurds and several other religious sects (e.g., Yezidis and the Ahl-i-Haqq) and *tarikats* or mystical orders (e.g., Nakşibendi and Kadiri) (see also van Bruinessen 1992, 2000a, and 2000b; White 2000; Entessar 2010; Watts 2010; Aydin and Emrence 2015).

More relevant to our debate in this study is the Alevi-Sunni cleavage or division among Kurds. As indicated in the introduction, although the majority of Kurds in Turkey subscribe to the Sunni *mezhep* (*madhap*), at least 10% of Kurds adhere to the Alevi *mezhep*. Compared to Sunnis,

Alevis are relatively more heterodox and secular and are more likely to vote for secular, left-oriented political parties (see Çarkoğlu 2005). As some earlier studies also acknowledge, internal diversity (e.g., the long-standing Alevi-Sunni division) tends to create tension within the Kurdish movement and constrain the ethnopolitical leadership (e.g., see van Bruinessen 2000a, 2000b; White 2000, 207). As van Bruinessen (2000a, 26) also observes, "Alevi Kurds, many of whom moreover speak Zaza, which is quite different from ordinary Kurdish, therefore have ambivalent attitudes towards the Kurdish movement: some play active and even leading roles in it, others prefer to stay aloof or even perceive it as a threat to their distinct identities."

Several circles of Alevi Kurds have also been highly concerned with the Islamic opening of the Kurdish movement. Some Alevi Kurdish leaders and activists have even publicly protested this initiative. For instance, Şerafettin Halis, chairperson of the BDP's Tunceli provincial branch, resigned from his position in April 2013, claiming that he had a difference of opinion with the party administration over certain issues.[22] As Tunceli is where most Alevi Kurds reside, Halis's resignation was viewed as a reflection of Alevis' uneasiness with the increasingly pro-Islamic actions and discourses of Kurdish ethnopolitical leadership.[23] Since his resignation, Halis has publicly admitted that he was disturbed about the movement's new approach toward Islam. He criticized the party leadership as follows: "Within the party, those who openly advocate *shariah* [Islamic law] at any opportunity get promoted or rewarded. But when I express Alevis' concerns about this new policy, they get disturbed. I do not know the reason for this intolerance."[24]

In May 2013, several Alevi organizations and federations also met in Ankara and publicly declared that they were disturbed by the movement's increasing references to such notions as the flag of Islam, Islamic unity, and Islamic brotherhood. Several Alevi leaders argued that a settlement of the Kurdish conflict should be based on equal citizenship rather than Islamic notions such as Muslim brotherhood.[25] Selahattin Özel, chairperson of the Alevi-Bektashi

Federation, also criticized the Kurdish ethnopolitical movement's Islamicized discourse and references to the idea of Islamic unity:

> We are offended and disappointed by the Kurdish movement. . . . It is impossible for us to accept the idea of "Islamic unity" that Öcalan referred to in his [March 2013] Nowruz message. We suffered a lot from the discourse of Turkish-Islamic unity. Now, they talk about Turkish-Kurdish Islamic unity. . . . We are concerned that we will continue to suffer in this new era as well. As an organization representing the people who have been discriminated against for years because of their beliefs, we would expect from them [Kurdish ethnopolitical leaders] a more inclusive framework or approach as a common denominator, not one based on Islamic unity.[26]

During my fieldwork in Tunceli, several interviewees also acknowledged that Alevis were disturbed by the increasing role of Islam within the Kurdish movement.[27] For instance, Sabit Menteşe, an assistant professor at Tunceli University, stated, "People in Tunceli identify themselves first as Alevi and then as Kurds, Zaza, or Turks. As a result, they approach increasing Islamic references within the Kurdish movement with great skepticism. Many people here in Tunceli think or perceive that the Kurdish movement has been shifting from the left to the right, and they are worried about this."[28] Activists close to the movement have also acknowledged such a disturbance or uneasiness among Alevis. For instance, Murat Polat, former chairperson of the Tunceli provincial branch of the pro-Kurdish BDP, said, "Yes, I do observe that the rise of the pro-Islamic approach and discourse within the Kurdish movement creates some disturbance among Alevis here in Tunceli and in other places. It is a well-known fact that Alevis are in general fearful of political Islam. Our main rival party in Tunceli [the secular CHP] also provokes such fears and concerns among Alevis. They, for instance, propagate that the Kurdish movement has turned into an Islamic one. This makes them even more worried about this development within the Kurdish movement."[29] During my interview, Halis, aforementioned former chairperson of

Tunceli provincial branch of the BDP, also emphasized that Alevis were highly concerned with the Kurdish movement's new approach toward Islam: "Let me emphasize that Alevis do not fear social Islam, but they are highly concerned with political Islam. In other words, it is a serious problem for them when Islam becomes a reference point within politics and state apparatus. It is simply because throughout history [Ottoman and Republican periods], Alevis have been persecuted in the name of Islam, and it still constitutes a major trauma in Alevi memory. Naturally, increasing emphasis on Islam within the Kurdish movement upsets Alevis."[30]

Having realized that the rise of an Islam-friendly approach within the Kurdish movement in general and Öcalan's 2013 Nowruz message in particular created a disturbance in Alevi circles, the Kurdish leadership felt the need to take conciliatory steps. For instance, in the aftermath of Öcalan's message, some BDP officials (e.g., cochair Gülten Kışanak and deputies İdris Baluken and Nursel Aydoğan) met with several Alevi leaders and representatives to discuss their complaints. Kışanak claimed that Öcalan's reference to the "flag of Islam" was misunderstood.

Moreover, Öcalan himself felt the need to send a new message from İmralı Island in April 2013, praising Alevis and Alevi beliefs and emphasizing the importance of Alevis for the Kurdish movement.[31] Similarly, in May of that year, Öcalan sent a message to the congress of the Democratic Alevi Federation, organized by pro-Kurdish groups in Germany, in which he claims that there are several similarities between the Kurdish movement and Alevi beliefs, rituals, and traditions: "I value very much *cem* [the main Alevi religious gathering, a ritual prayer, and a congregational ceremony] and *semah* [a ritual dance performed during the *cem*]. Our movement is very close to the *cem* and *semah*. Similar to the *cem*, our movement represents a congregation. . . . And the *semah* is a magical performance, constituting the essence of the *cem*. Our guerillas' march is akin to the *semah*. . . . We should be very respectful to both the *cem* and *semah*. . . . In a sense, the PKK movement stands for a modern *cem* movement."[32]

In addition to such appeasing statements, Kurdish ethnopolitical leaders have emphasized that their notion of Islam is based on democratic, libertarian, egalitarian, pluralist, and peaceful norms and values rather than radical understandings. In other words, by stressing that their version of Islam is much more pluralist and democratic than the understandings of radical Islamists, ethnopolitical leaders have tried to mitigate the fears and concerns in Kurdish Alevi circles. In theoretical terms, through such propitiatory discourses and actions, the Kurdish leadership has tried to contain internal boundary contestations by Alevis. Such efforts suggest that ethnic-group heterogeneity has a constraining impact on the strategies of boundary makers, which supports the second hypothesis presented in chapter 1. Boundary making is not a smooth process, and this reality is even more valid for relatively more heterogeneous ethnic groups and movements.

Although the Kurdish ethnopolitical leadership responded to Alevi criticisms and contestations by some symbolic gestures such as making conciliatory statements and praising Alevi community and beliefs, the movement did not change its course of action (i.e., accommodating Islamic ideas, discourses, and actors). For instance, Alevis were also highly disturbed by the statements of some pro-Islamic figures incorporated into pro-Kurdish parties in the recent period.[33] As a case in point, in April 2013, the Islamist Altan Tan, who was elected to parliament in 2011 for the pro-Kurdish BDP, stated that as a devout Muslim, he was against secularism and in favor of Sharia rule.[34] Several interviewees during my fieldwork in Tunceli indicated that Alevis were highly concerned with Tan's statements. Thus, during the candidate selection process before the 2015 general elections, there were rumors that Tan would not be nominated again. However, Tan and several other conservative figures (e.g., Hüda Kaya and Ayhan Bilgen) were included in the final list submitted to the High Council of Elections.[35] Thus, internal boundary contestations by some Alevi circles did not really reverse the boundary work by Kurdish ethnopolitical leadership. In fact, the leadership sometimes responded to leftist criticisms of the movement's increasingly Islamicized

FIGURE 3.5. HDP coleader Selahattin Demirtaş praying during civilian Friday prayers, March 4, 2016, Sümerpark, Diyarbakır. Courtesy of Mahmut Bozarslan.

discourse by putting forward countercriticisms. For instance, HDP leader Selahattin Demirtaş rebuffed those criticisms as follows:

> No offense, but those leftists who associate the leftist ideology with an antireligious attitude do not have much to offer to this country. This country suffered a lot from those circles [antireligious leftists]. They should understand that someone can believe in Allah but at the same time become a strong leftist person. . . . The reason for why the left does not enjoy much social popularity in this country is their enmity toward Islam. . . . I am a leftist and socialist. I have always defended leftist policies. But I am also a Muslim. My grandfather was a cleric from Palu. . . . My mother and my wife perform *namaz* five times a day. I grew up in a pious family.[36]

One main reason for the failure of such internal contestations is the highly hierarchic nature of the Kurdish movement. As White (2000,

136) suggests, one defining feature of the movement is "a Stalin-like personality cult around its leader, Abdullah Öcalan." White (2000, 137) observes,

> Öcalan stresses that, while the Kurdish personality is a "natural" personality, the Kurds must receive it from his party, or be unable to form themselves as a unified nation. This is almost religious—(Prophet) Apo receives [a] revelation, which he transmits to his chosen disciples, who alone can transmit it to the chosen people, provided they remain in communion with Prophet Apo. According to this scheme, while initiative and self-reliance (within limits) are praised in coping with adversity and scarce resources, it is essential for general success that all Kurds should be inculcated with the one, true, "national" personality.

Akkaya and Jongerden (2011, 147) also draw attention to the very centralized and hierarchic organizational structure of the Kurdish movement, using an interesting analogy:

> Today, the organization [the PKK] has grown even more complex, and what we refer to as the PKK is actually a party complex, a complex of parties and organizations comprising several parties (including the PKK as a party) and sister parties in Iraq, Syria and Iran, the co-party which separately organizes women, the armed organizations and the popular front Kongra-Gel. It is difficult to represent the organization with a traditional organizational flowchart. *As the members and sympathizers of the PKK refer to Abdullah Öcalan, as a sun (güneş), we may develop this analogy and compare the organization of the party-complex as a planetary system: The planets (PKK, KONGRA-GEL, KKK/KCK KNK, and guerilla forces) are in orbit around a sun (Abdullah Öcalan), and various moons (institutions, committees) are in orbit around these.* (emphasis added)

Although Öcalan has been imprisoned on İmralı Island since 1999, he remains the unchallenged, supreme, peerless leader and theoretician of the movement (see also Akkaya and Jongerden 2011; Gürbüz 2016).[37] Through meetings with and letters sent to his lawyers, family members, and officials and deputies from the pro-Kurdish parties, Öcalan has continued to exert substantial influence over the Kurdish movement.[38] Kurdish ethnopolitical activists also acknowledge Öcalan's importance. For instance, Fırat Anlı, a lawyer, former mayor of Yenişehir (Diyarbakır), and important figure within the Kurdish movement, states that "Öcalan is a highly important political figure. He is a phenomenon. For the majority of Kurds, he is even a mythical figure. . . . He has that much influence on Kurds. We should not forget that hundreds of Kurds set themselves on fire and thousands undertook a hunger strike to show their support for him."[39]

Since the beginning of the movement, it has been difficult to get away with criticizing Öcalan's position and instructions. Those who question or oppose his views, decisions, or orders face accusations of disloyalty and/or betrayal, which result in severe punishments, including execution (Gunter 1990; Birand 1992; Imset 1992; van Bruinessen 2000a; White 2000; Marcus 2007; Aydin and Emrence 2015). As Marcus (2007, 263) observes, "The PKK leader put protecting his leadership first, to the point that he would destroy his chief military commander. Öcalan did not consider that this might hurt the PKK's ability to wage war, because he believed that only his leadership mattered."

Aydin and Emrence (2015) suggest that such a strong leadership cult within the Kurdish movement has been maintained in several ways. First, the ideology of the movement regards internal opposition as a major threat to the party: "Öcalan eliminated political dissidents as 'traitors' who questioned his unchecked powers, authoritarian style, and ruthless guerilla tactics" (23). Second, the PKK leadership has created a mechanism of criticism and self-criticism, which has led to a trust deficit among PKK members: "[Öcalan] turned the 'criticism-self-criticism mechanism' into a political weapon for downgrading party members with high reputations and preventing alliances from being formed against him. Group approval gave the impression that political persecutions were not the leader's individual decisions but reflected a consensus" (23). White (2000, 141) also draws attention to how the mechanism of criticism and self-criticism promotes social control within the movement: "PKK members are expected to make a series of pledges, write regular reports on their own weaknesses and to submit to regular, frequent 'criticism and self-criticism' sessions. Combined, these generally seem adequate as a means of ensuring adherence to the ideal personality type, not to mention an ideal means of social control."

Third, Öcalan's control of access to power and authority within the organization has prevented the rise of alternative leaders: "His unchecked power [has] enabled him to make and break political careers, turning yesterday's hero into today's traitor" (Aydin and Emrence 2015, 23). In addition, presenting himself as the "Leadership" (Önderlik), Öcalan positioned himself above the party and the PKK members and so idealized and exalted his leadership and mission. In the words of Aydin and Emrence (2015, 24),

The rebel leader idealized his life experience as a model for insurgents. . . . In this view, the qualities of the rebel leader appeared as supreme from day one, and insurgents were depicted as lost souls without a cause who could not satisfy their leader regardless of how hard they tried. Öcalan was the sole driving force behind the PKK, the insurgents, and Kurdish society. He invented a new identity for insurgents, established the PKK to change the Kurds' misfortune, and built a Kurdish nation despite many obstacles. As such, he was the embodiment of Kurdistan and an unattainable role model for all Kurds.

In brief, the highly hierarchical structure of the Kurdish movement, strong leadership cult, and resultant high degree of elite unity did not create a favorable environment for internal dissension. Hence, internal boundary contestations by Alevi Kurds ended in failure. That is, such efforts by subordinate groups failed to reverse the movement's shifting attitude toward Islam and Islamic actors. This progression suggests that the organizational structure of ethnic movements conditions the processes and dynamics of internal boundary contestation. In the case of highly hierarchical ethnic movements, internal boundary contestation appears to have a limited chance of success, confirming the third and fourth hypotheses presented in chapter 1.

The Kurdish movement's boundary making (i.e., the Kurdish ethnopolitical leadership's expansion of symbolic and social boundaries of the movement to accommodate Islam and Islamic actors) also triggered external boundary contestations. Conservative and Islamic circles in particular responded to such efforts by challenging the redrawn boundaries. Their primary strategy in their response to the Kurdish movement's Islamic opening was to contract Islamic religious boundaries, excluding Kurdish ethnopolitical elites. In other words, pro-Islamic circles responded to changes in the Kurdish movement by treating Kurdish ethnopolitical elites as the religious "Other." For instance, on several occasions, Erdoğan harshly criticized and condemned the civilian Friday prayers initiated and promoted by the Kurdish movement. During his electoral campaign in Diyarbakır before the June 2011 general elections, Erdoğan addressed the Kurdish crowd as follows:

> We [Turks and Kurds] are eternal brothers. . . . We have the same *qibla*. When we perform *namaz* at Sülaymaniye mosque in İstanbul, at Selimiye mosque in Edirne, at Hacı Bayram mosque in Ankara, we turn our face to the same *qibla* that you turn here at Ulucami mosque in Diyarbakır. . . . However, in recent times we see a new practice. . . . The BDP officials and their supporters try to discourage my Kurdish Muslim brothers from attending Friday prayers at mosques and from praying behind the imams appointed by the state. . . . Those circles do not have anything to do with Islam, . . . Now they organize alternative civilian Friday prayers. These are all wrong. First of all, imams leading the Friday prayers should be trained and authorized for that job. You cannot pray behind any random

imam. Secondly, organizing an alternative Friday prayers would divide the Muslim community. Thirdly, men and women cannot perform *namaz* together. . . . Thus, all these efforts mean nothing but creating division, provocation, and conspiracy among Muslim brothers. But we know that they are not really religious. . . . They even consider Apo as a prophet. . . . My Kurdish brothers! Be aware that in order to gain your votes, they are trying to deceive you with religion.[40]

The AKP government also encouraged Diyanet to take countermeasures against civilian Friday prayers. For instance, in late 2011, Diyanet initiated a project targeting Kurdish *meles* in the southeast, which involved six months of official religious training and education for around 1000 *meles*.[41] After this period of instruction, the students were appointed as official imams to mosques in the region. It is widely believed that this project was politically motivated. By employing Kurdish *meles* as state imams within Diyanet, the AKP intended to prevent the co-option of *meles* by the Kurdish ethnonationalist movement (see Sarigil and Fazlioglu 2013). Diyanet also allowed sermons to be delivered in Kurdish by state imams in certain mosques in the region.[42] In addition, Diyanet translated the Koran into Kurdish.[43] Erdoğan also had a harsh reaction to the BDP's headscarf proposal in October 2011, which aimed to allow female deputies to wear headscarves during parliamentary sessions. He claimed that the pro-Kurdish party was not sincere about the proposal because it believes in Zoroastrianism but not in Islam: "Last week, one group within the parliament [the BDP] submitted a bill related to wearing headscarves during parliamentary sessions. They are not really sincere. . . . They just abuse the feelings and sensitivities of my sisters wearing headscarves! Actually, they do not have such a problem. How can those who believe in Zoroastrianism have such a problem or concern?"[44]

The Turkish nationalist and pro-Islamic Grand Unity Party (Büyük Birlik Partisi, BBP) also reacted harshly to Kurdish boundary expansion. In April 2011, then–party leader Yalçın Topçu stated, "Those separatists [referring to the Kurdish movement] are now playing with this nation's religion. With illogical, senseless justifications and unimaginable con-spiratorial accusations, they are inviting people not to stand behind state imams. Those who do not know anything about these separatists would look at their demands and think that they are indeed pious, conserva-tive people, performing *namaz* five times a day. I wonder how many times they have really visited a mosque with the region's conservative people. As if they are really conservative, they now demand praying in their mother tongue [Kurdish]."[45]

All such efforts and discourses by conservative circles or Turkish Is-lamists should be understood as a typical case of external boundary con-testation. Conservative or pro-Islamic circles (e.g., political elites and intellectuals) openly contest or challenge the Kurdish movement's ef-forts to accommodate Islam and Islamic figures. And in contesting such boundary work, they attempt to impose their alternative social categories onto the movement by declaring Kurdish ethnopolitical leaders as un-Islamic and thus illegitimate.

In the case of external boundary contestation, rival political groups attempt to enhance their own societal approval and popularity at the expense of the movement they are criticizing. In the Kurdish case, such rivals expect that denigrating or delegitimizing Kurdish eth-nopolitical actors in the eyes of conservative Kurds would enhance their electoral popularity among Kurds. It is not a coincidence that such efforts become more frequent and fiercer during electoral peri-ods, which confirms the first hypothesis presented in chapter 1. All these elements imply that a better understanding of external bound-ary contestation (what triggers it, how it happens, what form it takes) requires considering the broader sociopolitical context. Political fac-tors such as competition over material (e.g., power, economic gains) and/or ideational (e.g., prestige, legitimacy) resources substantially shape external boundary contestation.

It is also important to remember that, as discussed in chapter 1, external boundary contestation usually involves processes of *group* or *social cat-egorization*, which refers to the identification of *others* as a collectivity or group (R. Jenkins 2008, 56). Social categorization, however, is located within power relations and domination. In the words of R. Jenkins (2008, 23), social categorization is "intimately bound up with power relations and relates to the capacity of one group successfully to impose its categories of ascription upon another set of people, and to the resources which the categorized collectivity can draw upon to resist, if need be, that imposition." One particular form of group categorization is *nonrecognition* or *misrecognition*. As Taylor (1994, 100) also notes, "non-recognition or misrecognition can inflict harm, [and] can be a form of oppression, imprisoning someone in a false, distorted, reduced mode of being." Similar dynamics are also present in conservative circles' efforts to challenge the Kurdish movement's boundary expansion. By attempting to impose an alternative group identity onto the movement, such circles tried to present a distorted, reduced image of the Kurdish movement to the masses, particularly to conservative Kurds.

In brief, conservative circles, who have felt threatened by the increasingly Islam-friendly attitude of the Kurdish ethnopolitical movement, contest the latter's boundary expansion by categorizing or misrecognizing the Kurdish movement as atheist and/or un-Islamic. Although such efforts peak during electoral periods, the 2015 election results suggest that such labels did not resonate among the vast majority of the Kurdish electorate. As shown earlier in this chapter, the Kurdish ethnopolitical movement achieved its greatest electoral victory ever in the 2015 general elections, receiving the vast majority of Kurds' votes in the region (around 65%–70%).

Finally, we should acknowledge that conservative or Islamic circles are not the only external actors who have contested the Kurdish movement's boundary work. Some secular Turkish groups (intellectuals, writers, and political elites) also denounce the rise of an Islam-friendly approach within the Kurdish movement. For instance, CHP Istanbul deputy Ali Özgündüz criticized Öcalan's reference to Islam in the latter's 2013 Nowruz message by claiming that "socialist Apo" has become "Islamic Apo." Özgündüz also asked, "Since when has socialist Apo been taking Islam as a reference point?"[46] Similarly, columnist E. Attila Aytekin criticizes Öcalan's increasing references to Islam and claims that Öcalan and the conservative AKP government agree on reviving the Hamidian pan-Islamist project, which aimed at the political unity of Sunni-Islamic groups in Anatolia and the Middle East during the late Ottoman era. Aytekin warns that this is a dangerous path that would lead to new instabilities, conflicts, and catastrophes in the region.[47]

Alternative Considerations

With respect to alternative considerations, one might rightly raise the question of whether the Islamic opening of the secular Kurdish movement constitutes a superficial, cosmetic change or rather a genuine ideological transformation. To begin with, it would not be wise to claim that the Kurdish movement's boundary work has no strategic or instrumental motivations or expectations behind it. As Rieffer (2003, 229) suggests, "Religion is a useful resource to national leaders. Since religion is a powerful source of identity and one that can unify a group and create loyalty to the national movement, national leaders try to draw on religion to create a cohesive public body. . . . Religion in these cases can serve as a source of legitimacy to national leaders who are developing new political institutions." These points are valid in the Kurdish case as well. Kurdish ethnopolitical elites have discovered that Islam is a powerful tool to legitimize the Kurdish nationalist movement and demands. Islam has given the Kurdish ethnopolitical elites new ideas, discourses, symbols, customs, and rituals, and the movement's leaders have deployed these elements to advance ethnonationalist interests and objectives in the political arena and to strengthen ethnic cohesion and mobilization. A softening attitude toward Islam was expected to enhance the movement's popularity among Kurds, especially among pious Kurds. As a result, religion as a secondary aspect has been playing a supportive role in the Kurdish nationalist movement. For Abulof (2014), with such an interplay between religion and nationalism, religion becomes a resource for nationalism (i.e., an auxiliary religion). Similarly, Kurdish ethnopolitical elites have been treating Islam as an auxiliary element to enhance the legitimacy, prestige, and popularity of the ethnopolitical movement.

However, there are also several signs suggesting that it would not be fair to treat this shift as a mere strategic, instrumental usage of religion for political and/or social gains. For instance, the movement's systematic efforts to promote the notion of "democratic Islam" through various congresses, conferences, and meetings organized in Turkey and Europe since 2014 should be understood as sincere attempts to reinterpret Islam. Such efforts imply that beyond the mere strategic use of Islam for political gains, the movement is searching for a new, long-term relationship with Islam and Islamic actors. By developing an Islam-friendly approach in the past decades, the Kurdish movement has redrawn symbolic and social boundaries and so gained a new ideological character. In other words, such boundary work, which has transformed the ideational basis of the movement, represents a genuine ideological transformation. Instead of ignoring Islam, the movement has changed its attitude and decided to co-opt it. At the very least, the movement has modified its radical, antireligious, secularist understandings and adopted a more welcoming attitude toward Islam and Islamic actors and formations. Çakır shares these observations:

It is obvious that the secular-minded leadership of the Kurdish movement initiated this new approach toward Islam. But this initiative has been quite welcomed by Kurdish masses. Exactly because of this, this new approach toward Islam has definitely had a transformative impact on the movement itself. In other words, it is inevitable that this initiative would have Islamicized the Kurdish movement to a certain extent. . . . For instance, there are several districts in the East where the vast majority of women wear headscarves. Like it or not, you should somehow accommodate them. For instance, if you want to win the elections in those districts, you should nominate female candidates who wear headscarves. . . . Actually, the movement's previously held exclusionary attitude toward Islam was unusual and unnatural. This new initiative is quite a natural process or development. In other words, the movement has been getting normalized. In a sense, the Kurdish ethnonationalist movement has become more Kurdified.[48]

Ayhan Bilgen, a conservative political figure co-opted by pro-Kurdish political parties, also emphasized that this shift within the Kurdish movement should be interpreted as an ideological transformation, which "reduced the gap between the secular Kurdish ethnopolitical elites and conservative Kurdish masses."[49]

Conservative political and social circles are also represented within the movement. For instance, we see an increasing number of conservative or Islamic figures (e.g., politicians and activists and pro-Kurdish men of religion) in the high ranks of the movement. As members in the decision-making bodies of pro-Kurdish political parties (e.g., the BDP and the HDP) and civil society organizations (e.g., the DTK), they play an active role. Hence, the incorporation of such actors into the movement appears to be much more than window dressing. In brief, although the rise of an Islam-friendly approach within the secular Kurdish movement certainly involves strategic, instrumental motivations and expectations (e.g., to advance ethnopolitical objectives and interests such as electoral gains and societal recognition and legitimacy), it would be difficult to treat such a transformation as a short-term, solely strategic move. As Gürbüz (2016, 115) also states, "PKK's ideology was refined to embrace Kurdish Islamic repertoires through the symbolic localization process, a process in which Kurdish [ethnonationalist] activists gradually introduced local Islamic discourses and have constructed their own Kurdish-Islamic perspective in a dialectal opposition to Turkish-Islamic discourses."

Another important issue is that there is always a possibility that ethnopolitical leaders might undo their boundary work. In other words, they might shrink or contract the expanded boundaries. This scenario would be even more valid for hierarchically organized ethnic movements, in which ethnopolitical elites play the main role in boundary-making processes. Given this situation, we should ask ourselves whether this shift within the Kurdish movement is irreversible. Since the Kurdish movement is also elite dominated, one might expect that Kurdish ethnopolitical elites might easily reverse their Islamic opening. However, it would be difficult for the movement to turn its back on religion again simply because of how obviously Islam constitutes an important place in the lives of the Kurdish masses. For instance, our survey's results suggest that Kurds are relatively more religious than Turks. Regarding the measurement of religiosity, several empirical works indicate that religiosity involves multiple aspects such as belief (e.g., believing in an afterlife or God), attitude (e.g., support for Shariah law), and practice (e.g., performing daily *namaz*) (e.g., Çarkoğlu 2005; Çarkoğlu and Kalaycioğlu 2009; Yeşilada and Noordijk 2010). To better capture the multiple dimensions of religiosity, we included several religion-related items (e.g., belief in an afterlife and God, performing *namaz*, fasting, and support for headscarves and Sharia law) into our survey questionnaire. Using those survey items, I conducted principal-component analysis, engendering two additive indices capturing two different dimensions of religiosity: *faith* and *attitudinal/practical*. In terms of the faith dimension of religiosity, Turks and Kurds are not really distinguishable. However, as the box plot provided in figure 3.6 indicates, Kurds are relatively more religious in terms of the attitudinal-practical dimension (t = 16.472, df = 1811.2, p-value < 2.2e-16).[50]

Due to such a social structure (i.e., relatively higher level of religiosity among Kurds), the secular Kurdish movement's accommodative approach toward Islam and Islamic actors and formations in the past decades has resonated well with the Kurdish masses.[51] The incorporation of Islamic ideas and circles into the movement has also reduced the distance between the leftist, secularist ethnopolitical leadership and conservative Kurdish society. As a result, relations between the movement and the masses have been more concordant or harmonious in the past decades. This, in return, puts pressure on the movement to be more responsive to Kurds' religion-related demands. For instance, the pro-Kurdish BDP was pressured to organize its own *mawlid* meetings in 2014.[52] In other words, since the movement has opened itself to Islam and accommodated

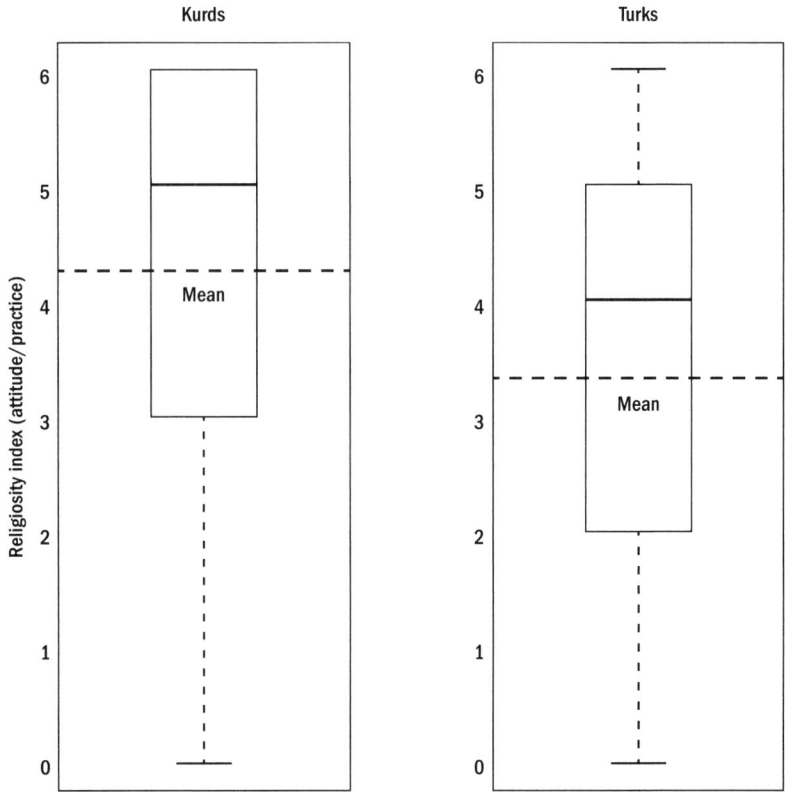

FIGURE 3.6. Box plot of religiosity (Kurds vs. Turks), 2013. *Note*: The data come from a 2013 survey funded by TEPAV.

Islamic circles, it has become more susceptible to pressures and demands originating from religious Kurdish circles.

Several interviewees also emphasized that it would be quite arduous for the Kurdish movement to adopt a hostile attitude toward Islam again.[53] For instance, the writer and journalist Oral Çalışlar explained, "The Kurdish movement cannot and will not turn its back on religion again. Several conservative figures and men of religion such as Kurdish *meles* now constitute an important power center within the pro-Kurdish political parties. They even occupy key posts in the high echelons of those parties. . . . If the movement reverses its friendly approach toward Islam, then this new policy would lead to lots of divisions and tensions within the movement. In addition, this would certainly marginalize the whole movement among Kurdish masses."[54] Hence, returning to an apathetic or antireligious attitude would be highly costly (e.g., electoral and/or legitimacy costs). As the electoral results also confirm (e.g., see table 3.1), the majority of Kurds in the region voted for pro-Kurdish political parties in the past three elections. The following observations by Lecours (2000, 121) would be valid for the Kurdish case as well: "Ethnonationalism is a movement with *leaders* and *followers*. It *cannot* exist unless the claims of political elites are supported by a substantial number of non-elites. In some cases, the nationalist fervor of the masses may exceed that of the elites. When the processes of ethnonationalism have been set in motion by specific patterns of elite interaction and the weight of political institutions, they may be difficult to control or reverse."

Conclusion

In sum, several endogenous and exogenous dynamics and factors have played a causal role in Kurdish boundary making (i.e., the rise of an Islam-friendly approach within the secular Kurdish movement). As shown in this chapter, we should particularly take into account the role of the declining influence of Marxism, the need to expand the movement's social basis and popularity, electoral competition and pressures, and legitimacy struggles against rival political movements and actors.

That being said, the Kurdish movement's boundary making has not been a smooth process. The Islamic opening of the secular Kurdish movement triggered both internal and external boundary contestations. Internally, relatively more secular Alevi Kurds expressed their concerns about the movement's increasing efforts to accommodate Islam and Islamic actors. Alevi discontent with the Kurdish movement's new approach toward Islam suggests that the heterogeneous structure of Kurdish society increases the likelihood of internal boundary contestations. Having hegemonic aspirations, the Kurdish ethnopolitical movement tries to mobilize a wide range of Kurdish groups (e.g., Alevis, Sunnis, conservatives, leftists, and liberal groups), which have diverse and sometimes conflicting interests and concerns. This point suggests that it is quite likely that the Kurdish ethnopolitical leadership's efforts of nationalist mobilization and boundary making will continue to face internal contestations or challenges in the future.

The boundary-making efforts of the Kurdish ethnopolitical leadership have also faced external contestations. Externally, conservative and Islamic circles have attempted to challenge the Islamic opening of the secular and leftist movement by openly condemning and denigrating Kurdish leaders' efforts to accommodate Islam and Islamic circles. The former's main counterstrategy has been to shrink Islamic boundaries (i.e., insisting that the Kurdish movement is still un-Islamic). The conclusion that follows first restates the key points and arguments of the book and then discusses the theoretical and practical implications of the Islamic opening of the secular Kurdish movement in Turkey.

Conclusions and Implications

To sum up the key points and arguments of the book, this work examines the attitude of the secular Kurdish movement in Turkey toward Islam and Islamic actors. As the empirical chapters detail, the Kurdish ethnonationalist movement, rooted in strong secularism and Marxism, has adopted an increasingly positive approach toward Islam since the early 1990s. As a result, Islam has played an increasing role in the discourses and actions of Kurdish ethnopolitical elites in the past decades. This study divides the evolving relations between the Kurdish movement and Islam into three different stages or periods: (1) an indifferent/apathetic and/or antagonistic attitude in the 1970s and 1980s, (2) an increasingly Islam-friendly approach in the 1990s, and (3) an accommodative attitude and the rise of a Kurdish-Islamic synthesis since the early 2000s. Approaching such a trajectory from the perspective of the boundary approach, this study treats the Islamic opening of the Kurdish movement in the past decades as a major case of boundary work and suggests that each of these periods is associated with a different boundary-making strategy: *boundary contraction, boundary expansion,* and *boundary reinforcement,* respectively.

With respect to the causes of Kurdish movement's boundary expansion (i.e., its Islamic opening), this study draws attention to the role of four causal factors: *the declining influence of Marxism; the need to expand its social basis and popularity; electoral politics;* and *legitimacy struggles against rival political actors.* The book further shows that the boundary expansion by Kurdish ethnopolitical elites triggered both internal and external boundary contestations. Internally, especially Alevi Kurds, who are relatively more liberal and secular than Sunni Kurds, raised some concerns and attempted to contest the rise of the movement's Islam-friendly approach. However, due to the highly centralized and hierarchical structure of the Kurdish movement and the high degree of elite unity, internal contestations did not have much impact on the Kurdish boundary work. Externally, rival political actors at local and national levels, such as conservative/Islamic and Turkish nationalist political circles, contested the Kurdish boundary making by harshly denouncing and disparaging Kurdish ethnopolitical elites' Islam-friendly discourses and actions. In criticizing and rebuffing the Kurdish boundary work, they claimed that the Kurdish ethnopolitical movement is still "Marxist," "atheist," and "un-Islamic." In other words, as a counterstrategy to the Kurdish boundary expansion, they sought to shrink religious boundaries.

Since this in-depth analysis of the Islamic opening of the secular Kurdish movement has major theoretical and practical ramifications for ethnicity and nationalism studies in general and for Kurdish ethnonationalism and Turkish politics in particular, we focus in this final chapter on the main theoretical and practical implications of this particular case of boundary making.

The Boundary Approach

To begin with the theoretical implications, this in-depth analysis of the Kurdish ethnopolitical movement's evolving relations with Islam provides some insights into boundary-making processes. As presented in chapter 1, the boundary approach initially disregarded the "cultural stuff" (Barth 1969b, 15) or contents of ethnic boundaries. However, it is now widely acknowledged that the "cultural stuff" matters for boundary processes. As R. Jenkins (2008, 126) also suggests, "boundaries and the interactions across them are intimately and indissolubly bound up with the cultural contents of ethnicity." Even Barth (1994, 18) himself admitted in his later works that "central and culturally valued institutions and activities in an ethnic group may be deeply involved in its boundary maintenance." The Kurdish case underscores that the cultural content of ethnic categories or movements, such as internal differences and divisions, do affect boundary-making processes.

Given the now-widespread acceptance of the significance of the cultural content of ethnic categories for boundary processes, we now leave that stale debate behind and shift our attention to more theoretically interesting and fruitful issues and questions, such as how the "cultural stuff" matters for boundary making. The case of the Islamic opening of the secular Kurdish movement provides us some answers to this question. First, as shown by empirical analyses, it shapes elites' strategies of boundary making. Ethnopolitical leaders should take into account possible divisions and cleavages within the ethnic category or movement as they make and remake symbolic and social boundaries. Second, cultural content molds the processes of boundary contestation. As the analyses indicate, ethnic group heterogeneity boosts the likelihood of internal boundary contestations.

In addition, this case study has examined the plausibility of several specific hypotheses concerning boundary processes. Empirical analyses suggest that the following propositions about boundary-making processes warrant further investigation through comparative case studies or large-N research:

1. Both the external (e.g., the larger sociopolitical and institutional contexts) and internal (e.g., intragroup cleavages) environments of a given ethnic category or movement shape boundary-making processes, including boundary-making styles and strategies.

2. Ethnopolitical elites' political legitimacy and survival concerns augment the likelihood of boundary work (e.g., boundary expansion or contraction).

3. Electoral periods increase the likelihood of boundary work in general and boundary contestation in particular.

4. In relatively more heterogeneous ethnic groups or movements, internal boundary contestation (struggle over boundaries among coethnics) becomes more likely.

5. In hierarchically organized ethnic groups or movements, internal boundary contestation is less likely to succeed.

6. In the case of a highly unified ethnopolitical leadership (i.e., limited elite competition or rivalry), internal boundary contestation is less likely to succeed.

The Primordialist versus the Circumstantialist/Constructionist/ Instrumentalist Debate

This research has also some ramifications for the theoretical debates around ethnicity and nationalism. As many scholars observe, the conventional theoretical division or rivalry in ethnicity and nationalism studies has been between and among the primordialist and circumstantialist/constructionist/instrumentalist perspectives (see Conversi 1995; Hutchinson and Smith 1996; Brubaker, Loveman, and Stamatov 2004; Hale 2004; Greenfeld 2006; Cornell and Hartmann 2007; Özkırımlı 2010; Keating 2011; Eriksen 2010; Chandra 2012a; Wimmer 2013). One major source of this division is related to the issue of to what extent ethnicity is situational, contextual, and fluid. As Brubaker, Loveman, and Stamatov (2004, 49) also observe, "this debate pits an understanding of ethnicity as rooted in deep-seated or 'primordial' attachments and sentiments against an understanding of it as an instrumental adaptation to shifting economic and political circumstances."

Such a division has its foundations in the agency-structure problem (also known as the agency-structure debate), which is one of fundamental dilemmas in social sciences. As Wendt (1987, 338–339) suggests, the problem emerges from two competing truisms about social life that shape most social scientific research: (1) "human beings and their organizations are purposeful actors whose actions help reproduce or transform the society in which they live," and (2) "society is made up of social relationships, which structure the interactions between these purposeful actors" (see also Dessler 1989). Thus, at the core of this debate is the question of whether agency (which refers to personal autonomy, choice, will, purposiveness, intentionality, reflexivity, creativity, learning, and transformative capacity)[1] or structure (e.g., material/actual and ideational/virtual entities such as resources, class, ideology, religion, institutions, world system, bureaucracy, and market)[2] is the most important factor in explaining and/or understanding political and social processes and outcomes (Carlsnaes 1992; Finnemore 1996; Peters 1998; O'Neill, Balsiger, and VanDeveer 2004; Halperin and Heath 2012, 92). In Finnemore's (1996, 14) words, the main issue in this debate is "whether, analytically, one treats actors (i.e. agents), capabilities, and preferences as given and derives social structures from their interaction, or whether one takes the social structures as given and treats actors, their preferences and powers, as defined by the social system(s) in which they are embedded."

Structuralist perspectives put greater emphasis on the role of factors and conditions, such as historical legacies, institutions, and power hierarchies, in analyzing social and political processes and outcomes. Such perspectives assert that humans do not act in a vacuum. Social, political, and economic environments and historical legacies condition or structure people's preferences, interests, actions, and interactions, and social and political structures exist independently of the actions and preferences of the people who occupy them (Clark 1998, 250). Therefore, it is claimed that human action cannot be understood simply by focusing on individual motivation and intention; these perspectives attribute ontological primacy to structure and treat it as "a fixed, enduring set of conditions that constrains and disposes, shapes and shoves behavior" (Dessler 1989, 466).

Agential approaches, on the other hand, consider human agents (either individual or collective) as prior to structures. Assuming that agents take autonomous, voluntary, and purposeful actions in sociopolitical life, these perspectives tend to treat human agency as an exogenous factor in social scientific research (e.g., behaviorism, utilitarianism, rational choice theory, game theory, poststructuralist theory). As Clark

(1998, 250) observes, for an agency-centered approach, "an explanation is not complete until the outcomes explained are traced back to the behavior of individuals. . . . Agency-centered theorists do not dismiss the explanatory import of structural factors, they maintain an a priori assumption that those structures are, themselves, to be viewed as the product of human agency." Similarly, O'Neill, Balsiger, and VanDeveer (2004, 151) note that "agent-centered (also called individualist or voluntarist) social theories consider structures epiphenomenal constructs that can be reduced to individuals and their interactions" (see also Carlsnaes 1992, 249).

Like all social scientific theories, theories of ethnicity and nationalism also adopt an implicit or explicit position on this debate (see also Eriksen 2010, 65–66). Some approaches or theories (e.g., primordialism and the sociobiological approach) put greater stress on factors such as consanguinity and inborn features (e.g., shared ethnic roots, kinship ties, phenotype, language, territory) and collective historical legacies, memories, symbols, and myths and so remain relatively more structural. For instance, van den Berghe (1995, 357), a prominent sociologist and anthropologist defending the sociobiological approach, asserts that "[human] behavior can only be understood within an evolutionary framework that gives equal weight to genes and environment." Such approaches tend to treat ethnicity as given, natural, persistent, and reified (e.g., Shils 1957; Geertz 1973; Isaacs 1975; van den Berghe 1981, 1995, 2001; Connor 1994; Grosby 1994, 1995; Van Evera 2001; Bayar 2009). On this point, it is worth quoting Eller and Coughlan (1993, 187) at length:

> Primordial identities or attachments are "given," *a priori*, underived, prior to all experience or interaction—in fact, all interaction is carried out *within* the primordial realities. Primordial attachments are "natural," even "spiritual," rather than sociological. Primordial attachments are *ab origine* and *causa sui*: they have no social source. . . . Primordial sentiments are "ineffable," overpowering, and coercive. They cannot be analysed in relation to social interaction. If an individual is a member of a group, he

or she *necessarily* feels certain attachments to that group and its practices (especially language and culture). The primordial realities are binding "in and of themselves . . . by virtue of some unaccountable absolute import attributed to the very tie itself."

Structural theories of ethnicity and nationalism, however, have some limitations. For instance, many of them often suffer from methodological holism. This orientation assumes that individual action takes place within a historical, social, political, and economic context. Therefore, behavior cannot be understood without taking into account the impact of the larger context or broader social structures. Thus, in social scientific inquiry, methodological holism prioritizes macro-level factors and variables (e.g., institutions, bureaucracies, classes, networks, market, culture, the state, the international system) and treats them as exogenous factors. As Halperin and Heath (2012, 82) state, "methodological holism assumes that social institutions, collectives, and organizations are prior to, and fundamentally independent of individuals and can therefore be taken as 'primitives' in social science explanations: they can serve as the primary independent variables determining individual and collective behavior and outcomes." However, since methodological holism treats structures as given, taken for granted (i.e., leaving them unexplained), and fixed or immutable, it falls into the trap of structural reification, which refers to the "tendency to treat macro-social entities as if they had a concrete, material existence; as analytically independent of their constituent elements; inert, unchanging, and unmediated by human agency" (Halperin and Heath 2012, 86; see also Sewell 1992, 2). Wendt (1987, 347) addresses a similar limitation: "Because it [the structuralist solution to the agent-structure problem] cannot 'explain anything but behavioral conformity to structural demands' it ultimately fails to provide a basis for explaining the properties of deep structures themselves." Considering structuralist orientations in ethnicity and nationalism studies, Lecours (2000, 110) observes that these approaches "tend to consider ethnic identities as 'givens' and are therefore unwilling and unable to explain how they are formed, transformed and crystallized" (see also Cederman 2002). Structural reification should be avoided because, as Bhaskar (quoted in Wendt 1987, 359) notes, "social structures, unlike natural structures, do not exist independently of the agents' conceptions of what they are doing in their activity."

A related problem is structural determinism, which is a direct result of the notion of weak, constrained, and limited agency that characterizes many structural theories. Structural determinism does not leave much room for the role of human agency in social processes and outcomes. It tends to reduce agents to being the "bearers of structures" and agency to "the predetermined outcome of structural imperatives" (Reed 1997, 31). However, as Dessler (1989, 444) also warns, "any social action is the product of both structural and agential forces, and therefore a strictly structural explanation of action . . . will necessarily be incomplete. Structural theory alone does not provide and is not capable of providing a complete explanation of action."

The great majority of approaches, however, treat ethnicity and nationality not as something atavistic, given, fixed, or static but as phenomena that are dynamic, fluid, malleable, contingent, situational, subjective, and socially constructed or even fabricated (e.g., see Barth 1969a; Lyman and Douglass 1973; Okamura 1981; Banton 1997; Brass 1979, 1991; Hobsbawm and Ranger 1983; Hobsbawm 1990; Eller and Coughlan 1993; Nagel 1994; Billig 1995; Haymes 1997; Lecours 2000; Brubaker 2002; Wodak 2006; Cornell and Hartman 2007; R. Jenkins 2008; Wodak et al. 2009; Eriksen 2010; Chandra 2012a). For instance, Brubaker (2002, 167–168) suggests that ethnicity, race, and nation should be understood in "relational, processual, dynamic, eventful and disaggregated terms." Associating these notions with "practical categories, cultural idioms, cognitive schemas, discursive frames, organizational routines, institutional forms, political projects and contingent events," Brubaker (2002, 174) claims that they are "not things *in* the world, but perspectives *on* the world. These include ethnicized ways of seeing (and ignoring), of construing (and misconstruing), of inferring (and misinferring), of remembering (and forgetting). . . . They include systems of classification, categorization and identification, formal and informal. And they include the tacit, taken-for-granted background knowledge . . . through which people recognize and experience objects, places, persons, actions or situations as ethnically, racially or nationally marked and meaningful" (see also Özkırımlı 2010, 214). Such accounts of ethnicity and nationalism involve a substantial degree of agency. By addressing the fluid and socially constructed nature of ethnicity and nationalism, they acknowledge, implicitly or explicitly, the role of agency (at either the elite or mass level) in ethnic and nationalist processes. Having relatively greater room for human agency, these approaches (e.g., constructionist, instrumentalist, and elite perspectives) emphasize the role of individual dispositions, choices, preferences, and actions and interactions in ethnonationalist processes. For instance, in Chandra's (2012b, 18) definition of constructivism, one notices a substantial degree of agency; constructivism refers "to the position that facts [e.g., ethnicity] that we take to be 'natural' are in fact *the product of some human attempt at creating and interpretation*" (emphasis added).

These perspectives highlight the role of agential factors in ethnonationalist processes because, as Calhoun (1997, 50) notes, "[(ethno)national] traditions are not simply inherited, they have to be reproduced: stories have to be told over and again [and] parts of traditions have to be adapted to new circumstances to keep them meaningful." For instance, in a defense of the constructionist account, Cornell and Hartmann (2007, 81) suggest, "Ethnicity and race are not simply labels forced upon people; they are also identities that people accept, resist, choose, specify, invent, redefine, reject, actively defend, and so forth. They involve an active 'we' as well as a 'they.' They involve not only circumstances but also active responses to circumstances by individuals and groups, guided by their own preconceptions, dispositions, and agendas." The authors claim that constructionist accounts are advantageous to analyze such processes because compared to structural accounts, which focus on the impact of external forces and conditions on ethnicity, the former have "a large dose of activism: the contribution groups make to creating and shaping their own—and others'—identities" (76).

Several orientations in the agential category pay particular attention to the role of cultural, intellectual, and political elites (e.g., ethnonationalist intellectuals, leaders, politicians) in creating, transforming, and crystallizing ethnic or national identities, in defining interests, and in politicizing and mobilizing ethnic or national identities (e.g., see Brass 1979, 1991; Haymes 1997; Lecours 2000). It is claimed that such elites not only interpret or reinterpret existing cultural materials (e.g., myths, memories, values, symbols, traditions, and historical legacies) but also invent cultural elements or groups to promote a certain ethnic or national identity (e.g., see Young 1985; Fardon 1987; Eriksen 2010; Chandra 2012a).[3] For instance, Lecours (2000, 118) points out that "elites are not only active in nationalist mobilization, but also in the construction, transformation, and politicization of ethnic identities, and in the definition of an ethnic group's interests. . . . These processes are enacted through the use of cultural markers, and the construction and manipulation of symbols. The subjective dimension of politics was stressed by classical theorists who argued that elites created and manipulated symbols, myths and ideas to build legitimacy for their power, and to pursue their own interests."

Thus, ethnicity and nationality, which are treated as exogenous factors by structural perspectives, are endogenized by agential perspectives (see also Chandra 2012a). Wimmer (2013) observes that by the end of the 1990s, approaches such as constructivism, instrumentalism, and circumstantialism had gained the upper hand over essentialist, primordialist, and perennialist perspectives. Brubaker (2009, 28) agrees: "Today, few if any scholars would argue that ethnic groups or races or nations are fixed or given; virtually everyone agrees that they are historically emergent and in some respects mutable. This holds even for those who, drawing on evolutionary and cognitive psychology, have sought to revive and respecify the primordialist position by explaining the deep roots of essentialist or primordialist thinking in everyday life. In this sense, we are all constructivists now."

That being said, agential theories also face several criticisms; a common one is that they overestimate or overstate the role of elites and elite manipulation in ethnonationalist processes, ignoring various structural factors constraining these elites (see Robinson 1977, 1979; O'Leary 2001). For instance, it is argued that nationalist discourses and movements are not constructed ex nihilo (Gorski 2006). Similarly, Smith (2006, 178) argues that in the absence of the necessary general processes and elements of nation formation (e.g., deep and pervasive cultural commonalities such as shared ethnic myths, memories, symbols, and traditions and a sense of the collective self), the political will of ethnopolitical leaders is not enough to sustain nations. Along the same lines, we see several criticisms against the constructionist account. Wimmer (2013, 26), for instance, warns against its radical versions and finds it problematic "to identify fluidity, situational variability and strategic malleability as the very nature of the ethnic phenomenon *as such*, as in radical versions of the constructivist paradigm . . . that treat ethnicity as a mere 'imagined community,' as a cognitive scheme of little consequence to the life chances of individuals, or as an individual 'identity choice' among many others" (emphasis in original). Eriksen (2010, 68) shares the same concern: "A one-sided emphasis on the manipulation of symbols, the situational selection of identity and the fleeting and indefinite character of culture seems to suggest that nothing really endures, that the social world is continuously re-created, and that constructivist analytical approaches may tell the whole story about human identification. This kind of view, which is rarely far away in contemporary studies of ethnicity and nationalism, would not just be methodologically individualist but also a rather strong expression of voluntarism."

As these statements also indicate, one source of the weakness of agential approaches is that these perspectives, in varying degrees, adhere to some form of methodological individualism, which regards individuals or groups as the primary unit of analysis and focuses on the beliefs, interests, preferences, intentions, actions, and interactions of human actors in social scientific inquiry (Peters 2012, 14; Kydd 2008). As Halperin and Heath (2012, 80) note, "Methodological individualism claims that, since all that it is possible for us to know are the actions of individuals, then explanations of social phenomena such as classes, power, or nations must ultimately be explicable in terms of facts about individuals. Unless we can account for an outcome in terms of individuals and their desires and beliefs, we do not have an explanation of that outcome."

However, methodological individualism remains limited due to atomistic or individualist reductionism (i.e., reducing sociopolitical processes and outcomes to individual properties, actions, and interactions) (Halperin and Heath 2012, 80). In addition, it has a tendency to treat human agency as a priori, given, and fixed. In the words of Kydd (2008, 427), methodological individualism "traces causality from the individual to larger social phenomena rather than from the structure to the individual. The actor, human or state, is taken as exogenous to the explanation. This conception assumes that the actor's identity and preferences are fixed." Exogenizing the individual also means having an asocial and ahistorical notion of the individual (Heywood 2005, 32). In brief, theories of ethnicity that are driven by methodological individualism neglect or underestimate the role of historical factors and sociopolitical structures in their accounts of ethnicity and nationalism.

An increasing number of scholarly works on ethnicity and nationalism, however, advocate transcending such dichotomous understandings (i.e., structure vs. agency; primordialism vs. constructivism) and instead emphasize the need to give due attention to both macro and micro factors and to durable and flexible aspects of ethnicity and nationalism (e.g., Laitin 1998; Hale 2004; Natali 2005; Smith 2005; Wolff 2006; Eriksen 2010; Wimmer 2013). Thus, believing in the causal role of both structural and agential factors in social and political processes and outcomes, several scholars have attempted to combine or link micro- and macro-level variables and factors as they study ethnicity and nationalism phenomena. Put differently, if we think about the structure-agency or primordialist-constructivist dichotomies on a continuum, many researchers occupy the middle ground. For instance, assuming that social life comprises both agency and structure simultaneously (or both individual dispositions, will, and choice and structural constraints), Eriksen (2010, 66) claims, "Ethnic identities are neither ascribed nor achieved: they are both. They are wedged between situational selection and imperatives imposed from without. . . . As Marx wrote, people make history, but not under circumstances of their own choosing." Similarly, treating cultural structures as "Janus-faced," Laitin (1998, 20) suggests that they have both a given, primordial, constraining dimension and a flexible, instrumental, constructed aspect (see also Smith 2005; Wolff 2006). As another example, Hale (2004) claims that neither the primordialist nor constructivist perspectives are fully accurate, and so he provides a micro-level account of why and how people tend to think and act in terms of macro-level identity categories.[4] Finally, Varshney (2007, 291) observes, "No one seriously argues any more that ethnic identity is primordial, nor that it is devoid of any intrinsic value and used only as a strategic tool. Pure essentialists or pure instrumentalists do not exist any longer."

The implications of this study are more in line with this third view. The analyses of the Kurdish case imply that, contrary to the assumptions of the primordialist perspective, which tends to treat ethnicity as a priori, given, natural, fixed, enduring, invariant, and timeless (e.g., see Shils 1957; Isaacs 1975; van den Berghe 1981, 1995; Grosby 1994, 1995; Van Evera 2001; Bayar 2009), ethnic identity and ethnic boundaries are more likely to be situational, interactional, and fluid. Thus, the Kurdish case provides confirming evidence for constructionists', situationalists', and transactionalists' main arguments that ethnic identifications and boundaries are socially constructed and situationally contingent, shaped by practices and interactions (e.g., see Barth 1969a; Conversi 1995, 1999; Brubaker et al. 2006; Cornell and Hartmann 2007; R. Jenkins 2008; Jackson 2015a, 2015b). As Cornell and Hartmann (2007, 87) summarize, "The constructionist approach . . . sees ethnic and racial identities as highly variable and contingent products of an ongoing interaction between on one hand, the circumstances groups encounter—including the conceptions and actions of outsiders—and, on the other, the actions and conceptions of group members—of insiders. It makes groups active agents in the making and remaking of their own identities, and it views construction not as a one-time event, but as continuous and historical. The construction of identity has no end point short of the disappearance of the identity altogether."

The case of the Islamic opening of the Kurdish movement also provides partial support for the famous instrumentalist perspective that ethnopolitical elites produce, reproduce, and manipulate ethnic identities and boundaries to achieve their material (e.g., security, political power, and economic resources) and/or ideational interests (e.g., social status, prestige, legitimacy) (e.g., see Brass 1991; Haymes 1997; Lecours 2000). In other words, this perspective suggests that in elites' competition and struggle for political and economic resources and gains, they instrumentalize ethnic identities and attachments. Brass (1991, 8), for instance, asserts that "ethnicity and nationalism are not 'givens,' but are social and political constructions. They are creations of elites, who draw upon, distort, and sometimes fabricate materials from the cultures of the groups they wish to represent in order to protect their wellbeing or existence or to gain political and economic advantage for their groups as well as for themselves." As illustrated by the empirical chapters, responding to political and economic developments and conditions, ethnopolitical elites may redraw symbolic and social boundaries of an ethnic group or movement to achieve their interests and objectives. This circumstance is even more valid for hierarchically organized ethnic groups or movements such as the Kurdish movement, which has been elite dominated. All these arguments suggest that ethnic boundaries should be understood not as reified or fixed frontiers but as somewhat flexible, ideational structures susceptible to both external and internal dynamics and factors (e.g., political survival, the legitimacy concerns of ethnopolitical leadership, internal cleavages).

That being said, this detailed analysis of the Kurdish case also suggests that ethnic boundaries and the "cultural stuff" they enclose constrain boundary makers as well. Instrumentalist perspectives tend to exaggerate the ability of ethnopolitical elites to construct or deconstruct ethnic identities. In reality, a variety of endogenous and exogenous factors and dynamics restrict political elites in their efforts at boundary work. In other words, it is problematic to treat ethnicity and ethnic boundaries as a toy in the hands of ethnopolitical elites. The Kurdish case indicates that ethnicity and nationalism involve a constant, dynamic interplay between agential and structural factors. Agents (e.g., ethnopolitical leaders, ethnonationalist intellectuals such as historians and linguists) definitely play a role in ethnic or national identity formation and mobilization, and several analyses have already implicitly or explicitly acknowledged the significance of such factors. It is, however, another fact that human agency operates in a historical, social, economic, and political context. In other words, diachronic (e.g., historical legacies and conditions) and synchronic factors (social, political, and economic structures, conditions) constrain or enable the agency of individuals. Hence, taking into account both structural *and* agential factors, as well as the aforementioned dynamics, would help us avoid the methodological holism traps of structure-based approaches and the methodological individualism pitfalls of agency-centered perspectives. As a result, theoretical frameworks of ethnicity and nationalism giving due analytical and explanatory weight to both agency and structure are relatively more advantageous with regard to having more comprehensive and robust explanations of ethnicity and nationalism, including ethnic boundary-making processes.

The Nexus between Religion and Nationalism

This case study also has some implications for the relationship between religion and nationalism. On the nexus between the two, we see competing approaches in the existing literature. The modernist view of nation and nationalism neglected the role of religion in nationalist movements (e.g., see Anderson 1991; Gellner 1983; Hobsbawm 1990). As Gorski

(2006) also observes, several proponents of the modernist view assert that genuine nationalism should be secular; it should not be contaminated with religious elements. Rieffer (2003, 216) also addresses this tendency of the modernist perspective: "[Modernist] authors such as Ernest Gellner, Benedict Anderson and Eric Hobsbawm, for example, have been largely silent on the interplay between religion and nationalism, instead focusing on economic conditions. . . . Many authors fail to adequately address the role that religion [plays], directly or indirectly, in this process." For instance, Anderson (1991) suggests that the decline of religion was one of the factors that promoted the rise of nationalism. Thus, treating nationalism as an essentially modern and secular phenomenon, the modernist view assumes a mutually exclusive relationship between religion and nationalism. As a result, the modernization approach expects that the rise of modern nationalism limits or decreases the influence of religion in the public sphere (e.g., see Gellner 1983; Hechter 2000). As Rieffer asserts (2003, 223), "The implication of a modern understanding of nationalism is that nationalism is secular. Modern societies are thought to be those societies that, inter alia, progressed past religion or at least past the influence of religion on political institutions. . . . If nationalism is associated with modernity and modernity is inherently thought to be secular, this explains why there have been few analyses of the effect of religion on nationalism."

Several scholars, however, reject the arguments and assumptions of the modernist view and claim that religion and nationalism can coexist, even empower each other. It is argued that the rise of religious nationalist movements around the world in the past decades constitutes a direct challenge to the modernization perspective (e.g., see Rieffer 2003). Hence, it is asserted that religion can be an integral part of nationalism (A. Hastings 1997). Similarly, Brubaker (2012, 16) draws attention to the possibility of the entanglement of religion and nationalism: "Nationalism and religion are often deeply intertwined; political actors may make claims both in the name of the nation and in the name of God. Nationalist politics can accommodate the claims of religion and nationalist rhetoric often deploys religious language, imagery, and symbolism; similarly, religion can accommodate the claims of the nation-state, and religious movements can deploy nationalist language." Smith (2008, 8) also addresses the complex interactions between religion and ethnicity and nationalism by noting the following: "It is clearly insufficient to argue that nations and nationalisms arose out of, and against, the great religious cultural systems of the medieval world. We have to recognize the complexity of continuing relations between religions and forms of the sacred, on the one hand, and national symbols, memories and traditions, on the other hand." Along the same lines, in the preface to Barker's *Religious Nationalism in Modern Europe*, Safran (2009, xiii) suggests that religion "was, and in many cases continues to be, a constitutive element of nationalism and an effective political mobilizing force. It may be instrumentalized to gain independence; to acquire political legitimacy; to create internal sociopolitical unity; to provide a political counter-ideology; and to fortify the cultural ramparts around a society." Juergensmeyer (2006, 182) also observes that "increasingly religious identities and ideologies have become the basis for strident new forms of nationalism and transnationalism in a globalized, postmodern world" (see also Abulof 2014; Stroup 2017).

The Islamic opening of the secular Kurdish movement in Turkey in the past decades supports the second view and shows that even secular, left-oriented ethnonationalist movements may resort to religious ideas and symbols to enhance their political and social legitimacy, approval, and popularity. Further, ethnonationalist movements could use religion for both internal and external consumption. Internally, ethnopolitical elites resort to religious beliefs, myths, and symbols to reinforce and sustain ethnic-group unity and cohesion. Externally, they might employ religious elements to expand the legitimacy and popularity of the ethnic movement within the larger social and political environment. In brief, religious beliefs, myths, and symbols might play an important role in ethnic and national continuity and survival (see also Smith 1992, 2008). Using the lexicon of the boundary approach, religion constitutes one of the major devices used by ethnopolitical leaders in their ethnic boundary work.

The Islamic Peace Hypothesis

The Kurdish case analyzed here also has some ramifications for the debates on the role of religion in solving the conflict. Regarding the nexus between Islam and Kurdish ethnonationalism, many people in conservative and Islamic circles embrace the Islamic peace hypothesis. Since the vast majority of Turks and Kurds self-identify as Muslim, Islam in Turkey is not a strong boundary marker. Instead, as a shared value among Turks and Kurds, Islam constitutes an overarching, superordinate identity. As a result, treating Islam as a bridge, as a social cement or glue connecting or binding two ethnic groups, proponents of the Islamic peace perspective attribute major social and political roles for Islam. Regarding its social role, assuming that a shared, superordinate identity would contain negative feelings toward out-group members and so improve interethnic relations, Islam is expected to promote social tolerance and thus peace and harmony between the two groups. Regarding its political role, assuming that Islam is incompatible with nationalism,[5] adherents of the Islamic peace hypothesis anticipate that promoting a shared Muslim identity would decrease the role of ethnicity in self-identification and so suppress Kurdish ethnonationalist orientations and demands. In brief, supporters of the Islamic peace hypothesis simply expect that promoting Islam and Islamic values would improve interethnic relations in the social landscape and contain Kurdish ethnonationalism in the political domain.[6] With such assumptions and expectations, many conservative and Islamic circles emphasize overarching identities and notions such as the Islamic brotherhood or *ummah*. As Houston (2001, 157) also observes, the "Islamist discourse on the Kurdish problem gives its assent to the existence and equality of Kurds as a *kavim* (people/nation) and to Kurdish as a language, but calls for the subordination of such an identity to an Islamic one" (see also Yavuz 1997; Duran 1998; Sakallioğlu 1998; Bahcheli and Noel 2011; Ünver 2015; Dag 2017).[7]

One can find numerous examples of such an understanding in scholarly, policy, and media analyses. For instance, Yavuz (1998, 12) claims that

"the Islamic layer of identity could be useful in terms of containing ethnic tensions and finding a peaceful solution" to the Kurdish issue. He
assumes a mutually exclusive relationship between religious and ethnic
identities and expects that promoting religious identities and attachments would weaken or suppress ethnic identities and consciousness.
Yavuz further contends that secularization reforms in the early Republic, such as the closure of Sufi religious orders, weakened religious ties
and values and so unintentionally promoted the rise of a Kurdish ethnic
consciousness. Yavuz (2003, 53) states, "In the long run, by removing
Sufi loyalties and leadership, which had made it relatively easy to blur
ethnic lines by stressing Islamic brotherhood between Turks and Kurds,
the ban consolidated Kurdish ethnic identity and politicized Kurdish
national consciousness." Van Bruinessen (2000a, 78) also draws attention to the unifying role of Islam: "The call for Muslim unity, sounded
during the War of Independence, had been more effective among the
Kurds than Kurdish nationalist agitation, but when Turkey set on a
course of secularization the very basis of this unity disappeared. The
Kemalists attempted to replace Islam as the unifying factor by a Turkey-
based nationalism. In so doing, they provoked the Kurdish nationalist
response that they feared." Updegraff (2012, 124) also claims that the notion of Islamic brotherhood promoted by conservative circles sells well
among conservative Kurds: "For the more religious among the large majority of Kurds who are Sunni Muslims, the AKP's framing of the issues
between Turks and Kurds as a matter between 'brothers' carries great
resonance" (see also A. Aslan 1996).[8]

Such an understanding (i.e., rejecting ethnic particularities in the
name of Muslim unity or brotherhood) is also quite widespread among
conservative and Islamic political actors in modern Turkish politics. For
instance, the political parties of the pro-Islamic National Outlook Movement (Milli Görüş Hareketi, MGH), which emerged on the Turkish political scene in the early 1970s, emphasize the notion of an Islamic or
Muslim brotherhood as a shared identity among Turkish citizens. On
several occasions, the leading figures of this movement have claimed

that Islamic identity, which surpasses particular ethnic identities and attachments, would be a cure for Kurdish ethnonationalism. For instance, Abdullah Gül, who was one of the key figures of the pro-Islamic Welfare Party (Refah Partisi, RP, 1983–1998), stated, "Racist approaches to the conflict are wrong, and may result in a civil war. The problem can only be solved by relying on one common denominator; Muslim brotherhood. This is not only a remedy to the problems of southeastern Turkey but also to the relations in the larger area concerned, i.e. relations between Turkey, Syria, Iraq and Iran" (quoted in Beriker-Atiyas 1997, 443).

Similarly, Mustafa Kamalak, who served as the leader of the Felicity Party (Saadet Partisi, SP), currently representing the MGH in Turkish party politics, claimed, "We believe that in order to solve the [Kurdish] problem, we should first disregard national or racial ideas and notions. Instead, we should focus on unifying concepts and common values between the Kurds and Turks. That would be Islam. Rather than race, Islam is the shared value between the Kurds and Turks and we should keep it powerful and alive. . . . Any proposal or initiative excluding or ignoring Islam and Islamic sentiments would not have much chance to solve the problem" (quoted in Sarigil and Fazlioglu 2013, 553–554).

The Islamic peace hypothesis is also shared by other conservative formations such as the AKP, whose officials also frequently refer to the Islamic brotherhood and *ummah* to appeal to the Kurdish masses and to discourage Kurds from ethnonationalist orientations. For instance, during a speech at Canterbury University in New Zealand in December 2005, Erdoğan stated, "There are around 30 different ethnic groups in Turkey, such as Turks, Kurds, Laz, Circassians, Georgians, Abhazians and Bosniaks, and they are all intermingled. . . . Ninety-nine percent of people living in Turkey are Muslim. Thus, these different ethnic groups are unified by shared Islamic bonds."[9] After his return to Turkey, Erdoğan reiterated those views, asserting that "Islam is a cement; it is the most important unifying factor among several ethnic groups in Turkey."[10]

Likewise, Numan Kurtulmuş, vice chair of the AKP, asserted that the Ottoman Empire was dissolved due to ethnic nationalisms and that, therefore, such nationalisms should be avoided. For Kurtulmuş, Turks and Kurds are part of the same *ummah*. Hence, the main unifying bond or common identity among multiple ethnic groups in Turkey is Islam, and it can play an important role in solving the Kurdish problem.[11] Another AKP official, Yasin Aktay, expressed similar views in Siirt during the AKP's 2015 electoral campaign: "It is a shame to call the people in the region as Kurds because as Turks, Kurds, Arabs and Circassion, we are the constituents of one single nation. Thanks to Allah, we are part of an honorable Islamic nation. By calling people Kurd or Arab we are creating divisions and discriminating against certain groups. . . . We should avoid ethnic nationalism [*kavmiyetçilik*]."[12]

As evident from these quotations, conservative AKP officials view Islam as a social cement or glue between different Muslim ethnic groups. With such an understanding, they anticipate that promoting overarching identities such as Islamic unity and Muslim brotherhood would contribute to improved interethnic relations and so empower social peace and harmony (see also Yavuz and Özcan 2006; Çiçek 2013). Particularly after the 2007 general elections, in which the AKP received the majority of Kurdish votes (see figure 3.3), we have seen an increasing emphasis on Islamic identity within AKP circles. As Aydin and Emrence (2015, xvii) also note, after the elections, "Islamic charities and civic society organizations [were] mobilized by the government to emphasize Muslim solidarity and downplay ethnic nationalism in the region."[13]

The results of our detailed analysis of the Kurdish case, however, raise doubts about the assumptions and expectations of the Islamic peace hypothesis. It appears that Islam is not the antidote to Kurdish ethnonationalism that it is touted as. Although the Islamic peace hypothesis assumes a mutually exclusive relationship between Islamic identity and ethnic particularities, religion and ethnonationalism can become entangled (Brubaker 2012). Gorski and Turkmen-Dervişoğlu (2013, 203) are in agreement: "nationalist rhetoric and ritual often borrow from religion."

Similarly, R Jenkins (2008, 124) remarks that "religious issues and motifs provide actors with a vocabulary and institutional arena through the medium of which that [ethnic, national] conflict may be waged."

The Kurdish case supports such observations. With the Islamic opening, the Kurdish movement has entangled itself with Islam and Islamic actors. Although conservative or Islamic circles refer to Islamic ideas, values, and principles when discussing the Kurdish issue to blur ethnic boundaries, Kurdish ethnonationalists use these principles to legitimize and assert ethnic differences (e.g., being Kurdish) and ethnonational demands (e.g., linguistic rights and local autonomy). In other words, they instrumentalize religion to promote ethnonationalist claims and demands.[14] Note that religion is instrumentalized for different goals and objectives by different political actors. Many conservative circles in Turkey resort to religious symbols and ideas to suppress or silence particular ethnic identities and demands; Kurdish ethnopolitical elites deploy such ideational and symbolic elements to promote ethnic particularities and rights.

Further, pro-Kurdish circles are highly critical of the notions of Islamic brotherhood and *ummah*, which are advocated and promoted by Islamic circles. The former think that Islamists instrumentalize such notions to silence Kurdish demands[15] and to control and subjugate Kurdish ethnic identity.[16] Hence, Kurdish ethnonationalist circles are highly disturbed by Islamists' efforts to subordinate Kurdish ethnic identity to an Islamic one. As Houston (2001, 178) also observes,

> Islamic *kardeşlik* [brotherhood] is a contested term. In Islamist discourse it implies the cessation of separatist claims in the name of Islamic unity (i.e. against the enemies of Islam). For Kurdish Islamism it demands the necessary (if as yet unforthcoming) support of Turkish Muslims in Kurds' struggle for God-given natural rights. "*Ne Türk, ne Kürt, biz Müslüman kardeşiz*" ("We are neither Turks nor Kurds, we are Muslim brothers"), say religious Turks. "*Biz üvey kardeşler olmak istemiyoruz*" ("We do not wish to be foster brothers") reply religious Kurds. That is, for Kurdish Islamism

Islamic fraternity involves not merely the acceptance of, but active support for, the protection of ethnic difference, not its cancellation in some meta-Islamic identity. (See also Çiçek 2013)

In brief, since ethnopolitical actors do use certain ideas and principles within religion (in our case, Islam) to legitimize ethnic differences and demands, it is not realistic to expect that promoting Islamic ideas and values among Kurds would suppress Kurdish ethnic consciousness and ethnonationalist orientations and demands. As I asserted earlier, then, Islam does not really serve as an antidote to Kurdish ethnonationalism, and therefore, stressing religious brotherhood between Turk and Kurds is not a realistic strategy to contain Kurdish ethnonationalism.[17]

Secularism and the Left in Turkey

This particular case has also significant implications for the debates on secularism among leftist groups in Turkey. It is widely accepted that most, if not all, of the leftist formations in Turkey have been skeptical toward religion. For instance, Çiçek notes that the Turkish left subscribes to an Orthodox secularist understanding, which tends to treat religion as an archaic or primitive phenomenon. Consequently, many leftist circles tend to associate religion with backwardness.[18] The prevalence of such a staunch secularist approach among many leftist circles was primarily due to the left's strong commitment to traditional modernization theory, which expects that socioeconomic progress (e.g., industrialization, urbanization, the rise of education and income levels) would gradually expand the secularization process and so reduce the influence of religion in sociopolitical life.[19] As Jung (2011) also suggests, such an approach assumes a zero-sum relationship between religion and modernity.

Given this reality, the secularist, leftist Kurdish movement's efforts to reconcile with Islam and Islamic actors in the past decades constitute an important development. By expanding symbolic and social boundaries to include Islamic ideas, principles, and actors, the movement renounced its antireligious, authoritarian secularist understanding and embraced a more moderate secularist outlook. This suggests that the movement has not turned into an Islamic one. It is still a secular movement but with a much more moderate and religion-friendly orientation.

As an unprecedented development, the rise of more moderate, religion-friendly secularist understandings among Kurdish leftist circles in the Turkish political sphere has the potential to encourage several other leftist circles and groups to be much more attentive to religious issues as well. In other words, this shift in the Kurdish left is likely to incite several antireligious Turkish leftist groups to reconsider their negative stance toward religion. At the very least, the reconciliation between the Kurdish left and Islam has substantial potential to trigger similar debates and efforts within antireligious leftist formations in Turkish polity.

Islam and Democracy

The Kurdish movement's boundary making also has some ramifications for the debate on the nexus between Islam and democracy, which has revived in the post–Cold War era. As Hashemi (2013) observes, the existing literature provides two competing approaches on that relationship: pessimist and optimist views. The proponents of the pessimist view argue that Islam is not really compatible with secular, modern, and democratic values (e.g., see Gellner 1981, 1992; Huntington 1984, 1991, 1996; Kedourie 1992; Lewis 2010). Francis Fukuyama provided a vivid expression of this understanding. In the aftermath of the Al-Qaeda attacks on the United States on September 11, 2001, Fukuyama stated, "There does seem to be something about Islam, or at least the fundamentalist versions of Islam that have been dominant in recent years, that makes Muslim societies particularly resistant to modernity. Of all contemporary cultural systems, the Islamic world has the fewest democracies (Turkey alone qualifies), and contains no countries that have made the transition from Third to First World status in the manner of South Korea or Singapore."[20]

As Fukuyama's statement also indicates, adherents of this view draw attention to the empirical fact that there is still a limited number of democracies among Muslim-majority countries. For instance, according to a report published in 2015 by Freedom House, a nongovernmental organization assessing and ranking countries around the world by their democratic development, the percentage of nondemocratic regimes is the highest among Muslim-majority countries.[21] In other words, Muslim countries are less likely to have democratic regimes (see also Rowley and Smith 2009; Potrafke 2012). The rise of ruthless violence by radical jihadist Islamic groups (e.g., Al-Qaeda, Taliban, Boko Haram, and ISIS) across several parts of the world (e.g., the Middle East, Africa, and Europe) in the past decades and the fact that by 2016 most Arab Spring uprisings failed to generate democracy raise further doubts, especially in Western circles, about Islam's compatibility with secular, democratic, and modern values and norms.

Those who have a more optimistic outlook on this issue, however, find the pessimist view highly essentialist (e.g., Cesari 2004; Hashemi 2013). They claim that both Islam and democracy can be interpreted in several ways and so might take different forms across space and time. For instance, Hashemi (2013, 83) notes,

Religion is not a monolithic and unchanging category that speaks with one voice throughout history. It is shaped by changing political and socioeconomic contexts and can be interpreted in a myriad of different ways. One need only think about the multiple uses to which the Bible has been put throughout history: justifying both the divine right of kings and democracy, slavery and abolitionism, misogyny and gender equality, colonialism and third world struggles for self-determination, and Jim Crow laws and the US Civil Rights Movement. . . . Like other religious traditions whose origins lie in the premodern era and that are scripturally based, Islam is neither more nor less compatible with modern democracy than Christianity or Judaism. . . . The key interpretive point here is that religious traditions are highly complex [bodies] of ideas, assumptions, and doctrines that . . . contain sufficient ambiguity and elasticity to be read in a variety of different ways—both in support of and in opposition to democracy.

In addition, optimists draw attention to a different empirical fact that some Muslim-majority countries, such as Indonesia, Turkey, and Tunisia, have achieved a relatively higher degree of democracy. Thus, taking into account the diversity of Muslim societies and of Islamic movements and groups, optimists put forward that there is nothing intrinsic about Islam that can be regarded as the reason for the weakness of democracy in Muslim-majority countries. Instead, it is claimed that this condition in the Muslim world is more related to historical circumstances and the domestic, regional, and international economic and political contexts (e.g., the legacy of Western colonialism and imperialism, and power politics among elites) than to the essence or nature of Islam (e.g., see Voll and Esposito 1994; Eickelman and Piscatori 1996; Esposito and Voll 1996; Filali-Ansary 2003; Cesari 2004, 2014; Feldman 2004; Nasr 2005; Esposito, Sonn, and Voll 2016). For instance, Cesari (2004, 5) warns against the risk of "taking Islam out of context, reducing it to a series of essentialized symbols and principles" and proposes, "In order to break through the iron cage of stereotypical Islamic images and representations . . . one must consider discursive practices of religion in general, and of Islam in particular. No religion or culture can be taken as a given. Instead of trying to discover what constitutes the essential quality of Islam, one must examine the social and historical contexts within which Muslims create their discourse on what is important or unimportant in Islam, in *their* Islam."

Given this debate on the nexus between Islam and democracy, the leftist Kurdish movement's recent efforts to promote a more liberal, democratic, and pluralist interpretation of Islam carries a substantial degree of importance. At the very least, it would be interesting to see to what extent the Kurdish ethnopolitical leadership will be able to promote a more democratic interpretation of Islam that would be appealing to the conservative Sunni-Shafi and the secular Alevi Kurdish masses. The success of the Kurdish movement in such a challenging endeavor would not only affect the future of Kurdish ethnopolitics in the Middle East but also shape the broader debate about the compatibility of Islam with secular, democratic, and modern values. Hence, it is worthwhile to follow closely the secular Kurdish ethnopolitical movement's experience with Islam and Islamic actors.

ACKNOWLEDGMENTS

Writing this book has been fulfilling though laborious. However, I am sure it would have been even more difficult without the invaluable support and encouragement of many mentors, colleagues, friends, and academic institutions. As I worked on this research project over the years (between 2011 and 2016), I incurred many debts to several people, all of whom provided enormous support. Colleagues and friends who shared their insightful comments and suggestions on the earlier versions of this study include Mücahit Bilici, Sinan Ciddi, Michael Cook, Berk Esen, Kristin Fabbe, Nathan Gonzalez, Şebnem Gümüşçü, Mehmet Gürses, Şükrü Hanioğlu, Lisel Hintz, Ekrem Karakoç, Yalçın Murgul, Elisabeth Özdalga, Güneş Murat Tezcür, and Andreas Wimmer. Two reviewers for NYU Press read the entire manuscript and provided useful comments and suggestions. I am grateful to Rana Nelson, who carefully edited the initial versions of the book chapters. I am also grateful to B. Guy Peters, Metin Heper, and Ersel Aydınlı for their continuous and generous support and encouragement. Last but not least, I thank Ilene R. Kalish and Maryam Arain from NYU Press for their help and support throughout the publication process.

My appreciation also goes to all the interviewees, who gave up their valuable time to answer my questions. The information and insights they provided enriched my understanding and analyses enormously. In particular, I am grateful to Muhammed Akar, Ayhan Bilgen, Mahmut Bozarslan, Vahap Coşkun, Tahir Elçi (1966–2015), and Ahmet Faruk Ünsal, who met with me several times, shared their thoughts about the Kurdish issue, and put me in contact with several other very helpful informants.

As I worked on this research project, I benefited from the financial assistance provided by several institutions through various stages of this study, including data collection and the writing process. For financial support, I would like to thank the Fulbright Commission, the Scientific and Technological Research Council of Turkey (Türkiye Bilimsel ve Teknolojik Araştırma Kurumu, TUBITAK), the Science Academy (Bilim Akademisi), and the Economic Policy Research Foundation of Turkey (Türkiye Ekonomi Politikaları Araştırma Vakfı, TEPAV).

Most of the book was written at Princeton University when I was on leave from Bilkent University during the 2014–2015 academic year with the support of fellowships from Fulbright and TUBITAK. During my stay at the Department of Near Eastern Studies of Princeton University as a visiting scholar, I had the opportunity to exchange views and ideas with several faculty members from the Department of Near Eastern Studies, the Department of Politics, and the Department of Sociology. In addition, Princeton libraries contributed significantly to my research. Hence, I am quite thankful to the Department of Near Eastern Studies and my mentor, Şükrü Hanioğlu, for providing me an inspiring and productive academic environment. I also thank for Yuki and Jeffrey Laurenti, who made my stay in Princeton especially pleasant.

I benefited from the opportunity to present earlier versions of this study at various venues (e.g., conferences and colloquia), such as the Institute of Turkish Studies, Georgetown University, Washington, DC, March 17, 2015; Faculty Lunch Seminar Series, Department of Near Eastern Studies, Princeton University, Princeton, NJ, April 9, 2015; Midwest Political Science Association (MPSA), 73rd Annual Conference, Chicago, April 16–19, 2015; Association for the Study of Nationalities (ASN) World Convention, Columbia University, New York, NY, April 23–25, 2015; POLS TALKS, the Department of Political Science, Bilkent University, Ankara, Turkey, December 2, 2015; Department of Political Science, Middle East Technical University, Ankara, March 30, 2016; and American Political Science Association (APSA), 112th

Annual Meeting, Philadelphia, PA, September 1–4, 2016. I would like to thank all those who participated in those presentations and shared their valuable comments and suggestions, which helped me improve my research.

Finally, I have deep gratitude for my wife, Burcu Özdemir, who offered her continuous support and kindness over the course of the research and writing of this book. As an expression of my special thanks, I dedicate this book to her.

APPENDIX

List of Interviewees

Number	Surname	First name	Position/background	Interview location(s)	Interview date(s)
1	Aday	Ahmet	Chairperson of Kurdish Democracy and Solidarity Association (Kürt Demokrasi ve Dayanışma Derneği, Kurd-Der)	Ankara	August 19, 2011
2	Akar	Muhammed	Lawyer; Azadi Initiative	Diyarbakır	May 21, 2011; February 17, 2012; March 20, 2013; January 27, 2014
3	Akçınar	Seher	Sociologist, Diyarbakır Branch of the Association for Human Rights and Solidarity for the Oppressed (İnsan Hakları ve Mazlumlar İçin Dayanışma Derneği, Mazlumder)	Diyarbakır	January 29, 2014; May 12, 2014
4	Akıncılar	Murad	Researcher, Diyarbakır Institute for Political and Social Research (Diyarbakır Siyasal ve Sosyal Araştırmalar Enstitüsü, DİSA)	Diyarbakır	January 30, 2014
5	Aktar	Mehmet Emin	Chairperson of Diyarbakır Bar Association	Diyarbakır	May 23, 2011
6	Aktoprak	Mehmedi	Social psychologist, Mazlumder Diyarbakır Branch	Diyarbakır	March 22, 2013
7	Altaç	Aydın	Chairperson of the Diyarbakır Provincial Branch of the AKP	Diyarbakır	January 29, 2014
8	Anlı	Fırat	Lawyer	Diyarbakır	March 23, 2013
9	Ari	Arjin	Poet, writer; Kürt-Pen	Diyarbakır	February 18, 2012

(continued)

Number	Surname	First name	Position/background	Interview location(s)	Interview date(s)
10	Aslan	Mehmet	Chairperson of the Diyarbakır Chamber of Commerce and Industry (Diyarbakır Ticaret ve Sanayi Odası)	Diyarbakır	May 23, 2011
11	Avcı	Hilal	Sociologist, Center for Political and Social Research (Siyasal ve Sosyal Araştırmalar Merkezi, SAMER)	Diyarbakır	February 1, 2014
12	Ay	Abdürrahim	Lawyer; chairperson of Mazlumder Diyarbakır Branch	Diyarbakır	May 24, 2011
13	Ay	Welat	Researcher, SAMER	Diyarbakır	January 31, 2014
14	Aygün	Hüseyin	Tunceli deputy of the CHP	Tunceli	August 3, 2013
15	Aytaç	Veli	Tunceli Provincial Branch of the BDP	Tunceli	August 2, 2013
16	Batmanlı	Muhittin	Tigris-Euphrates Dialogue Group (Dicle Fırat Diyalog Grubu)	Diyarbakır	May 23, 2011
17	Beşikçi	İsmail	Sociologist; researcher; writer	Ankara	July 23, 2014
18	Beştaş	Meral Danış	Lawyer	Diyarbakır	February 18, 2012
19	Bilgen	Ayhan	Mazlumder; the BDP	Ankara	July 13, 2011; August 20, 2014
20	Bilici	Mücahit	Assoc. Prof. Dr., John Jay College, Department of Sociology, CUNY	Washington, DC	November 25, 2014
21	Bilici	Raci	Chairperson of Human Rights Association (IHD) Diyarbakır Branch	Diyarbakır	January 30, 2014
22	Bozarslan	Hamit	École des Hautes Études en Sciences Sociales (EHESS)	Ankara	January 28, 2014
23	Bozarslan	Mahmut	Journalist	Diyarbakır	May 23, 2011; February 18, 2012; March 22, 2013; May 12, 2014
24	Bozkurt	Kemal	Chairperson of the Tunceli Provincial Branch of the CHP	Tunceli	August 2, 2013

Number	Surname	First name	Position/background	Interview location(s)	Interview date(s)
25	Bozyel	Bayram	Chairperson of Rights and Freedoms Party (Hak ve Özgürlükler Partisi, HAK-PAR)	Ankara	August 7, 2011
26	Bulut	Faik	Journalist; writer	Istanbul	February 22, 2015
27	Burkay	Kemal	HAK-PAR	Ankara	May 4, 2012
28	Çakır	Ruşen	Journalist; writer	Istanbul	February 23, 2015
29	Çalışlar	Oral	Journalist; writer	Istanbul	February 24, 2015
30	Çandar	Cengiz	Journalist; writer	Email	February 26, 2015
31	Çelik	Doğan	Tunceli Provincial Branch of the BDP	Tunceli	August 2, 2013
32	Çiçek	Rauf	Lawyer; Nübihar Journal	Diyarbakir	January 29, 2014
33	Çiftkuran	Zahit	Mele; chairperson of the Association for the Solidarity of Imams and Religious Scholars (Din Alimleri Yardımlaşma Derneği, DİAYDER)	Diyarbakir	February 18, 2012; January 28, 2014
34	Çoban	Selahattin	Lawyer; vice chair of Mazlumder; Zehra Group	Diyarbakır	February 17, 2012; January 31, 2014
35	Coşkun	Vahap	Associate professor, Law School, Dicle University	Ankara, Diyarbakir	January 21, 2012; March 22, 2013; January 28, 2014
36	Demirbaş	Abdullah	Mayor of Sur (Diyarbakır); the BDP	Diyarbakir	May 24, 2011; February 18, 2012
37	Doğru	Ergin	Chairperson of the Tunceli Provincial Branch of the BDP	Tunceli	August 2, 2013
38	Elçi	Tahir	Lawyer; chairperson of Diyarbakır Bar Association	Diyarbakir	March 22, 2013
39	Erdem	Fazıl Hüsnü	Professor, Law School, Dicle University	Diyarbakir	January 30, 2014
40	Ergün	Lokman	Chairperson of Ankara Provincial Branch of the HDP	Ankara	February 27, 2015
41	Erkan	Rüstem	Professor, Sociology Department, Dicle University	Diyarbakir	January 31, 2014
42	Erkol	Ahmet	Associate professor, Faculty of Divinity, Dicle University	Diyarbakir	February 19, 2012

(continued)

Number	Surname	First name	Position/background	Interview location(s)	Interview date(s)
43	Ersanlı	Büşra	Professor, Department of Political Science and International Relations, Marmara University	Email	October 29, 2014
44	Fırat	Adnan	Rewşen Group	Ankara	July 29, 2011
45	Fırat	Kasım	Businessman; grandson of Sheikh Said	Ankara	January 24, 2014
46	Fırat	Seydi	Peace Assembly (Barış Meclisi)	Ankara, Diyarbakır	September 13, 2011; May 12, 2014
47	Geyik	Seyfi	Chairperson of the Hozat (Tunceli) District Branch of the CHP	Tunceli	August 5, 2013
48	Göçer	Atalay	DİSA researcher	Diyarbakır	January 30, 2014
49	Gönden (Kawari)	Mehmet	*Mele*; the BDP Diyarbakır Provincial Party Assembly	Diyarbakır	February 18, 2012
50	Güler	Nuri	Association of Solidarity with the Disadvantaged (Mustazaflar İle Dayanışma Derneği, Mustazaf-Der)	Diyarbakır	May 24, 2011
51	Gün	Özden Eren Başkavak	Vice chair of Tunceli Bar Association	Tunceli	August 2, 2013
52	Halis	Şerafettin	Former chairperson of the Tunceli Provincial Branch of the BDP	Tunceli	August 3, 2013
53	İdikut	Recep	Chairperson of Diyarbakır Branch of IHH Association for Humanitarian Aid (İHH İnsani Yardım Derneği)	Diyarbakır	May 23, 2011
54	İpekyüz	Necdet	Chairperson of DİSA	Diyarbakır	January 30, 2014
55	Kamalak	Mustafa	Chairperson of Felicity Party (Saadet Partisi, SP)	Ankara	May 13, 2012
56	Kaya	Hüda	Party Assembly of the HDP	İstanbul	February 22, 2015
57	Kaya	Mehmet	Chairperson of Tigris Social Research Center (Dicle Toplumsal Araştırmalar Merkezi, DİTAM)	Diyarbakır	March 23, 2013
58	Kaya	Muhittin	*Nübihar Journal*; Zehra Group	Ankara	August 6, 2011

Number	Surname	First name	Position/background	Interview location(s)	Interview date(s)
59	Kışanak	Gülten	Cochair of the BDP	Ankara	February 26, 2012
60	Koç	Abdullah Hadi	*Mele*, DIAYDER	Diyarbakır	January 28, 2014
61	Koçuk	Ali Asker	Chairperson of the Ovacık (Tunceli) District Branch of the CHP	Tunceli	August 4, 2013
62	Lale	Ferzende	Association for Bright Future, Rights and Freedoms, Education, Culture, and Solidarity (Aydınlık Yarınlar için Hak ve Özgürlükler, Eğitim Kültür ve Yardımlaşma Derneği, AYDER)	Diyarbakır	May 24, 2011
63	Menteşe	Sabit	Assistant professor, Department of Public Administration, Tunceli University	Email	August 7, 2013
64	Mert	Nuray	Journalist; writer; professor, Department of Political Science and International Relations, Istanbul University	Diyarbakır	May 11, 2014
65	Nemir	Kawa	PEN Turkey	Ankara	September 15, 2011
66	Öneş	Cevat	Retired senior advisor, National Intelligence Organization (Milli İstihbarat Teşkilatı, MİT)	Ankara	August 22, 2011
67	Özcaner	Adem	Teacher; Azadi Initiative	Diyarbakır	January 28, 2014
68	Özsoy	Felat	Grandson of Sheikh Said	Diyarbakır	January 29, 2014
69	Polat	Murat	Former chairperson of the Tunceli Provincial Branch of the BDP	Tunceli	August 2, 2013
70	Sancar	Mithat	Professor, Law School, Ankara University	Ankara	July 22, 2014
71	Sayım	Muzaffer	Chairperson of the Diyarbakir Provincial Branch of the CHP	Diyarbakır	January 28, 2014

(continued)

Number	Surname	First name	Position/background	Interview location(s)	Interview date(s)
72	Soylu	Cesim	Chairperson of the İstanbul Provincial Branch of the HDP	İstanbul	February 24, 2015
73	Tan	Altan	Candidate of the BDP for the parliament from Diyarbakır	Diyarbakır	May 23, 2011
74	Tuncer	Ali Serdar	Chairperson of Gönül Köprüsü Derneği	Diyarbakır	February 17, 2012
75	Türkdoğan	Öztürk	Chairperson of Human Rights Association (İnsan Hakları Derneği, İHD)	Ankara	July 12, 2011
76	Ünsal	Ahmet Faruk	Chairperson of Mazlumder	Ankara	Haziran 28, 2011; Aralık 27, 2011; Ocak 22, 2014
77	van Bruinessen	Martin	Emeritus professor, Utrecht University, Religious Studies	Online	August 24, 2014
78	Yıldırım	Barış	Lawyer; chairperson of the Tunceli Branch of the IHD	Tunceli	August 2, 2013
79	Yıldırım	Kadri	Professor, vice rector, Mardin Artuklu University	Diyarbakır	May 11, 2014
80	Yıldız	Dursun	Chairperson of the Pertek (Tunceli) District Branch of the CHP	Tunceli	August 5, 2013
81	Yılmaz	Hüseyin	Chairperson of Mustazaf-Der	Diyarbakır	February 19, 2012
82	Yılmaz	İbrahim	Retired imam	Diyarbakır	February 17, 2012
83	Yılmaz	Kamil	Professor; the Directorate of Religious Affairs (Diyanet İşleri Başkanlığı)	Ankara	September 15, 2011
84	Yılmaz	Serdar Bülent	Chairperson of Özgür-Der	Diyarbakır	May 23, 2011
85	Yüksel	Mehmet	Washington representative of the HDP	Washington, DC	May 23, 2014
86	Yurttaş	Sedat	Lawyer	Diyarbakır	February 17, 2012
87	Zilan	Bilal	Dil-Der; Zazaki	Diyarbakır	May 24, 2011
88	Zilan	Sıdkı	Lawyer; writer; activist; Azadi Initiative	Diyarbakır	January 28, 2014

Note: 104 interviews were conducted with 88 participants between 2011 and 2015.

NOTES

INTRODUCTION

1. *Meles* or *melas* (mullahs) are Kurdish religious scholars and teachers, highly respected by the people living in Turkey's Kurdish region (i.e., the east and southeast). Since most of them have received unofficial *madrasa* (religious school) education and training (around seven years), they are regarded as nonstate imams. Although madrasas were closed down in 1924 as part of secularization reforms, some of them continued to operate as clandestine organizations, especially in Kurdish areas (see also van Bruinessen 2000b).
2. Quoted in "BDP Going after the Religious Vote," *Turkish Politics in Action*, April 7, 2011, www.turkishpoliticsinaction.com.
3. See "Turkish PM Slams Pro-Kurdish BDP in Bingöl," *Hürriyet Daily News*, June 8, 2011, www.hurriyetdailynews.com.
4. "Erdogan'dan dindar Kurtlere cok agir ifadeler," *Fırat News Agency*, May 10, 2011, www.firatnews.com.
5. In the Islamic belief system, *iftar* refers to the evening meal that ends the daily fast during Ramadan, the holy month for Islam.
6. Despite worldwide Islamic revival, there are also some shifts in the opposite direction (i.e., a shift away from Islamism to secular nationalism). For instance, Aspinall (2007, 2009) illustrates that, in contrast to much of the Islamic world, a shift from Islamism to nationalism took place in the context of Indonesia's Aceh province. Aspinall shows that in the 1950s, an Islamic rebellion (Darul Islam) emerged with a goal of transforming Indonesia into an Islamic state. However, in the mid-1970s, the Free Aceh Movement (Gerakan Aceh Merdeka, GAM) was established as a successor movement. Downplaying Islamic ideology, symbols, and goals, GAM embraced secular and nationalist orientations and sought independence for Aceh province.
7. I also conducted a few interviews abroad (e.g., in Washington, DC). Moreover, four informants answered my questions through email.
8. In this study, I use interview data for illustrative purposes (i.e., to elucidate or clarify the causes and mechanisms of the rise of the Islam-friendly approach within the secular Kurdish movement and to illustrate other elite groups' general perceptions of and attitudes toward such a transformation within secular Kurdish ethnopolitics). With regard to sampling interviewees, since random sampling "runs against the logic of the process tracing method, as it risks excluding

important respondents from the sample purely by chance" (Tansey 2007, 765), I combined two nonprobability sampling techniques (i.e., purposive and snowball sampling) to reach the most appropriate and useful informants. As I progressed in my research, I needed to revisit some of the informants. Hence, I interviewed several of them two or three times (for a full list of the interviewees, see the appendix).

9. The notions of *descent* and *descent-based attributes* (e.g., attributes acquired through genetic, cultural, and historical inheritance such as phenotype, language, and place of birth) constitute the basic component of ethnicity in almost all existing definitions (e.g., see Horowitz 1985; Hutchinson and Smith 1996; Fearon 2003). As Chandra (2012b, 10) also observes, "Virtually all social science definitions of an ethnic identity emphasize the role of descent in some way. But they specify it differently, to mean a common ancestry, or a myth of common ancestry, or a common region of origin, or a myth of a common region of origin, or a 'group' descent rule—and they typically combine descent with other features such as a common culture, a common language, a common history and a common territory."

10. One can also find studies claiming that Kurds in Turkey comprise higher percentages of the total population, such as roughly 20% (e.g., see Romano and Gurses 2014b, 11) or 20% to 28% (Gunes 2012b, 1).

11. The survey data that this study utilizes come from three public opinion surveys conducted in 2011, 2013, and 2015. The surveys were conducted as part of a comprehensive research project on the Kurdish issue, which was fully funded by TEPAV (The Economic Policy Research Foundation of Turkey). The primary goal of the surveys was to identify Kurdish demands and Turkish attitudes toward those demands. The surveys were administered by a professional public opinion research company based in Istanbul. The first survey (November 2011) was implemented through face-to-face interviews with 6,516 respondents, aged 18 and above, from seven regions, 48 provinces, and 369 districts and villages. In April 2013, we repeated the same survey with slight modifications. The second survey involved face-to-face interviews with 7,103 participants from seven regions, 50 provinces, and 398 districts and villages. In April 2015, we made slight changes to the 2013 survey and repeated it with a representative sample of 7,100 participants. In all the surveys, households were selected using a multistage stratified, cluster-sampling procedure. Once households were selected randomly, age and gender quotas were applied to choose one respondent from each household. This study utilizes some of the survey findings to further enrich the analyses of the evolving attitude of the secular Kurdish movement toward Islam and Islamic actors.

12. Kurds constitute the majority of the population in the following eastern and southeastern provinces: Diyarbakır, Van, Siirt, Şanlıurfa, Muş, Mardin, Hakkari, Şırnak, Batman, Bitlis (see Mutlu 1996).

13. At least 10% of Kurds in Turkey subscribe to the Alevi *mezhep*.

14. Regarding Turks, the vast majority (95%) of Sunni Turks adhere to the Hanefi school, which was the official school of law during the Ottoman Empire and has been upheld during the Republican period. The Diyanet (the Directorate of Religious Affairs), for instance, is based on Hanefi teachings and understandings, which creates resentment among certain sections of Alevi Turks and Kurds and Shafi Kurds in Turkey.

15. It is important to indicate at this point that the first Kurdish ethnonationalist movements emerged during the late-Ottoman period. The Ottomans had created several locally autonomous emirates in Kurdish regions; however, centralization efforts in the nineteenth century (e.g., curbing the power of Kurdish chiefs and emirs) and competing territorial claims made by the Armenians triggered some local revolts against the Ottoman administration (e.g., Skeikh Ubaydullah of Nehri Revolt, 1880–1881) (see McDowall 2004; Natali 2005). Regarding the Republican period, Kurds revolted several times against the Turkish state's suppression and denial of Kurdish ethnic identity during the early Republic (e.g., Sheikh Said Revolt, 1925; the Ağrı Revolt, 1926–1930; Dersim (Tunceli) Revolt, 1936–1938). Most of those revolts involved both ethnic and religious elements. After a relative calm period in the 1940s and 1950s, Kurdish ethnonationalism revived in the 1960s and 1970s (see also McDowall 2004; Natali 2005).

16. Thus, the unit of analysis in this study is an ethnonationalist movement, rather than masses. Focusing on the case of the Islamic opening of the secular, leftist Kurdish movement in the past decades, this study treats the Kurdish movement's evolving attitudes toward Islam and Islamic actors as a major case of boundary work and investigates the causes, mechanisms, and consequences of Kurdish movement's boundary making. Readers who are interested in discussion on various other aspects and dimensions of the Kurdish ethnopolitics in the Turkish setting might consult the following works: Gunter 1990, 1997; Entessar 1992, 2010; van Bruinessen 1992, 2000a, 2000b; Olson 1996; Yeğen 1996, 2007, 2011; Kirişçi and Winrow 1997; Barkey and Fuller 1998; Yavuz 1998, 2001; N. Özcan 1999; Watts 1999, 2006, 2010; White 2000; Bozarslan 2001; Houston 2001; Saatci 2002; McDowall 2004; Natali 2005; Somer 2005; Taspinar 2005; Jwaideh 2006; A. Özcan 2006; Romano 2006; Heper 2007; Lundgren 2007; Marcus 2007; Tezcür 2009, 2010, 2015; Casier and Jongerden 2011; Gunes 2012b; Özkırımlı 2013; Sarigil 2010, 2012; Sarigil and Fazlioglu, 2013, 2014; Sarigil and Karakoc 2016; Bengio 2014; Romano and Gurses 2014; Aslan 2015; Aydin and Emrence 2015; Ünver 2015; Gürbüz 2015, 2016.

17. The parliamentary commission responsible for human rights prepared a report on the conflict and casualties in 2013. It is available at www.tbmm.gov.tr (accessed June 21, 2016). Some other studies, however, suggest that the death toll is around 40,000 (e.g., see Marcus 2007, 1; Watts 2010, 22; Aydin and Emrence 2015, 2).

18. See also an interview with PKK leader Öcalan in the *Hürriyet* daily (April 1, 1993).

19. Such arrangements proposed by Öcalan are based on the principle of "radical democracy" (see Akkaya and Jongerden 2011, 2012; Jongerden and Akkaya 2011). Öcalan's thinking about the notion of radical democracy is heavily shaped by the works of Murray Bookchin (1921–2006), who was an American anarchist, environmentalist, and socialist author and theoretician. Influenced by Bookchin's concepts of "libertarian municipalism" and "social ecology," Öcalan attempts to dissociate the notion of democracy from the nation-state and statehood. Instead, he advocates self-governing, nonhierarchical bodies and institutions such as assemblies, councils, and committees in villages, towns, and neighborhoods. These bodies would be based on grassroots-based democracy. That is, people would democratically and directly manage their own affairs at the local level (see Akkaya and Jongerden 2011, 152–153; Leverink 2015).

20. Major pro-Kurdish political parties were as follows: People's Labor Party (Halkın Emek Partisi, HEP; 1990–1993; the first legal Kurdish party); Freedom and Democracy Party (Özgürlük ve Demokrasi Partisi, ÖZDEP; 1992–1993); Democracy Party (Demokrasi Partisi, DEP; 1993–1994); Democracy Party of the People (Halkın Demokrasi Partisi, HADEP; 1994–2003); Democratic People's Party (Demokratik Halk Partisi, DEHAP; 1997–2005); Democratic Society Party (Demokratik Toplum Partisi, DTP; 2005–2009); Peace and Democracy Party (Barış ve Demokrasi Partisi, BDP; 2008–2014); the Democratic Regions Party (Demokratik Bölgeler Partisi, DBP; 2008 onward); and the Peoples' Democratic Party (Halkların Demokratik Partisi, HDP; 2012 onward).

21. For two preliminary attempts, see Tezcür 2009; and Aydin and Emrence 2015.

CHAPTER 1. THE BOUNDARY APPROACH TO ETHNICITY
AND NATIONALISM

1. For other illustrative studies of the boundary-making approach, see, for instance, Wallman 1978, 1986; Lamont 1992, 2000; Conversi 1995, 1999; Zolberg and Woon 1999; Fuller 2003; Alba 2005; Tilly 2005; Bail 2008; R. Jenkins 2008; Wimmer 2008a, 2008b, 2009, 2013; Jackson and Molokotos-Liederman 2015; and Goalwin 2017. See also Lamont and Molnár 2002; and Pachucki, Pendergrass, and Lamont 2007 for useful reviews of the notion of boundaries in various social science fields.

2. With respect to the evolution of the notion of boundary, Terrier (2015, 28) observes that in the twentieth century its meaning shifted from the objective and concrete (i.e., dividing line, geographical borders) to the abstract (the principle of differentiation or an object's set of distinctive features). Conversi (1999) labels such a shift as the "deterritorialisation" of the concept of boundary.

3. Readers interested in territorial boundary-making processes in the context of the Kurdish issue might consult Aydin and Emrence 2015.

4. With regard to the nexus between symbolic and social boundaries, the former is treated as a necessary but insufficient condition for the existence of the latter (Lamont and Molnár 2002, 169; see also Lamont 1992).

5. Wimmer (2013, 9) makes a similar distinction, differentiating between *categorical* and *social/behavioral* dimensions of a boundary. In his words, "The former refers to acts of social classification and collective representation, the latter to everyday networks of relationships that result from individual acts of connecting and distancing. . . . One divides the social world into social groups—into 'us' and 'them'—and the other offers scripts of action—how to relate to individuals classified as 'us' and 'them' under given circumstances." For Wimmer, the former refers to "ways of seeing the world" and the latter to "ways of acting in the world." But for a critique of such conceptualizations, see R. Jenkins 2015.

6. In the Barthian framework, the notion of "cultural stuff" refers to language, religion, customs and laws, tradition, material culture, etc. (R. Jenkins 2008, 111). Thus, the cultural stuff and symbolic boundaries are closely related.

7. On the notion of boundary shifting, see also Zolberg and Woon (1999).

8. Jackson (2015b, 206–211) adds further strategies to the list of boundary work: "concealing" and "avoiding." In the case of concealing, actors hide which group they belong to. To prevent possible tension, conflict or discrimination during interaction with others, actors may simply obstruct boundary markers (e.g., name, neighborhood, region, language, religion, etc.) that would reveal their group membership. Avoiding involves conscious efforts to circumvent interacting with out-group members. As Jackson (2015b, 208) states, "The avoiding strategy refers to cases where the backgrounds or population affiliation of the respondents are already known by the actors involved. With this information on the table, respondents seek to circumvent contention by pursuing avoidance, for example by avoiding specific topics of conversation, or avoiding specific locations or spaces."

9. For one recent work that takes boundary struggles or contestations much more seriously, see Wimmer 2013.

10. Brubaker (2009, 28) defines such a tendency as "groupism" or "groupist social ontology," that is, treating "various categories of people as if they were *internally homogenous, externally bounded groups, even unitary collective actors with common purposes*; and [taking] ethnic and racial groups and nations as basic constituents of social life, chief protagonists of social conflicts, and fundamental units of social analysis" (emphasis added). For Wimmer, this tendency in ethnicity and national-ism studies is partly due to a Herderian legacy. As Wimmer (2013, 16) notes, in the social ontology of the philosopher Johann Gottfried Herder (1744–1803), "the world is made up of peoples distinguished by a unique culture, held together by communitarian solidarity, and bound by shared identity."

CHAPTER 2. THE ISLAMIC OPENING OF THE KURDISH MOVEMENT

1. These hypothetical categories or types should be understood as ideal types in the Weberian sense. Thus, in real-life situations, a certain political movement or actor may not fit any of these categories perfectly. Nevertheless, by helping us categorize different types of interplay between religion and nationalism, these analytical

constructs contribute to our understanding of political actors' varying attitudes toward or positions on religion and nationalism.

2. For more discussion on this issue, see Salt 1995; Sakallioğlu 1996; Yavuz 1997; Cetinsaya 1999; van Bruinessen 2000a; Houston 2001; Taspinar 2005; Cagaptay 2006; Casier and Jongerden 2011; and Kadıoğlu and Keyman 2011.

3. Although these political actors can all be included within the category of Turkish Islamism, there are major differences among them. For more on this topic, see Coşar 2011.

4. Readers interested in a discussion on how actors in areas xy (i.e., Turkish Islamists), y (i.e., Islamists), and/or zy (i.e., Kurdish Islamists) approach the Kurdish issue can consult Houston 2001.

5. This transition was partly because of agricultural mechanization (e.g., the introduction of tractors) and burgeoning industrialization in Turkey in the 1950s and 1960s.

6. These Kurdish activists constituted the so-called group of "Easterners" within the TİP (S. Aslan 2015, 125).

7. Due to suppression of Kurdish ethnic identity and legal restrictions, the group avoided using terms such as "Kurd" or "Kurdistan." The word "*Doğu*" in DDKO, however, implied Kurdish areas (Yanarocak 2014, 140).

8. Both the DDKO and TİP were accused of communist propaganda and of Kurdish separatism and banned in the early 1970s. Several of their leaders and members were imprisoned, staying in prison until 1974, when the coalition government led by Bülent Ecevit passed an amnesty law, which released political prisoners.

9. Founded by Kemal Burkay in late 1974 as a relatively moderate group, this party rejected the use of violence in national struggles. In 1992, during its third congress, the party renamed itself as the Socialist Party of Kurdistan (*Partiya Sosyalista Kurdistan*, PSK).

10. We should also note that there were a few other pro-Kurdish formations in the 1960s. The most prominent one was the relatively more right-oriented, conservative Kurdistan Democratic Party of Turkey (Türkiye Kürdistan Demokrat Parti, TKDP), which was established by the lawyer Faik Bucak and the accountant Said Elçi in 1965. It was a clandestine formation sympathetic to Mullah Mustafa Barzani (1903–1979), who led the Kurdish ethnonationalist movement in northern Iraq against the Baghdad administration. The TKDP defended the recognition of political, economic, and cultural rights for Kurds and a kind of regional autonomy within Turkish borders. In 1968, many of its leading members were arrested, and the party split in two in 1969 (see van Bruinessen 2000b; Natali 2005; Gunes 2012b; Tezcür 2015).

11. Initially, the group was known as Apocular (meaning the "followers of Apo," Öcalan's nickname).

12. One emblematic case of PKK attacks against landlords or tribal leaders was the July 1979 armed attack on Mehmet Celal Bucak, a powerful local landlord and Justice Party deputy, in Siverek (Urfa).

13. Several PKK attacks against Kurdish villagers were motivated by revenge on paramilitary village guards (*köy korucuları*). Introduced in 1985 and still used today, village guards are composed of local people, armed and paid by the state to increase the security of villages in the region and to fight against the PKK (van Bruinessen 2000a, 252; White 2000, 172–173; McDowall 2004, 423–424).

14. The PKK reorganized itself in Lebanon and Syria. In the Beqaa Valley, located in eastern Lebanon, and in certain parts of Syria, the PKK was able to find bases and facilities for ideological and armed training. In 1982, the PKK also established training camps in the mountainous areas in northern Iraq, referred to as "Southern Kurdistan" (Başûr). After Turkey's transition back to a civilian regime in 1983, PKK members infiltrated Turkey and initiated an armed struggle against the Turkish state in 1984.

15. ADYÖD was accused of propagating communism and banned in 1975.

16. For an interview with Tan, see "Ümmetçi kalınabilseydi Kürt sorunu çözülürdü," *Radikal*, July 11, 2011, available at www.radikal.com.tr.

17. For instance, author's interviews with Murat Polat, Tunceli, August 2, 2013; Sıdkı Zilan, Diyarbakır, January 28, 2014; Rauf Çiçek, Diyarbakır, January 29, 2014; Raci Bilici, Diyarbakır, January 30, 2014; Fazıl Hüsnü Erdem, Diyarbakır, January 30, 2014; Selahattin Çoban, Diyarbakır, January 31, 2014; Welat Ay, Diyarbakır, January 31, 2014; Nuray Mert, Diyarbakır, May 11, 2014; Kadri Yıldırım, Diyarbakır, May 11, 2014; Büşra Ersanlı, email interview, August 21, 2014; Mücahit Bilici, Washington, DC, November 25, 2014; Ruşen Çakır, Istanbul, February 23, 2015; Oral Çalışlar, Istanbul, February 24, 2015; Hüdya Kaya, Istanbul, February 22, 2015; and Cengiz Çandar, email interview, February 26, 2015.

18. Author's interview, Istanbul, February 23, 2015. The quotations from interviews are the author's translations.

19. Author's interview, Washington, DC, November 25, 2014.

20. Author's interview, Diyarbakır, January 31, 2014.

21. Author's email interview, May 20, 2014.

22. See "Sivil cuma, sivil imam," *Özgür Gündem*, April 8, 2011, www.ozgur-gundem .com; "Diyarbakır'da 4 bin kişilik sivil cuma namazı!," *Haber Türk*, April 22, 2011, www.haberturk.com; "Sivil cuma ve İmralı'ya idama dair," *Radikal*, June 11, 2011, www.radikal.com.tr.

23. Established in 1924, Diyanet is Turkey's highest religious public body, which oversees religious services and controls religious institutions, including nearly 85,000 mosques. Diyanet also appoints state imams and prepares Friday *khutbahs* or sermons.

24. See "Devletsiz Cuma!," *Özgür Gündem*, July 9, 2011, www.ozgur-gundem.com.

25. Although the Kurdish ethnopolitical movement ended the campaign of civilian Friday prayers in summer 2013, they occasionally organize similar prayers to deliver their political views and messages under the guise of Islam.

26. All these candidates, except Nesrin Hilal Şanlı, were elected to parliament in the 2015 general elections.

27. In the aftermath of that congress, similar meetings (e.g., symposiums, panels, conferences) were organized in other cities in Turkey and in Europe. For instance, in late May 2014, a similar congress was organized in Hagen, Germany, by the Federation of Kurdish Islamic Communities.

28. See "Demirtaş'tan Said Nursi'li açıklama: Peygamberimizin Medine Sözleşmesi re feranslarımızdan biridir," *Haber Sol*, October 24, 2015, http://haber.sol.org.tr. Also author's interview with Hüda Kaya, Istanbul, February 22, 2015.

29. See "Demokratik İslam Kongresi sonuç bildirgesi açıklandı," *IMCTV*, December 20, 2015, www.imctv.com.tr.

30. See "BDP'den türban ve kravat önergesi," *Sabah*, October 12, 2011, www.sabah .com.tr.

31. See "BDP Going after the Religious Vote?," *Turkish Politics in Action*, April 7, 2011, www.turkishpoliticsinaction.com.

32. See, for instance, "AYM eski raportörü Aydın: Danıştay cuma genelgesini iptal etmelidir," *Haber sol*, January 6, 2016, http://haber.sol.org.tr.

33. See "Demirtaş'tan Davutoğlu'na 'Cuma namazı' desteği," *Haber sol*, January 6, 2016, http://haber.sol.org.tr.

34. The word *mawlid* refers either to the birth of the Prophet Muhammad or to the observance of the birthday of the Prophet, which takes place in the third month of the Islamic calendar.

35. See "İki farklı Kutlu Doğum etkinliği," *Radikal*, April 21, 2014, www.radikal.com.tr.

36. The meetings were organized by the Platform of the Lovers of the Prophet (Peygamber Sevdalıları Platformu), which is composed of several Islamic groups, including Mustazaf-Der, and is known as being sympathetic to Kurdish Hezbollah.

37. In April 2014, the *mawlid* meeting organized by pro-Kurdish groups took place one day before the *mawlid* meeting organized by the Platform of the Lovers of the Prophet.

38. See "BDP'ten Şeyh Sait'e anma," *NTV*, June 30, 2011, www.ntv.com.tr.

39. It is, however, important to note that although Turkish Islamists tend to disregard Said Nursi's Kurdish ethnic origin, Kurdish ethnonationalists emphasize his Kurdishness. For instance, they refer to him as "Said-i Kürdi" (Kurdish Said) rather than "Said Nursi" (Said from the Nurs village of Bitlis) (see also Gürbüz 2015, 2016). In other words, Kurdish ethnonationalists attempt to promote a much more Kurdified image of the cleric Said Nursi.

40. *Surah* refers to a chapter or section of the Koran. The Koran has 114 chapters in total.

41. See the translation by Arthur J. Arberry (1990).

42. Similarly, *Mele* Mehmet Gönden, a member of the Diyarbakir-Sur municipal assembly, noted, "If we look at the Koran, we see that Allah created different races

and languages equally. Allah does not distinguish among them. . . . If so, then how can you ignore or suppress a nation and its language? If you do that, then you would violate the Koran" (quoted in Sarigil and Fazlioglu 2013, 558).

43. See "Demirtaş: Ölen askere de gerillaya da ağlayacaksınız," *Radikal*, October 14, 2012, www.radikal.com.tr.
44. Author's interview, Diyarbakır, May 11, 2014.
45. See "'Ya Allah bismillah seroke me Öcalan' diye yürüdüler," *Radikal*, September 13, 2009, www.radikal.com.tr.
46. Author's translation. Original message is available at Hurriyet, "Öcalan'ın mesajının şifreleri," accessed April 4, 2015, www.hurriyet.com.tr.
47. See also "Öcalan-BDP görüşmesinin zabıtları ortaya çıktı," *Radikal*, February 28, 2013, www.radikal.com.tr.
48. For instance, author's interviews with Tahir Elçi, Diyarbakır, March 22, 2013; Fırat Anlı, Diyarbakır, March 23, 2013; Ahmet Faruk Ünsal, Ankara, January 22, 2014; Kasım Fırat, Ankara, January 24, 2014; Muhammed Akar, Diyarbakır, January 27, 2014; Vahap Coşkun, Diyarbakır, January 28, 2014; Zahit Çiftkuran, Diyarbakır, January 28, 2014; Aydın Altaç, Diyarbakır, January 29, 2014; Rauf Çiçek, Diyarbakır, January 29, 2014; Raci Bilici, Diyarbakır, January 30, 2014; Fazıl Hüsnü Erdem, Diyarbakır, January 30, 2014; Rüstem Erkan, Diyarbakır, January 31, 2014; Selahattin Çoban, Diyarbakır, January 31, 2014; Seher Akçınar, Diyarbakır, January 29, 2014, and May 12, 2014; Hamit Bozarslan, Ankara, April 28, 2014; Mahmut Bozarslan, Diyarbakır, May 12, 2014; Nuray Mert, Diyarbakır, May 11, 2014; Kadri Yıldırım, Diyarbakır, May 11, 2014; Martin van Bruinessen, email interview, May 20, 2014; İsmail Beşikçi, Ankara, July 23, 2014; Ayhan Bilgen, Ankara, August 20, 2014; Büşra Ersanlı, email interview, August 21, 2014; Mehmet Yüksel, Washington, DC, November 23, 2014; Mücahit Bilici, Washington, DC, November 25, 2014; Hüda Kaya, Istanbul, February 22, 2015; Ruşen Çakır, Istanbul, February 23, 2015; and Cengiz Çandar, email interview, February 26, 2015.
49. Author's interview, Washington, DC, November 23, 2014.
50. Author's interview, Diyarbakır, January 30, 2014. Vahap Coşkun shared similar points (author's interview, Diyarbakır, March 22, 2013).
51. Author's interview, Diyarbakır, January 28, 2014.
52. This point was also emphasized by Seher Akçınar (author's interview, Diyarbakır, May 12, 2014).
53. See HDP, "Demirtaş'tan Erdoğan'a: Sana kalsa Kürt de yok," April 29, 2015, www.hdp.org.tr. Also author's interview with Cesim Soylu, Istanbul, February 24, 2015.

CHAPTER 3. EXPLAINING THE KURDISH MOVEMENT'S BOUNDARY MAKING

1. "PKK amblemini değiştirdi," *Cumhuriyet*, July 17, 1995, 7.
2. Author's interview, Ankara, July 22, 2014.

3. Along the same lines, Romano (2006, 92) notes, "by offering goals that mattered to the people, selective (dis)incentives, astute organization and coordination, and the establishment of credibility with the local Kurdish population through ideology, self-sacrifice, and demonstrative actions against Turkish security forces, the founders of the PKK were able to turn their movement into a mass-based, significant challenge to the Turkish state." Dag (2014) makes similar observations: "This movement flourished from armed groups to a fully-fledged institutional industry. This includes armed organisations (PKK and HPG), cultural, political, and social works (human rights associations, educational support centres, job training courses and the Democratic Society Congress), dozens of pro-Kurdish political parties, and recently even an attempt at forming an economic association consisting of ethnic Kurds."

4. For more discussion on the transformation of the PKK movement into a mass movement, see Romano 2006; Marcus 2007.

5. In addition to the HEP's pro-Kurdish stance, it had a social-democratic orientation. For a detailed discussion of the establishment of the HEP, see Watts 2010.

6. At this point, we should note that Öcalan was arrested by the Turkish National Intelligence Agency (MIT), aided by the US Central Intelligence Agency (CIA), in Nairobi, Kenya, in February 1999. After his trial, he was sentenced to death in June 1999. When Turkey abolished the death penalty as part of the EU reform process in 2002, Öcalan's sentence was commuted to life imprisonment.

7. This point was also emphasized by several interviewees, such as Cesim Soylu, Istanbul, February 24, 2015.

8. See also an interview with Mehmet Kurt on Kurdish Hezbollah, "Hizbullah devlet güdümünde kurulmadı, ama devlet tarafından kullanılmakla yüzleşmeli," published by T24 on March 27, 2015. It is available at http://t24.com.tr.

9. It is believed that the Turkish state provided intelligence and logistics support for Hezbollah and ignored or tolerated several of its armed actions (G. Jenkins 2008; also author's interview with Ismail Beşikçi, Ankara, July 23, 2014). Some former state officials even confessed state support for Hezbollah. For instance, see an interview with Ismet Sezgin, a Turkish politician, who has held various positions in government, such as president of the Turkish Grand National Assembly (Türkiye Büyük Millet Meclisi, TBMM), and has worked in several ministries, including the Ministry for Internal Affairs. The interview is available at BBC News, Türkçe, "90'larda ne olmuştu? İsmet Sezgin: Birtakım öldürmeler, hapsetmeler, bir mücadele," accessed September 4, 2015, www.bbc.com.

10. In 2000, the state finally took action against Kurdish Hezbollah. Founder Hüseyin Velioğlu was killed during a police operation in Istanbul, and several other leading members were arrested (G. Jenkins 2008). Having experienced the state's crackdown, Hezbollah decided to abandon its armed struggle and instead focus on empowering and expanding its social base among Kurds by setting up legal civil society organizations, associations, and foundations, publishing books and

magazines, and organizing through the media (e.g., initiating radio and TV broadcasting and various websites) (see also Gürbüz 2016). In 2004, the sympathizers of Kurdish Hezbollah set up an Islamic charity association called Mustazaf-Der (Association of Solidarity with the Disadvantaged). In 2012, the Mustazaf-Der was banned by a court decision. It was accused of being linked to illegal Kurdish Hezbollah. The shutdown of Mustazaf-Der spurred the movement to organize itself in legal party politics. As a result, in December 2012, the Hezbollah movement established a legal, pro-Islamic Kurdish party called the Free Cause Party (Hür Dava Partisi, Hüda-Par). The acronym Hüda-Par means "the Party of Allah" in Kurdish (Hezbollah in Arabic). The party competed in the March 2014 local elections but received only 0.22% of the national vote.

11. See "Zerdüşt," *Milliyet*, October 22, 2012, available at http://siyaset.milliyet.com.tr. See also "Kandil'de ilk kez bir başörtülü," *En Son Haber*, June 23, 2011, www.ensonha ber.com. Zoroastrianism is an ancient, pre-Islamic religion, which was popular in Persia. Based on the teachings of the prophet Zoroaster, it regards Ahura Mazda as the creator and sole God.

12. "La ilahe illallah diyen, terör örgütüyle aynı yere bakamaz," *Haber Türk*, December 6, 2012, www.haberturk.com.

13. See "Çiçek'ten Ermeni PKK'lılar iması," *Radikal*, August 21, 2010, www.radikal .com.tr.

14. For the whole speech, see AK Party, "1 Haziran Diyarbakır mitingi konuşmasının tam metni," June 2, 2011, www.akparti.org.tr.

15. The speech is available at Vikikaynak, "Recep Tayyip Erdoğan'ın 8 Haziran 2011 tarihli Bingöl mitinginde yaptığı konuşma," accessed January 15, 2016, http:// tr.wikisource.org.

16. According to the 1982 constitution, the president should be politically neutral or impartial. However, Erdoğan, who was elected as the 12th president of Turkey in August 2014 by popular vote, campaigned on the AKP's behalf before the 2015 general elections.

17. See "Erdoğan Diyarbakır'dan Demirtaş'a seslendi: Devletin parasıyla buraya çıkıyorum, yasal hakkım," *T24*, May 2, 2015, http://t24.com.tr.

18. See "Batman'da önemli açıklamalar," *Hürriyet*, May 2, 2015, www.hurriyet.com.tr. See also "Erdoğan Siirt'te: Ben Kuran'la büyüdüm," *Radikal*, 4 May 2015, www .radikal.com.tr; "Erdoğan: Bunlar ateist, bunlar zerdüşt," *Cumhuriyet*, May 28, 2016, www.cumhuriyet.com.tr.

19. The state has also attempted to promote Sunni-Islamic understandings among Alevis. See, for instance, "Darbeciler 5 bin çocuğu imam hatibe sürdü," *Radikal*, October 26, 2012, www.radikal.com.tr.

20. During the author's fieldwork, several interviewees such as Raci Bilici (Diyarbakır, January 30, 2014), Necdet İpekyüz (Diyarbakır, January 30, 2014), Fazıl Hüsnü Erdem (Diyarbakır, January 30, 2014), and İsmail Beşikçi (Ankara, July 23, 2014) also stressed that the state has attempted to use Islam against the Kurdish

movement. They noted that the state hopes to retard Kurdish ethnonationalism by promoting Islamic identity and values among the Kurdish masses.

21. This point was also emphasized by İsmail Beşikçi (author's interview, Ankara, July 23, 2014) and Faik Bulut (author's interview, Istanbul, February 22, 2015).

22. See "Şerafettin Halis BDP'deki görevinden istifa etti," *Radikal*, April 2, 2013, www .radikal.com.tr.

23. See "CHP'li Aygün'den Öcalan'a 'Alevi' tepkisi," *Haber 7*, March 22, 2013, www .haber7.com; "Alevilerden 'süreç kurultayı,'" *Radikal*, April 4, 2013, www.radikal .com.tr.

24. See "Şerafettin Halis: Dersim'in vicdanına ve izanına ipotek konulamaz," *Radikal*, April 28, 2013, www.radikal.com.tr.

25. See "Alevi Kurultayı'ndan 'Barış' çıktı," *Radikal*, May 12, 2013, www.radikal.com.tr; "Üçüncü büyük Alevi kurultayı yapıldı," *Haber soL*, May 12, 2013, http://haber.sol .org.tr. For an analysis of Alevis' criticisms of the Kurdish movement's references to Islam, see "Kürtlerin Alevi sorunu," *Radikal 2*, April 14, 2013, www .radikal.com.tr.

26. See "Kürt hareketinin Aleviler için ne yaptığını bilmiyorum," *Radikal*, May 6, 2013, www.radikal.com.tr. For another Alevi critique, see "İslam çimento mu?" *Güneş*, April 25, 2013, www.gunes.com.

27. For instance, author's interviews with Özden Eren Başkavak Gün, Tunceli, August 2, 2013; Ergin Doğru, Tunceli, August 2, 2013; Murat Polat, Tunceli, August 2, 2013; Hüseyin Aygün, Tunceli, August 3, 2013; Şerafettin Halis, Tunceli, August 3, 2013; Ali Asker Koçuk, Ovacık-Tunceli, August 4, 2013; Seyfi Geyik, Hozat-Tunceli, August 5, 2013; Dursun Yıldız, Tunceli, August 5, 2013; Sabit Menteşe, email interview, August 7, 2013.

28. Author's email interview, August 7, 2013.

29. Author's interview, Tunceli, August 2, 2013.

30. Author's interview, Tunceli, August 3, 2013.

31. See Öcalan'dan, "Aleviler ve Ermeniler için 'özel' mesajlar," *T24*, April 4, 2013, http://t24.com.tr.

32. See "Alevilere tarihi çağrı," *Özgür Gündem*, May 12, 2013, http://ozgur-gundem .com.

33. Author's interview with Murat Polat, Tunceli, August 2, 2013.

34. See "Altan Tan şeriatçı çıktı!," *Milliyet*, April 23, 2013, www.milliyet.com.tr.

35. See "HDP karar değiştirdi: Altan Tan Diyarbakır adayı," *Radikal*, April 7, 2015, www.radikal.com.tr; "HDP'nin sıradışı adayı: Hüda Kaya," *Radikal*, April 7, 2015, www.radikal.com.tr.

36. "Selahattin Demirtaş'tan 'İslami söylem' açıklaması," *Haber soL*, May 28, 2015, http://haber.sol.org.tr.

37. During the third congress of the PKK, which took place in October 1986 in Bekaa Valley, Lebanon, Öcalan was granted special status within the PKK. Since then, he has been referred to as the "Leadership" (*Önderlik*) (Jongerden and Akkaya 2011, 137).

38. We should, however, note that the government occasionally prevents or limits visits to Öcalan at İmralı Island. In addition, all his meetings with visitors take place under strict surveillance (see also Akkaya and Jongerden 2011, 146).
39. See "Gerçek 2. Cumhuriyet dönemi şimdi başladı," *Radikal*, March 25, 2013, www .radikal.com.tr.
40. See "Diyarbakır'a helalleşmeye geldim," *TimeTurk*, June 1, 2011, www.timeturk .com.
41. See "Doğuya bin mele atandı," *NTV*, June 21, 2012, www.ntv.com.tr.
42. See "Görmez: Alevilik Sünniliğin zıttı değil," *NTV*, February 19, 2013, www.ntv .com.tr.
43. See *Diyanet* Kürt Kuran'ı Kerim meali çalışmasını tamamladı," *Radikal*, April 30, 2015, www.radikal.com.tr.
44. See "Dini Zerdüştlük olanın böyle bir derdi olabilir mi?," *Milliyet*, October 15, 2011, www.milliyet.com.tr.
45. See "BBP, BDP'ye din uyarısı yaptı," *Milli Gazete*, April 7, 2011, www.milligazete .com.tr.
46. See "Akıllı sosyalist niye İslam'ı karşısına alsın?," *T24*, March 26, 2013, http://t24 .com.tr. For similar criticisms, see also "Yeni Abdülhamit'in yeni Hamidiye Alayları," *BirGün*, February 4, 2013, http://birgunarsiv.net.
47. See "Kürt sorununa Abdülhamitçi çözüm," *Haber soL*, March 17, 2013, http:// haber.sol.org.tr.
48. Author's interview, Istanbul, February 23, 2015. Several other interviewees also emphasized that although the rise of an Islam-friendly approach within the Kurdish movement might involve pragmatic or strategic concerns or motivations, it should be understood as a long-term, ideational shift (e.g., Tahir Elçi, Diyarbakır, March 22, 2013; Fırat Anlı, Diyarbakır, March 23, 2013; Fazıl Husnu Erdem, Diyarbakır, January 30, 2014; Welat Ay, Diyarbakır, January 31, 2014; Hamit Bozarslan, Ankara, April 28, 2014; Nuray Mert, Diyarbakır, May 11, 2014; Seher Akçınar, Diyarbakır, May 12, 2014; Mithat Sancar, Ankara, July 22, 2014; and Cengiz Çandar, email interview, February 26, 2015).
49. Author's interview, Ankara, August 20, 2014.
50. For a similar conclusion, see also "Kürt bölgesindeki seçmenle ilgili müthiş araştırma (1)," *Radikal*, May 25, 2015, available at www.radikal.com.tr (accessed on January 22, 2016).
51. Ayhan Bilgen (author's interview, Ankara, August 20, 2014) and Kadri Yıldırım (author's interview, Diyarbakır, May 11, 2014) also made similar observations.
52. This information was shared by Ayhan Bilgen (author's interview, Ankara, August 20, 2014).
53. For instance, author's interview with Oral Çalışlar, Istanbul, February 24, 2015; Kadri Yıldırım, Diyarbakır, May 11, 2014; Seher Akçınar, Diyarbakır, May 12, 2014; Mahmut Bozarslan, Diyarbakır, May 12, 2014; Mithat Sancar, Ankara, July 22, 2014.
54. Author's interview, Istanbul, February 24, 2015.

CONCLUSIONS AND IMPLICATIONS

1. For a general discussion of the notion of agency, see Emirbayer and Mische 1998.
2. For a general discussion of the notion of structure, see Sewell 1992.
3. Such a process is also known as *ethnogenesis* (see Roosens 1989; Wimmer 2013, 52–55).
4. Most of these studies are influenced in varying degrees by the structuration approach (see Giddens 1979, 1986). As a conceptual framework or metatheory, this approach attributes agents and structures equal ontological status and provides a dialectical synthesis of the two (Wendt 1987). Giddens's dialectical synthesis of the agent and structure is based on the ontological notion of the "duality of structure," which asserts that structures are both the medium and the outcome of social actions or practices (Giddens 1986, 25). For Giddens, structural factors exert a causal impact on the actions of human agents, but they are also caused or constituted by human agents' actions. Human agents are *knowledgeable* and *reflexive* and so have the ability to create and re-create structures. Thus, this perspective asserts that agency and structure are dependent on each other; they mutually constitute or codetermine each other (see also Wendt 1987; Dessler 1989; Sewell 1992; Clark 1998). With these premises and arguments (i.e., a dualist or binary social ontology; a dynamic, reciprocal relationship between agency and structure), the structuration perspective avoids the tendencies of the reductionism, reification, and determinism of agential and structural approaches and so provides a better resolution to the long-standing debate concerning the relationship between structure and agency. For another attempt at resolving the agency-structure problem, see the morphogenetic approach offered by Margaret Archer (1995, 2007).
5. As Jacoby and Tabak (2015) observe, for many religious scholars, the Islamic belief system, which promotes the notion of the *ummah*, rejects nationalist ideologies and movements (e.g., Babanzade Ahmet Naim, 1872–1934).
6. It is observed that such an instrumentalist approach to Islam was also present during Ottoman times. It is argued that Ottoman legitimacy among different Muslim ethnic groups was partially based on an overarching Muslim identity. For instance, White (2000, 55) notes, "The diverse tribes under Ottoman control were unified politically through the medium of Islam. That is, their religion provided them with their primary identity. At the head of this polity stood the Ottoman sultan, who was, in theory, simultaneously its spiritual authority and temporal leader." During the reign of Abdulhamid II (1876–1909), we saw an increasing emphasis on the unifying role of Islam among diverse Muslim ethnic communities. Believing that Ottomanism failed to achieve unity and solidarity among diverse ethnic groups of the empire, Abdulhamid II embraced and promoted pan-Islamist ideas and principles, which emphasized and preached *ummah*, Islamic political unity (*ittihad-i Islam*), and the institution of the Caliphate (e.g., see Deringil 1991; Mardin 2006; Campo 2009).

7. Several Muslim thinkers also claim that Islam and nationalism are not compatible. For example, it is worth quoting the Moroccan thinker Abd al-Salam Yasin (1928–2012) on this subject: "Both the allegiance to Allah and the allegiance between His believers are diametrically opposed to racial or nationalist (*qawmi*) allegiance. Nationalism is our scourge and our plague, for it sows divisiveness among Muslims, based upon a presumed ethnic affiliation. It further leads to political, internecine fights initiated by the nationalist statelets. . . . The Prophet himself has declared solidarities predicated upon blood and ethnicity to be *jahili*, dregs of the past, which must be combated and erased" (quoted in Aspinall 2009, 11–12).

8. Several Islamist writers and columnists also occasionally express similar ideas. See, for instance, "Silahlı ve Sivil PKK," *Vahdet*, January 1, 2016, www.gazetevahdet.com.

9. See "Erdoğan: Kürtlerin de Türklerin de sorunları aynı," *Hürriyet*, December 6, 2005, www.hurriyet.com.tr.

10. See "Erdoğan: Din Türkiye'nin çimentosudur," *Hürriyet*, December 11, 2005, www.hurriyet.com.tr. See also "Erdoğan: Babama Laz mıyız Türk müyüz diye sordum," *Hürriyet*, April 17, 2016, www.hurriyet.com.tr.

11. See "Çözümün çimentosu İslam," *Akşam*, April 22, 2013, www.aksam.com.tr.

12. See "Süreçte 'Kürt sorunu yoktur'dan sonraki aşama: Yöre insanına Kürt demek ayıptır," *Diken*, May 11, 2015, www.diken.com.tr.

13. Emphasis on Islamic ideas and symbols such as Islamic brotherhood and *ummah* against ethnic nationalisms and separatisms is not limited to conservative circles in Turkey. For instance, government officials in Indonesia's Aceh province also emphasized such Islamic ideas to defend the unitary state against Acehnese separatists (see Aspinall 2007, 2009).

14. The instrumental usage of religion in Turkish politics is not restricted to the Kurdish ethnopolitical movement. Other secular, nationalist formations have also instrumentalized religion. For instance, a similar strategy was pursued by Kemalist nationalists during the formative years of the Republic. During the War of Independence against the Greeks, Armenians, and the Allied powers, Mustafa Kemal framed the nationalist struggle in religious terms to secure Kurdish support. As Romano (2006, 30) observes, "Ataturk was thus able to paint the ongoing struggle as a contest between the infidel Western powers who supported the Christian Armenians and Greeks, and Muslim-Ottoman Turks and Kurds fighting to save the Sultan, Caliph, and homeland" (see also Natali 2005, 73). Thus, the Turkish nationalist leadership deployed the bond of Islam and Islamic attachments and loyalties to mobilize Muslim ethnic groups, including Kurds, against the invading powers.

15. Author's interview with Lokman Ergün, Ankara, February 27, 2015.

16. See, for instance, Mücahit Bilici's comments on this issue: "Türklüğün şartları üçten ikiye indi: Kültürel anayasa ve Kürtler," *Taraf*, February 27, 2013,

http://arsiv.taraf.com.tr; "Iki Hazine: Benlik ve Milliyet," *Taraf*, July 23, 2015, www .taraf.com.tr; "Kürdleri İslam'la kandırmak," *Yeni Yüzyıl*, March 20, 2016, www .gazeteyeniyuzyil.com.

17. There are several other studies (quantitative or qualitative) reaching similar conclusions. For instance, see Aspinall 2009; Sarigil and Fazlioglu 2013, 2014; Gurses 2015; Somer and Glüpker-Kesebir 2016; Gurses and Rost 2017.

18. See "Kürt hareketi ve İslami meydan okuma," *Radikal 2*, November 3, 2013, www .radikal.com.tr. Several interviewees also expressed quite similar points, for instance, Ruşen Çakır, Istanbul, February 23, 2015; Nuray Mert, Diyarbakır, May 11, 2014; Mithat Sancar, Ankara, July 22, 2014.

19. For a critique of modernization theory in the Turkish setting, see Kosebalaban 2007.

20. See Francis Fukuyama, "History Is Still Going Our Way," *Wall Street Journal*, October 5, 2001, www.wsj.com.

21. The report is available at Freedom House, "Discarding Democracy: Return to the Iron Fist," *Freedom in the World 2015*, accessed February 11, 2016, http://freedom house.org.

REFERENCES

Abulof, Uriel. 2014. "The Roles of Religion in National Legitimation: Judaism and Zionism's Elusive Quest for Legitimacy." *Journal for the Scientific Study of Religion* 53 (3): 515–533.

Ahmad, Feroz. 1993. *The Making of Modern Turkey*. London: Routledge.

Akkaya, Ahmet H., and Joost Jongerden. 2011. "The PKK in the 2000s: Continuity through Breaks?" In *Nationalism and Politics in Turkey: Political Islam, Kemalism and the Kurdish Issue*, edited by Marlies Casier and Joost Jongerden, 143–162. New York: Routledge.

———. 2012. "Reassembling the Political: The PKK and the Project of Radical Democracy." *European Journal of Turkish Studies* 14.

Alba, Richard. 2005. "Bright vs. Blurred Boundaries: Second-Generation Assimilation and Exclusion in France, Germany, and the United States." *Ethnic and Racial Studies* 28 (1): 20–49.

Almond, Gabriel A., R. Scott Appleby, and Emmanuel Sivan. 2003. *Strong Religion: The Rise of Fundamentalisms around the World*. Chicago: University of Chicago Press.

Anderson, Benedict. 1991. *Imagined Communities: Reflections on the Origin and Spread of Nationalism*. Rev. ed. New York: Verso Books.

Arberry, Arthur J. 1990. *The Koran*. Oxford: Oxford University Press.

Archer, Margaret S. 1995. *Realist Social Theory: The Morphogenetic Approach*. New York: Cambridge University Press.

———. 2007. "The Trajectory of the Morphogenetic Approach." *Sociologia, Problemas e Práticas* 54:35–47.

Aslan, Abdurrahman. 1996. *Kürt Sorunu Nasıl Çözülür*. Istanbul: Nübihar.

Aslan, Senem. 2015. *Nation-Building in Turkey and Morocco: Governing Kurdish and Berber Dissent*. New York: Cambridge University Press.

Aspinall, Edward. 2007. "From Islamism to Nationalism in Aceh, Indonesia." *Nations and Nationalism* 13 (2): 245–263.

———. 2009. *Islam and Nation: Separatist Rebellion in Aceh, Indonesia*. Stanford, CA: Stanford University Press.

Aydin, Aysegul, and Cem Emrence. 2015. *Zones of Rebellion: Kurdish Insurgents and the Turkish State*. Ithaca, NY: Cornell University Press.

Bahcheli, Tozun, and Sid Noel. 2011. "The Justice and Development Party and the Kurdish Question." In *Nationalisms and Politics in Turkey: Political Islam, Kemalism and the Kurdish issue*, edited by Marlies Casier and Joost Jongerden, 101–120. London: Routledge.

Bail, Christopher A. 2008. "The Configuration of Symbolic Boundaries against Immigrants in Europe." *American Sociological Review* 73 (1): 37–59.

Banton, Michael. 1997. *Ethnic and Racial Consciousness*. 2nd ed. New York: Longman.

Barker, Philip W. 2009. *Religious Nationalism in Modern Europe: If God Be for Us*. New York: Routledge.

Barkey, Henri J., and Graham E. Fuller. 1998. *Turkey's Kurdish Question*. New York: Rowman and Littlefield.

Barth, Fredrik, ed. 1969a. *Ethnic Groups and Boundaries: The Social Organization of Culture Difference*. London: Allen and Unwin.

———. 1969b. Introduction to *Ethnic Groups and Boundaries: The Social Organization of Culture Difference*, edited by Fredrik Barth, 9–38. London: Allen and Unwin.

———. 1994. "Enduring and Emerging Issues in the Analysis of Ethnicity." In *The Anthropology of Ethnicity*, edited by Hans Vermeulen and Cora Govers, 11–32. Amsterdam: Het Spinhuis.

Bayar, Murat. 2009. "Reconsidering Primordialism: an Alternative Approach to the Study of Ethnicity." *Ethnic and Racial Studies* 32 (9): 1639–1657.

Bengio, Ofra, ed. 2014. *Kurdish Awakening: Nation Building in a Fragmented Homeland*. Austin: University of Texas Press.

Beriker-Atiyas, Nimet. 1997. "The Kurdish Conflict in Turkey: Issues, Parties and Prospects." *Security Dialogue* 28 (4): 439–452.

Billig, Michael. 1995. *Banal Nationalism*. Thousand Oaks, CA: Sage.

Birand, Mehmet Ali. 1992. *Apo ve PKK*. Istanbul: Milliyet Yayınları.

Bora, Tanil. 2003. "Nationalist Discourses in Turkey." *South Atlantic Quarterly* 102 (2): 433–451.

Bourdieu, Pierre. 1984. *Distinction: A Social Critique of the Judgement of Taste*. Cambridge, MA: Harvard University Press.

Bozarslan, Hamit. 2001. "Human Rights and the Kurdish Issue in Turkey: 1984–1999." *Human Rights Review* 3 (1): 45–54.

Brady, Henry E., and David Collier. 2010. *Rethinking Social Inquiry: Diverse Tools, Shared Standards*. 2nd ed. Lanham, MD: Rowman and Littlefield.

Brass, Paul R. 1979. "Elite Groups, Symbol Manipulation and Ethnic Identity among the Muslims of South Asia." In *Political Identity in South Asia*, edited by David Taylor and Malcolm Yapp, 35–68. London: Curzon.

———. 1991. *Ethnicity and Nationalism: Theory and Comparison*. Thousand Oaks, CA: Sage.

Breuilly, John. 1993. *Nationalism and the State*. 2nd ed. Manchester: Manchester University Press.

Brubaker, Rogers. 2002. "Ethnicity without Groups." *Archives Europeennes de Sociologie* 43 (2): 163–189.

———. 2009. "Ethnicity, Race, and Nationalism." *Annual Review of Sociology* 35:21–42.

———. 2012. "Religion and Nationalism: Four Approaches." *Nations and Nationalism* 18 (1): 2–20.

———. 2014. "Beyond Ethnicity." *Ethnic and Racial Studies* 37 (5): 804–808.

Brubaker, Rogers, Margit Feischmidt, Jon Fox, and Liana Grancea. 2006. *Nationalist Politics and Everyday Ethnicity in a Transylvanian Town*. Princeton, NJ: Princeton University Press.

Brubaker, Rogers, Mara Loveman, and Peter Stamatov. 2004. "Ethnicity as Cognition." *Theory and Society* 33 (1): 31–64.

Bryman, Alan. 2004. "Triangulation." In *The Sage Encyclopedia of Social Science Research Methods*, edited by Michael S. Lewis-Beck, Alan Bryman, and Tim Futing Liao, 1143–1144. Thousand Oaks, CA: Sage.

Cagaptay, Soner. 2006. *Islam, Secularism and Nationalism in Modern Turkey: Who Is a Turk?* New York: Routledge.

Calhoun, Craig J. 1993. "Nationalism and Ethnicity." *Annual Review of Sociology* 19:211–239.

———. 1997. *Nationalism*. Buckingham, UK: Open University Press.

Campo, Juan E. 2009. "Pan-Islamism." In *Encyclopedia of Islam*, edited by Juan E. Campo, 545–546. New York: Facts on File.

Çarkoğlu, Ali. 1998. "The Turkish Party System in Transition: Party Performance and Agenda Change." *Political Studies* 46 (3): 544–571.

———. 2005. "Political Preferences of the Turkish Electorate: Reflections of an Alevi-Sunni Cleavage." *Turkish Studies* 6 (2): 273–292.

Çarkoğlu, Ali, and Ersin Kalaycioğlu. 2009. *The Rising Tide of Conservatism in Turkey*. New York: Palgrave Macmillan.

Carlsnaes, Walter. 1992. "The Agency-Structure Problem in Foreign Policy Analysis." *International Studies Quarterly* 36 (3): 245–270.

Casier, Marlies, and Joost Jongerden. 2011. *Nationalisms and Politics in Turkey: Political Islam, Kemalism, and the Kurdish Issue*. New York: Routledge.

Cederman, Lars-Erik. 2002. "Nationalism and Ethnicity." In *Handbook of International Relations*, edited by Walter Carlsnaes, Thomas Risse, and Beth A. Simmons, 409–429. Thousand Oaks, CA: Sage.

Cesari, Jocelyne. 2004. *When Islam and Democracy Meet: Muslims in Europe and in the United States*. New York: Palgrave Macmillan.

———. 2014. *The Awakening of Muslim Democracy: Religion, Modernity, and the State*. New York: Cambridge University Press.

Cetinsaya, Gokhan. 1999. "Rethinking Nationalism and Islam Some Preliminary Notes on the Roots of Turkish-Islamic Synthesis in Modern Turkish Political Thought." *Muslim World* 89 (3–4): 350–376.

Chai, Sun-Ki. 2005. "Predicting Ethnic Boundaries." *European Sociological Review* 21 (4): 375–391.

Chandra, Kanchan. 2006. "What Is Ethnic Identity and Does It Matter?" *Annual Review of Political Science* 9:397–424.

———, ed. 2012a. *Constructivist Theories of Ethnic Politics*. Oxford: Oxford University Press.

———. 2012b. Introduction to *Constructivist Theories of Ethnic Politics*, edited by Kanchan Chandra, 1–48. Oxford: Oxford University Press.

———. 2012c. "What Is Ethnic Identity? A Minimalist Definition." In *Constructivist Theories of Ethnic Politics*, edited by Kanchan Chandra, 51–97. Oxford: Oxford University Press.

Çiçek, Cuma. 2013. "The Pro-Islamic Challenge for the Kurdish Movement." *Dialectical Anthropology* 37 (1): 159–163.

Cizre, Ümit, ed. 2008. *Secular and Islamic Politics in Turkey: The Making of the Justice and Development Party*. New York: Routledge.

Clark, William R. 1998. "Agents and Structures: Two Views of Preferences, Two Views of Institutions." *International Studies Quarterly* 42 (2): 245–270.

Conforti, Yitzhak. 2015. "Ethnicity and Boundaries in Jewish Nationalism." In *Nationalism, Ethnicity and Boundaries: Conceptualising and Understanding Identity through Boundary Approaches*, edited by Jennifer Jackson and Lina Molokotos-Liederman, 142–162. New York Routledge.

Connor, Walker. 1994. *Ethnonationalism: The Quest for Understanding*. Princeton, NJ: Princeton University Press.

Conversi, Daniele. 1995. "Reassessing Current Theories of Nationalism: Nationalism as Boundary Maintenance and Creation." *Nationalism and Ethnic Politics* 1 (1): 73–85.

———. 1999. "Nationalism, Boundaries, and Violence." *Millennium: Journal of International Studies* 28 (3): 553–584.

Cornell, Stephen. 1996. "The Variable Ties That Bind: Content and Circumstance in Ethnic Processes." *Ethnic and Racial Studies* 19 (2): 265–289.

Cornell, Stephen, and Douglas Hartmann. 2007. *Ethnicity and Race: Making Identities in a Changing World*. 2nd ed. Thousand Oaks, CA: Sage.

Coşar, Simten. 2011. "Turkish Nationalism and Sunni Islam in the Construction of Political Party Identities." In *Symbiotic Antagonisms Competing Nationalisms in Turkey*, edited by Ayse G. Kadıoğlu and Fuat Keyman, 162–198. Salt Lake City: University of Utah Press.

Cox, Julie W., and John Hassard. 2010. "Triangulation." In *Encyclopedia of Case Study Research*, edited by Albert J. Mills, Gabrielle Durepos, and Elden Wiebe, 945–949. Thousand Oaks, CA: Sage.

Criss, Nur Bilge. 1995. "The Nature of PKK Terrorism in Turkey." *Studies in Conflict & Terrorism* 18 (1): 17–37.

Dag, Rahman. 2014. "Democratic Islam Congress and the Middle East." openDemocracy, last modified June 13. www.opendemocracy.net.

———. 2017. *Ideological Roots of the Conflict Between Pro-Kurdish and Pro-Islamic Parties in Turkey*. Newcastle upon Tyne, UK: Cambridge Scholars.

Denny, Frederick M. 1977. "Ummah in the Constitution of Medina." *Journal of Near Eastern Studies* 36 (1): 39–47.

Deringil, Selim. 1991. "Legitimacy Structures in the Ottoman State: The Reign of Ab-dülhamid II (1876–1909)." *International Journal of Middle East Studies* 23:345–359.

Dessler, David. 1989. "What's at Stake in the Agent-Structure Debate?" *International Organization* 43 (3): 441–473.

Duran, Burhanettin. 1998. "Approaching the Kurdish Question via Adil Düzen: An Islamist Formula of the Welfare Party for Ethnic Coexistence." *Journal of Muslim Minority Affairs* 18 (1): 111–128.

Eckstein, Harry. 1975. "Case Studies and Theory in Political Science." In *Handbook of Political Science*, edited by Fred I. Greenstein and Nelson W. Polsby, 79–138. Reading, MA: Addison-Wesley.

Eickelman, Dale F., and James P. Piscatori. 1996. *Muslim Politics*. Princeton, NJ: Princeton University Press.

Elitsoy, Z. Asli. 2013. "The Changing Dynamics of Islamic and Nationalist Discourse among the Kurds of Turkey." MA thesis, Tel Aviv University.

Eller, Jack David, and Reed M. Coughlan. 1993. "The Poverty of Primordialism: the Demystification of Ethnic Attachments." *Ethnic and Racial Studies* 16 (2): 183–202.

Emerson, Michael O., and David Hartman. 2006. "The Rise of Religious Fundamentalism." *Annual Review of Sociology* 32:127–144.

Emirbayer, Mustafa, and Ann Mische. 1998. "What Is Agency?" *American Journal of Sociology* 103 (4): 962–1023.

Entessar, Nader. 1992. *Kurdish Ethnonationalism*. Boulder, CO: Lynne Rienner.

———. 2010. *Kurdish Politics in the Middle East*. Plymouth, UK: Lexington Books.

Eriksen, Thomas Hylland. 2010. *Ethnicity and Nationalism: Anthropological Perspectives*. 3rd ed. New York: Pluto.

Esman, Milton Jacob. 1994. *Ethnic Politics*. Ithaca, NY: Cornell University Press.

Esposito, John L., Tamara Sonn, and John O. Voll. 2016. *Islam and Democracy after the Arab Spring*. New York: Oxford University Press.

Esposito, John L., and John O. Voll. 1996. *Islam and Democracy*. New York: Oxford University Press.

Fardon, Richard. 1987. "African Ethnogenesis: Limits to the Comparability of Ethnic Phenomena." In *Comparative Anthropology*, edited by Ladislav Holy, 168–188. Oxford, UK: Blackwell.

Fearon, James D. 2003. "Ethnic and Cultural Diversity by Country." *Journal of Economic Growth* 8 (2): 195–222.

Feldman, Noah. 2004. *After Jihad: America and the Struggle for Islamic Democracy*. New York: Farrar, Straus and Giroux.

Filali-Ansary, Abdou. 2003. "Muslims and Democracy." In *Islam and Democracy in the Middle East*, edited by Larry Diamond, Marc Plattner and Daniel Brumberg, 193–207. Baltimore: Johns Hopkins University Press.

Finnemore, Martha. 1996. *National Interests in International Society*. Ithaca, NY: Cornell University Press.

Flick, Uwe. 2004. "Triangulation in Qualitative Research." In *A Companion to Qualitative Research*, edited by Uwe Flick, Ernst von Kardoff, and Ines Steinke, 178–183. Thousands Oaks, CA: Sage.

Fuller, Sylvia. 2003 "Creating and Contesting Boundaries: Exploring the Dynamics of Conflict and Classification." *Sociological Forum* 18 (1): 3–30.

Geertz, Clifford. 1973. *The Interpretation of Cultures: Selected Essays*. New York: Basic Books.

Gellner, Ernest. 1981. *Muslim Society*. Cambridge: Cambridge University Press.

———. 1983. *Nations and Nationalism*. Ithaca, NY: Cornell University Press.

———. 1992. *Postmodernism, Reason and Religion*. New York: Routledge.

George, Alexander L., and Andrew Bennett. 2005. *Case Studies and Theory Development in the Social Sciences*. Cambridge, MA: MIT Press.

Gerring, John. 2007. *Case Study Research: Principles and Practices*. Cambridge: Cambridge University Press.

Giddens, Anthony. 1979. *Central Problems in Social Theory: Action, Structure and Contradiction in Social Theory*. Berkeley: University of California Press.

———. 1986. *The Constitution of Society: Outline of the Structuration Theory*. Paperback ed. Cambridge, UK: Polity.

Goalwin, Gregory J. 2017. "Understanding the Exclusionary Politics of Early Turkish Nationalism: An Ethnic Boundary-Making Approach." *Nationalities Papers*, 1–17. doi: 10.1080/00905992.2017.1315394.

Göle, Nilüfer. 1997. "Secularism and Islamism in Turkey: The Making of Elites and Counter-elites." *Middle East Journal* 51 (1): 46–58.

Gorski, Philip S. 2006. "Premodern Nationalism: An Oxymoron? The Evidence from England." In *The Sage Handbook of Nations and Nationalism*, edited by Gerard Delanty and Krishan Kumar, 143–156. London: Sage.

Gorski, Philip S., and Gülay Türkmen-Dervişoğlu. 2013. "Religion, Nationalism, and Violence: An Integrated Approach." *Annual Review of Sociology* 39:193–210.

Gottlieb, Gidon. 1994. "Nations without States." *Foreign Affairs* 73 (3): 100–112.

Greenfeld, Liah. 2006. "Modernity and Nationalism." In *The Sage Handbook of Nations and Nationalism*, edited by Gerard Delanty and Krishan Kumar, 157–169. London: Sage.

Grosby, Steven. 1994. "Debate: The Verdict of History: The Inexpungeable Tie of Primordiality—A Response to Eller and Coughlan." *Ethnic and Racial Studies* 17 (2): 164–171.

———. 1995. "Territoriality: The Transcendental, Primordial Feature of Modern Societies." *Nations and Nationalism* 1 (2): 143–162.

Gunes, Cengiz. 2012a. "Explaining the PKK's Mobilization of the Kurds in Turkey: Hegemony, Myth and Violence." *Ethnopolitics* 12 (3): 247–267.

———. 2012b. *The Kurdish National Movement in Turkey: From Protest to Resistance*. New York: Routledge.

Gunter, Michael M. 1990. *The Kurds in Turkey: A Political Dilemma*. Boulder, CO: Westview.

———. 1997. *The Kurds and the Future of Turkey*. New York: St. Martin's.

———. 2004. "The Kurdish Question in Perspective." *World Affairs* 166 (4): 197–205.

Gürbüz, Mustafa E. 2015. "Ideology in Action: Symbolic Localization of Kurdistan Workers' Party in Turkey." *Sociological Inquiry* 85 (1): 1–27.

———. 2016. *Rival Kurdish Movements in Turkey: Transforming Ethnic Conflict*. Amsterdam: Amsterdam University Press.

Gurses, Mehmet. 2015. "Is Islam a Cure for Ethnic Conflict? Evidence from Turkey." *Politics and Religion* 8 (1): 135–154.

Gurses, Mehmet, and Nicolas Rost. 2017. "Religion as a Peacemaker? Peace Duration after Ethnic Civil Wars." *Politics and Religion* 10 (2): 339–362.

Hale, Henry E. 2004. "Explaining Ethnicity." *Comparative Political Studies* 37 (4): 458–485.

Halperin, Sandra, and Oliver Heath. 2012. *Political Research: Methods and Practical Skills*. New York: Oxford University Press.

Handler, Richard. 1988. *Nationalism and the Politics of Culture in Quebec*. Madison: University of Wisconsin Press.

Hashemi, Nader. 2013. "Islam and Democracy." In *Islam and Politics*, edited by John L. Esposito and Emad E. Shahin, 68–88. Oxford: Oxford University Press.

Hastings, Adrian. 1997. *The Construction of Nationhood: Ethnicity, Religion and Nationalism*. Cambridge: Cambridge University Press.

Hastings, Sarah L. 2010. "Triangulation." In *Encyclopedia of Research Design*, edited by Neil J. Salkind, 1538–1541. Thousand Oaks, CA: Sage.

Haymes, Thomas. 1997. "What Is Nationalism Really? Understanding the Limitations of Rigid Theories in Dealing with the Problems of Nationalism and Ethnonationalism." *Nations and Nationalism* 3 (4): 541–557.

Hechter, Michael. 2000. *Containing Nationalism*. Oxford: Oxford University Press.

Heper, Metin. 2007. *The State and Kurds in Turkey: The Question of Assimilation*. New York: Palgrave Macmillan.

Heywood, Andrew. 2005. *Political Theory: An Introduction*. 4th ed. New York: Palgrave Macmillan.

Hobsbawm, Eric. 1990. *Nations and Nationalism since 1780: Programme, Myth, Reality*. Cambridge: Cambridge University Press.

Hobsbawm, Eric, and Terence Ranger, eds. 1983. *The Invention of Tradition*. Cambridge: Cambridge University Press.

Horowitz, Donald L. 1985. *Ethnic Groups in Conflict*. Berkeley: University of California Press.

Houston, Christopher J. 2001. *Islam, Kurds and the Turkish Nation State*. Oxford, UK: Berg.

Huntington, Samuel P. 1984. "Will More Countries Become Democratic?" *Political Science Quarterly* 99 (2): 193–218.

————. 1991. *The Third Wave: Democratization in the Late Twentieth Century*. Norman: University of Oklahoma Press.

————. 1996. *The Clash of Civilisations and the Remaking of the Modern World*. New York: Simon and Schuster.

Hutchinson, John, and Anthony D. Smith. 1996. *Ethnicity*. Oxford: Oxford University Press.

Imset, Ismet G. 1992. *The PKK: A Report on Separatist Violence in Turkey, 1973–1992*. Ankara: Turkish Daily News Publications.

————. 1996. "The PKK: Terrorists or Freedom Fighters?" *International Journal of Kurdish Studies* 10 (1–2): 45–100.

Isaacs, Harold Robert. 1975. *Idols of the Tribe: Group Identity and Political Change*. Cambridge, MA: Harvard University Press.

Jackson, Jennifer. 2015a. Introduction to *Nationalism, Ethnicity and Boundaries: Conceptualising and Understanding Identity through Boundary Approaches*, edited by Jennifer Jackson and Lina Molokotos-Liederman, 1–8. New York: Routledge.

————. 2015b. "Negotiating National Identity in Northern Ireland and Quebec: Youth Perspectives." In *Nationalism, Ethnicity and Boundaries: Conceptualising and Understanding Identity through Boundary Approaches*, edited by Jennifer Jackson and Lina Molokotos-Liederman, 192–219. New York: Routledge.

Jackson, Jennifer, and Lina Molokotos-Liederman, eds. 2015. *Nationalism, Ethnicity and Boundaries: Conceptualising and Understanding Identity through Boundary Approaches*. New York: Routledge.

Jacoby, Tim, and Hüsrev Tabak. 2015. "Islam, Nationalism, and Kurdish Ethnopolitics in Turkey." *Peace Review: A Journal of Social Justice* 27:346–353.

Jenkins, Gareth. 2008. *Political Islam in Turkey: Running West, Heading East?* New York: Palgrave Macmillan.

Jenkins, Richard. 1986. "Social Anthropological Models of Inter-ethnic Relations." In *Theories of Race and Ethnic Relations*, edited by John Rex and David Mason, 170–187. Cambridge: Cambridge University Press.

————. 2008. *Rethinking Ethnicity*. 2nd ed. London: Sage.

————. 2015. "Boundaries and Borders." In *Nationalism, Ethnicity and Boundaries: Conceptualising and Understanding Identity through Boundary Approaches*, edited by Jennifer Jackson and Lina Molokotos-Liederman, 11–27. New York: Routledge.

Jensen, Sune Qvotrup. 2011. "Othering, Identity Formation and Agency." *Qualitative Studies* 2 (2): 63–78.

Jongerden, Joost, and Ahmet H. Akkaya. 2011. "Born from the Left: The Making of the PKK." In *Nationalism and Politics in Turkey: Political Islam, Kemalism and the Kurdish Issue*, edited by Marlies Casier and Joost Jongerden, 123–142. New York: Routledge.

Juergensmeyer, Mark. 1993. *The New Cold War? Religious Nationalism Confronts the Secular State*. Berkeley: University of California Press.

———. 2006. "Nationalism and Religion." In *The Sage Handbook of Nations and Nationalism*, edited by Gerard Delanty and Krishan Kumar, 182–191. London: Sage.

———. 2008. *Global Rebellion: Religious Challenges to the Secular State, from Christian Militias to al Qaeda*. Berkeley: University of California Press.

Jung, Dietrich. 2011. *Orientalists, Islamists and the Global Public Sphere: A Genealogy of the Modern Essentialist Image of Islam*. Sheffield, UK: Equinox.

Jwaideh, Wadie. 2006. *The Kurdish National Movement: Its Origins and Development*. Syracuse, NY: Syracuse University Press.

Kadıoğlu, Ayşe G., and Fuat Keyman, eds. 2011. *Symbiotic Antagonisms: Competing Nationalisms in Turkey*. Salt Lake City: University of Utah Press.

Kasfir, Nelson. 1979. "Explaining Ethnic Political Participation." *World Politics* 31 (3): 365–388.

Keating, Michael. 2011. "Nationalism." In *International Encyclopedia of Political Science*, edited by Bertrand Badie, Dirk Berg-Schlosser, and Leonardo Morlino, 1654–1659. Thousand Oaks, CA: Sage.

Kedourie, Elie. 1960. *Nationalism*. London: Hutchinson.

———. 1992. *Democracy and Arab Political Culture*. Washington, DC: Washington Institute for Near East Policy.

Kellas, James G. 1998. *The Politics of Nationalism and Ethnicity*. 2nd ed. Basingstoke, UK: Macmillan.

Kirişçi, Kemal, and Gareth M Winrow. 1997. *The Kurdish Question and Turkey: An Example of a Trans-state Ethnic Conflict*. Portland, OR: Frank Cass.

Koc, Ismet, Attila Hancioglu, and Alanur Cavlin. 2008. "Demographic Differentials and Demographic Integration of Turkish and Kurdish Populations in Turkey." *Population Research and Policy Review* 27 (4): 447–457.

Kosebalaban, Hasan. 2007. "The Rise of Anatolian Cities and the Failure of the Modernization Paradigm." *Critique: Critical Middle Eastern Studies* 16 (3): 229–240.

Kramer, Heinz. 2000. *A Changing Turkey: The Challenge to Europe and the United States*. Washington, DC: Brookings Institution Press.

Kurt, Mehmet. 2015. *Türkiye'de Hizbullah: Din, Şiddet ve Aidiyet*. Istanbul: İletişim.

Kydd, Andrew H. 2008. "Methodological Individualism and Rational Choice." In *The Oxford Handbook of International Relations*, edited by Christian Reus-Smit and Duncan Snidal, 425–443. New York: Oxford University Press.

Laitin, David D. 1998. *Identity in Formation: The Russian-Speaking Populations in the Near Abroad*. Ithaca, NY: Cornell University Press.

Lamont, Michèle. 1992. *Money, Morals, and Manners: The Culture of the French and American Upper-Middle Class*. Chicago: University of Chicago Press.

———. 2000. *The Dignity of Working Men: Morality and the Boundaries of Race, Class and Immigration*. New York: Russell Sage Foundation Press.

———. 2014. "Reflections Inspired by Ethnic Boundary Making: Institutions, Power, Networks by Andreas Wimmer." *Ethnic and Racial Studies* 37 (5): 814–819.

Lamont, Michèle, and Virág Molnár. 2002. "The Study of Boundaries in the Social Sciences." *Annual Review of Sociology* 28:167–195.

Lecours, André. 2000. "Ethnonationalism in the West: A Theoretical Exploration." *Nationalism and Ethnic Politics* 6 (1): 103–124.

Leverink, Joris. 2015. "Murray Bookchin and the Kurdish Resistance." *ROAR*, August 9.

Levy, Jack S. 2008. "Case Studies: Types, Designs, and Logics of Inference." *Conflict Management and Peace Science* 25 (1): 1–18.

Lewis, Bernard. 2010. *Faith and Power: Religion and Politics in the Middle East.* New York: Oxford University Press.

Loveman, Mara, and Jeronimo O. Muniz. 2007. "How Puerto Rico Became White: Boundary Dynamics and Intercensus Racial Reclassification." *American Sociological Review* 72:915–939.

Lundgren, Asa. 2007. *The Unwelcome Neighbour: Turkey's Kurdish policy.* London: I. B. Tauris.

Lyman, Stanford M., and William A. Douglass. 1973. "Ethnicity: Strategies of Collective and Individual Impression Management." *Social Research* 40 (2): 344–365.

Marcus, Aliza. 2007. *Blood and Belief: The PKK and the Kurdish Fight for Independence.* New York: NYU Press.

Mardin, Şerif. 2006. *Religion, Society, and Modernity in Turkey.* Syracuse, NY: Syracuse University Press.

McDowall, David. 2004. *A Modern History of the Kurds.* 3rd ed. London: I. B. Tauris.

Meijer, Roel, ed. 2009. *Global Salafism: Islam's New Religious Movement.* New York: Columbia University Press.

Moustakis, Fotios, and Rudra Chaudhuri. 2005. "Turkish-Kurdish Relations and the European Union: An Unprecedented Shift in the Kemalist Paradigm?" *Mediterranean Quarterly* 16 (4): 77–89.

Mutlu, Servet. 1996. "Ethnic Kurds in Turkey: A Demographic Study." *International Journal of Middle East Studies* 28 (4): 517–541.

Nagel, Joane. 1978. "The Conditions of Ethnic Separatism: The Kurds in Turkey, Iran, and Iraq." *Ethnicity* 7 (3): 1–33.

———. 1994. "Constructing Ethnicity: Creating and Recreating Ethnic Identity and Culture." *Social Problems* 41 (1): 152–176.

Nash, Manning. 1989. *The Cauldron of Ethnicity in the Modern World.* Chicago: University of Chicago Press.

Nasr, Seyyed Vali Reza. 2005. "The Rise of 'Muslim Democracy.'" *Journal of Democracy* 16 (2): 13–27.

Natali, Denise. 2005. *The Kurds and the State: Evolving National Identity in Iraq, Turkey, and Iran.* Syracuse, NY: Syracuse University Press.

Öcalan, Abdullah. 1994. *Kürdistan Devriminin Yolu (Manifesto).* 6th ed. Köln: Weşanen Serxwebun.

———. 1995. *Diriliş Tamamlandı, Sıra Kurtuluşta.* Istanbul: Güneş Ülkesi Yayıncılık.

———. 2001. *Kürt Hümanizmi ve Yeni İnsan.* Istanbul: Mem Yayınları.

———. 2007. *Prison Writings: The Roots of Civilization.* Translated by Klaus Happel. London: Pluto.

———. 2008. *Din Sorununa Devrimci Yaklaşım.* 3rd ed. Cologne: Weşanen Serxwebun.

———. 2015. *Demokratik Kurtuluş ve Özgür Yaşamı İnşa (İmralı Notları).* Cologne: Weşanen Mezopotamya.

Okamura, Jonathan Y. 1981. "Situational Ethnicity." *Ethnic and Racial Studies* 4 (4): 452–465.

O'Leary, Brendan. 2001. "Instrumentalist Theories of Nationalism." In *Encyclopedia of Nationalism,* edited by Athena S. Leoussi, 148–153. New Brunswick, NJ: Transaction.

Olson, Robert. 1989. *The Emergence of Kurdish Nationalism and the Sheikh Said Rebellion, 1880–1925.* Austin: University of Texas Press.

———, ed. 1996. *The Kurdish Nationalist Movement in the 1990s: Its Impact on Turkey and the Middle East.* Lexington: University Press of Kentucky.

Olzak, Susan. 1992. *The Dynamics of Ethnic Competition and Conflict.* Stanford, CA: Stanford University Press.

O'Neill, Kate, Jörg Balsiger, and Stacy D. VanDeveer. 2004. "Actors, Norms, and Impact: Recent International Cooperation Theory and the Influence of The Agent-Structure Debate." *Annual Review of Political Science* 7:149–175.

Özbudun, Ergun. 2000. *Contemporary Turkish Politics: Challenges to Democratic Consolidation.* Boulder, CO: Lynne Rienner.

Özcan, Ali Kemal. 2006. *Turkey's Kurds: A Theoretical Analysis of the PKK and Abdullah Öcalan.* London: Routledge.

Özcan, Nihat Ali. 1999. *PKK (Kurdistan Isci Partisi) Tarihi, Ideolojisi, Ve yontemi,* Ankara: ASAM.

Özkırımlı, Umut. 2010. *Theories of Nationalism: A Critical Introduction.* New York: Palgrave Macmillan.

———. 2013. "Vigilance and Apprehension: Multiculturalism, Democracy, and the 'Kurdish Question' in Turkey." *Middle East Critique* 22 (1): 25–43.

Pachucki, Mark A., Sabrina Pendergrass, and Michèle Lamont. 2007. "Boundary Processes: Recent Theoretical Developments and New Contributions." *Poetics* 35 (6): 331–351.

Peters, B. Guy. 1998. *Comparative Politics: Theory and Methods.* New York: NYU Press.

———. 2012. *Institutional Theory in Political Science: The New Institutionalism.* 3rd ed. New York: Continuum.

PKK (Partiya Karkaren Kurdistan). 1984. *PKK (Partiya Karkaren Kurdistan) Kuruluş Bildirgesi.* Cologne: Weşanen Serxwebun.

———. 1995. *PKK 5. Kongre Kararları.* 2nd ed. Cologne: Weşanen Serxwebun.

Potrafke, Niklas. 2012. "Islam and Democracy." *Public Choice* 151 (1–2): 185–192.

Reed, Michael I. 1997. "In Praise of Duality and Dualism: Rethinking Agency and Structure in Organizational Analysis." *Organization Studies* 18 (1): 21–42.

Rieffer, Barbara-Ann J. 2003. "Religion and Nationalism Understanding the Consequences of a Complex Relationship." *Ethnicities* 3 (2): 215–242.

Robinson, Francis. 1977. "Nation Formation: The Brass Thesis and Muslim Separatism." *Journal of Commonwealth & Comparative Politics* 15 (3): 215–230.

———. 1979. "Islam and Muslim Separatism." In *Political Identity in South Asia*, edited by David Taylor and Malcolm Yapp, 78–112. London: Curzon.

Romano, David. 2006. *The Kurdish Nationalist Movement: Opportunity, Mobilization and Identity*. Cambridge: Cambridge University Press.

Romano, David, and Mehmet Gurses, eds. 2014a. *Conflict, Democratization, and the Kurds in the Middle East: Turkey, Iran, Iraq, and Syria*. New York: Palgrave Macmillan.

———. 2014b. "Introduction: The Kurds as Barrier or Key to Democratization." In *Conflict, Democratization, and the Kurds in the Middle East: Turkey, Iran, Iraq, and Syria*, edited by David Romano and Mehmet Gurses, 1–14. New York: Palgrave Macmillan.

Roosens, Eugeen E. 1989. *Creating Ethnicity: The Process of Ethnogenesis*. Frontiers of Anthropology 5. Thousand Oaks, CA: Sage.

Rothbauer, Paulette M. 2008. "Triangulation." In *The Sage Encyclopedia of Qualitative Research Methods*, edited by Lisa M. Given, 893–895. Thousand Oaks, CA: Sage.

Rothschild, Joseph. 1981. *Ethnopolitics: A Conceptual Framework*. New York: Columbia University Press.

Rowley, Charles K., and Nathanael Smith. 2009. "Islam's Democracy Paradox: Muslims Claim to Like Democracy, So Why Do They Have So Little?" *Public Choice* 139 (3–4): 273–299.

Roy, Olivier. 2004. *Globalized Islam: The Search for a New Ummah*. New York: Columbia University Press.

Saatci, Mustafa. 2002. "Nation-states and Ethnic Boundaries: Modern Turkish Identity and Turkish-Kurdish Conflict." *Nations and Nationalism* 8 (4): 549–564.

Safran, William. 2009. Preface to *Religious Nationalism in Modern Europe: If God Be for Us*, by Philip W. Barker, xii–xiii. New York: Routledge.

Sakallioğlu, Ümit Cizre. 1996. "Parameters and Strategies of Islam-State Interaction in Republican Turkey." *International Journal of Middle East Studies* 28 (2): 231–251.

———. 1998. "Kurdish Nationalism from an Islamist Perspective: The Discourses of Turkish Islamist Writers." *Journal of Muslim Minority Affairs* 18 (1): 73–89.

Salt, Jeremy. 1995. "Nationalism and the Rise of Muslim Sentiment in Turkey." *Middle Eastern Studies* 31 (1): 13–27.

Sarigil, Zeki. 2010. "Curbing Kurdish Ethno-nationalism in Turkey: An Empirical Assessment of Pro-Islamic and Socio-economic Approaches." *Ethnic and Racial Studies* 33 (3): 533–553.

———. 2012. "Ethnic Groups at 'Critical Junctures': The Laz vs. Kurds." *Middle Eastern Studies* 48 (2): 269–286.

Sarigil, Zeki, and Omer Fazlioglu. 2013. "Religion and Ethno-nationalism: Turkey's Kurdish Issue." *Nations and Nationalism* 19 (3): 551–571.

——. 2014. "Exploring the Roots and Dynamics of Kurdish Ethno-nationalism in Turkey." *Nations and Nationalism* 20 (3): 436–458.

Sarigil, Zeki, and Ekrem Karakoc. 2016. "Who Supports Secession? The Determinants of Secessionist Attitudes among Turkey's Kurds." *Nations and Nationalism* 22 (2): 325–346.

Schermerhorn, Richard A. 1970. *Comparative Ethnic Relations: A Framework for Theory and Research*. New York: Random House.

Segal, Daniel A., and Richard Handler. 2006. "Cultural Approaches to Nationalism." In *The Sage Handbook of Nations and Nationalism*, edited by Gerard Delanty and Krishan Kumar, 57–65. London: Sage.

Sewell, William H., Jr. 1992. "A Theory of Structure: Duality, Agency, and Transformation." *American Journal of Sociology* 98 (1): 1–29.

Shils, Edward. 1957. "Primordial, Personal, Sacred and Civil Ties: Some Particular Observations on the Relationships of Sociological Research and Theory." *British Journal of Sociology* 8 (2): 130–145.

Smith, Anthony D. 1992. "Chosen Peoples: Why Ethnic Groups Survive." *Ethnic and Racial Studies* 15 (3): 436–456.

——. 2005. "The Genealogy of Nations: An Ethno-symbolic Approach." In *When Is the Nation? Towards an Understanding of Theories of Nationalism*, edited by Atsuko Ichijo and Gordana Uzelac, 94–112. New York: Routledge.

——. 2006. "Ethnicity and Nationalism." In *The Sage Handbook of Nations and Nationalism*, edited by Gerard Delanty and Krishan Kumar, 169–179. London: Sage.

——. 2008. *The Cultural Foundations of Nations: Hierarchy, Covenant, and Republic*. New York: Wiley.

Somer, Murat. 2005. "Resurgence and Remaking of Identity Civil Beliefs, Domestic and External Dynamics, and the Turkish Mainstream Discourse on Kurds." *Comparative Political Studies* 38 (6): 591–622.

Somer, Murat, and Gitta Glüpker-Kesebir. 2016. "Is Islam the Solution? Comparing Turkish Islamic and Secular Thinking toward Ethnic and Religious Minorities." *Journal of Church and State* 58 (3): 529–555.

Stoker, Laura. 2011. "Triangulation." In *International Encyclopedia of Political Science*, edited by Bertrand Badie, Dirk Berg-Schlosser, and Leonardo Morlino, 2670–2672. Thousand Oaks, CA: Sage.

Stroup, David R. 2017. "Boundaries of Belief: Religious Practices and the Construction of Ethnic Identity in Hui Muslim Communities." *Ethnic and Racial Studies* 40 (6): 988–1006.

Tansey, Oisín. 2007. "Process Tracing and Elite Interviewing: A Case for Non-probability Sampling." *PS: Political Science & Politics* 40 (4): 765–772.

Tarrow, Sidney. 2010. "Bridging the Quantitative-Qualitative Divide." In *Rethinking Social Inquiry: Diverse Tools, Shared Standards*, edited by Henry E. Brady and David Collier, 101–111. Lanham, MD: Rowman and Littlefield.

Taspinar, Omer. 2005. *Kurdish Nationalism and Political Islam in Turkey: Kemalist Identity in Transition*. Philadelphia: Psychology Press.

Taylor, Charles. 1994. *Multiculturalism and the Politics of Recognition*. Princeton, NJ: Princeton University Press.

Terrier, Jean. 2015. "Aspects of Boundary Research from the Perspective of *Longue Duree*." In *Nationalism, Ethnicity and Boundaries: Conceptualising and Understanding Identity Through Boundary Approaches*, edited by Jennifer Jackson and Lina Molokotos-Liederman, 28–56. New York: Routledge.

Tezcür, Güneş Murat. 2009. "Kurdish Nationalism and Identity in Turkey: A Conceptual Reinterpretation." *European Journal of Turkish Studies* 10. http://journals.openedition.org.

———. 2010. "When Democratization Radicalizes: The Kurdish Nationalist Movement in Turkey." *Journal of Peace Research* 47 (6): 775–789.

———. 2015. "Violence and Nationalist Mobilization: The Onset of the Kurdish Insurgency in Turkey." *Nationalities Papers* 43 (2): 248–266.

Tilly, Charles. 2005. *Identities, Boundaries and Social Ties*. Boulder, CO: Paradigm.

Ünver, H. Akin. 2015. *Turkey's Kurdish Question: Discourse and Politics since 1990*. New York: Routledge.

Updegraff, Ragan. 2012. "The Kurdish Question." *Journal of Democracy* 23 (1): 119–128.

van Bruinessen, Martin. 1992. *Agha, Shaikh, and State: the Social and Political Structures of Kurdistan*. Atlantic Highlands, NJ: Zed Books.

———. 2000a. *Kurdish Ethno-nationalism versus Nation-Building States: Collected Articles*. Istanbul: Isis.

———. 2000b. *Mullahs, Sufis and Heretics: The Role of Religion in Kurdish Society: Collected Articles*. Istanbul: Isis.

van den Berghe, Pierre L. 1981. *The Ethnic Phenomenon*. New York: Elsevier.

———. 1995. "Does Race Matter?" *Nations and Nationalism* 1 (3): 357–368.

———. 2001. "Sociobiological Theory of Nationalism." In *Encyclopedia of Nationalism*, edited by Athena S Leoussi, 273–279. New Brunswick, NJ: Transaction.

Van Evera, Stephen. 2001. "Primordialism Lives!" *APSA-CP* 12 (1): 20–22.

Varshney, Ashutosh. 2007. "Ethnicity and Ethnic Conflict." In *Oxford Handbook of Comparative Politics*, edited by Carles Boix and Susan C. Stokes, 274–296. Oxford: Oxford University Press.

Voll, John O., and John L. Esposito. 1994. "Islam's Democratic Essence." *Middle East Quarterly* 1 (3): 3–11.

Wallman, Sandra. 1978. "The Boundaries of 'Race': Processes of Ethnicity in England." *Man* 13 (2): 200–217.

———. 1986. "Ethnicity and the Boundary Process in Context." In *Theories of Race and Ethnic Relations*, edited by John Rex and David Mason, 226–245. Cambridge: Cambridge University Press.

Watts, Nicole F. 1999. "Allies and Enemies: Pro-Kurdish Parties in Turkish Politics, 1990–94." *International Journal of Middle East Studies* 31 (4): 631–656.

———. 2006. "Activists in Office: Pro-Kurdish Contentious Politics in Turkey." *Ethno-politics* 5 (2): 125–144.

———. 2010. *Activists in Office: Kurdish Politics and Protest in Turkey*. Seattle: University of Washington Press.

Weber, Max. 1968. *Economy and Society*. Berkeley: University of California Press.

Weis, Lois. 1995. "Identity Formation and the Processes of 'Othering': Unraveling Sexual Threads." *Educational Foundations* 9 (1): 17–33.

Wendt, Alexander E. 1987. "The Agent-Structure Problem in International Relations Theory." *International Organization* 41 (3): 335–370.

White, Paul J. 2000. *Primitive Rebels or Revolutionary Modernizers? The Kurdish National Movement in Turkey*. London: Zed Books.

Wimmer, Andreas. 2008a. "Elementary Strategies of Ethnic Boundary Making." *Ethnic and Racial Studies* 31 (6): 1025–1055.

———. 2008b. "The Making and Unmaking of Ethnic Boundaries: A Multilevel Process Theory." *American Journal of Sociology* 113 (4): 970–1022.

———. 2009. "Herder's Heritage and the Boundary-Making Approach: Studying Ethnicity in Immigrant Societies." *Sociological Theory* 27 (3): 244–270.

———. 2013. *Ethnic Boundary Making: Institutions, Power, Networks*. Oxford: Oxford University Press.

Wodak, Ruth. 2006. Discourse-Analytic and Socio-linguistic Approaches to the Study of Nation(alism)." In *The Sage Handbook of Nations and Nationalism*, edited by Gerard Delanty and Krishan Kumar, 104–117. London: Sage.

Wodak, Ruth, Rudolf de Cillia, Martin Reisigl, and Karin Liebhart. 2009. *The Discursive Construction of National Identity*. Edinburgh: Edinburgh University Press.

Wolff, Stefan. 2006. *Ethnic Conflict: A Global Perspective*. Oxford: Oxford University Press.

Yanarocak, Hay Eytan Cohen. 2014. "A Tale of Political Consciousness: The Rise of a Nonviolent Kurdish Political Movement in Turkey." In *Kurdish Awakening: Nation Building in a Fragmented Homeland*, edited by Ofra Bengio, 138–154. Austin: University of Texas Press.

Yavuz, M. Hakan. 1997. "Political Islam and the Welfare (Refah) Party in Turkey." *Comparative Politics* 30 (1): 63–82.

———. 1998. "A Preamble to the Kurdish Question: The Politics of Kurdish Identity." *Journal of Muslim Minority Affairs* 18 (1): 9–18.

———. 2001. "Five Stages of the Construction of Kurdish Nationalism in Turkey." *Nationalism and Ethnic Politics* 7 (3): 1–24.

———. 2003. *Islamic Political Identity in Turkey*. Oxford: Oxford University Press.

———. 2009. *Secularism and Muslim Democracy in Turkey*. Cambridge: Cambridge University Press.

Yavuz, M. Hakan, and Nihat Ali Özcan. 2006. "The Kurdish Question and Turkey's Justice and Development Party." *Middle East Policy* 13 (1): 102–119.

Yeğen, Mesut. 1996. "The Turkish State Discourse and the Exclusion of Kurdish Identity." *Middle Eastern Studies* 32 (2): 216–229.

———. 2007. "Turkish Nationalism and the Kurdish Question." *Ethnic and Racial Studies* 30 (1): 119–151.

———. 2011. "The Kurdish Question in Turkey: Denial to Recognition." In *Nationalisms and Politics in Turkey: Political Islam, Kemalism and the Kurdish Issue*, edited by Marlies Casier and Joost Jongerden, 67–85. New York: Routledge.

Yeğen, Mesut, Uğraş Ulaş Tol, and Mehmet Ali Çalışkan. 2016. *Kürler Ne İstiyor? Kürdistan'da Etnik Kimlik, Dindarlık, Sınıf ve Seçimler.* Istanbul: İletişim.

Yeşilada, Birol A., and Peter Noordijk. 2010. "Changing Values in Turkey: Religiosity and Tolerance in Comparative Perspective." *Turkish Studies* 11 (1): 9–27.

Yin, Robert K. 2009. *Case Study Research: Design and Methods.* 4th ed. Thousand Oaks, CA: Sage.

Young, Crawford. 1985. "Ethnicity and the Colonial and Post-Colonial State in Africa." In *Ethnic Groups and the State*, edited by Paul R. Brass, 59–93. Totowa, NJ: Barnes and Noble.

Zolberg, Aristide R., and Long Litt Woon. 1999. "Why Islam Is Like Spanish: Cultural Incorporation in Europe and the United States." *Politics & Society* 27 (1): 5–38.

INDEX

accommodative attitude towards Islam: the secular Kurdish movement, 72–85

agency, 137

agency-structure problem (debate), 136–137

agential approach, 137–138; in ethnicity and nationalism studies, 140–142

AKP (Adalet ve Kalkınma Partisi), 1, 17–18, 32, 53, 54, 80, 104–105, 107–108, 123, 126, 151–153

Al-Hujraat (Surah), 82

Al-Qaeda, 21, 77, 88, 156–157

Alevi Kurds, 18, 43, 88, 90, 114, 121, 131, 133; reaction to Islamic opening of the Kurdish movement, 114–118

Alevi-Sunni cleavage, 113–114

anesthetic effect: of Islam, 66

antireligious attitude: of the secular Kurdish movement, 65–69

Arab Spring uprisings, 157

Azadi Movement, 54, 75

Barth, Fredrik, 26–27, 29, 134, 175n6

Baydemir, Osman, 85

BBP (Büyük Birlik Partisi), 54, 123

BDP (Barış ve Demokrasi Partisi), 1, 14, 73, 75, 77, 79–83, 99, 101, 105, 108–109, 116, 112, 123, 129, 174n20

Bilgen, Ayhan, 75, 117, 128

boundary, 28–29; approach, 14–15; blur-ring, 35; contraction, 34, 86; crossing, 34–35; equalization, 34; expansion, 34, 86; making, 25–38; normative inversion, 34; positional move, 34;

reinforcement 86; social boundaries, 29–32; symbolic boundaries, 29–32; transvaluation, 34

boundary contestations, 18–20, 38–43, 112–126; external, 39–42, 122–126; internal, 42–43, 112–122

boundary making: the bounded nature of, 36–38

case study, 5

Charter of Medina (Constitution of Medina/the Medina Contract), 2, 36, 78–79, 89

CHP, 54, 105, 115; Istanbul deputy, 125

Çiftkuran, Zahit, 73, 82, 85

civilian Friday prayers, 1, 2, 73–74, 80, 122–123, 177n25

co-opting conservative figures, the secular Kurdish movement, 75–76

conceptual issues, 7–14

constructivism, 141–142

cultural stuff, 26, 30–31, 34, 87, 134–135, 146, 175n6

data sources, 6

DDKO (Devrimci Doğu Kültür Ocakları), 60

Demirtaş, Selahattin, 1, 76, 78, 80, 82, 90, 109, 118; namaz, 118

Democratic Islam Congress, 2, 6, 77–79, 88

DIAYDER, 73, 75–77, 80, 82, 85, 90

Diyanet, 73, 82, 90–91, 109–110, 123, 177n23

DTK (Demokratik Toplum Kongresi), 77, 80

ABOUT THE AUTHOR

Zeki Sarigil is Associate Professor of Political Science at Bilkent University (Ankara, Turkey). His research interests include ethnicity, ethnonationalism, ethnic conflict, civil-military relations, institutional theory (e.g., institutional change, path dependence, informal institutions), Turkish politics, and Kurdish ethnopolitics. He has published articles in such journals as *European Political Science Review, European Journal of International Relations, Nations and Nationalism, Ethnic and Racial Studies, Armed Forces & Society,* and *South European Society and Politics.* Sarigil has received scholarships, grants, and awards from various institutions, including Fulbright, TUBITAK, and the Science Academy of Turkey. He spent the 2014–2015 academic year at Princeton University as Fulbright Visiting Scholar.